Stuart Peckham

The Triumph of Humanism

A Visual Survey of the Decorative Arts of the Renaissance

Introduction by

D. Graeme Keith

Curator-in-Charge, Department of Decorative Arts
The Fine Arts Museums of San Francisco

With Contributions by

Charles Avery
Deputy Keeper, Department of Architecture and Sculpture, Victoria and Albert Museum, London

Jessie McNab Dennis
Associate Curator, Western European Arts
The Metropolitan Museum of Art, New York

David DuBon
Curator of Medieval and Renaissance Arts, Philadelphia Museum of Art

Stephen V. Grancsay
Curator Emeritus, Arms and Armor, The Metropolitan Museum of Art, New York

Yvonne Hackenbroch
Curator, Western European Arts, The Metropolitan Museum of Art, New York

Paul Needham
Curator of Books and Bindings, The Pierpont Morgan Library, New York

Clare Vincent
Associate Curator, Western European Arts,
The Metropolitan Museum of Art, New York

William D. Wixom
Curator of Medieval and Renaissance Decorative Arts, Cleveland Museum of Art

This catalogue was printed on the occasion of the exhibition *The Triumph of Humanism* at the California Palace of the Legion of Honor, San Francisco, October 22, 1977, to January 8, 1978.

This project is supported by The Museum Society

Library of Congress Catalogue Card No. 77-81221
ISBN 0-88401-030-9

Front cover:
Albrecht Altdorfer
THE HOLY FAMILY ON THE FLIGHT INTO EGYPT AT A FOUNTAIN
Lent by Yale University Art Gallery,
New Haven, Connecticut.
Gift of Mr. and Mrs. Christopher Tunnard (Cat no. 255).

Flyleaf:
Detail from Italian fifteenth century COPE

Back cover:
Hans Sebald Beham
ORNAMENT WITH SEA MONSTERS
The Fine Arts Museums of San Francisco,
Achenbach Foundation for Graphic Arts (Cat. no. 261).

Edited by Ann Heath Karlstrom
Designed by Linnea J. West and Ron Rick
Typesetting by Petrographics/Typeworld
Printed by Cal Central Press

Table of Contents

Preface

Not so long ago an art dealer from New York visiting San Francisco offered our museums an opportunity to purchase at an exorbitant price a tiny pair of panel paintings said to have been the work of Raphael. They each depicted a single figure in monochrome on a plain dark background. Since no other paintings by Raphael are on view in the public collections of Northern California, if we had acquired these paintings I wonder what impression a museum-goer — perhaps a high school student on a first visit to an art museum — would have had of the work of the Renaissance master who at twenty-seven years had created the *School of Athens* frescoes to decorate the library of Pope Julius II. Might it not be better to delay that firsthand glimpse of Raphael's genius till the day that young person should be fortunate enough to visit Rome? In the meantime, although limited to the decorative arts, such an exhibition as *The Triumph of Humanism* may provide preferable insights into the development of western civilization which emanated from Italy in the fifteenth and sixteenth centuries.

When Graeme Keith proposed the project, it was with this conviction in mind that we all urged him on. It was destined to be his last official endeavor before retiring after nineteen years at the de Young Museum. It is San Francisco's loss that the museum was so understaffed during those years that there could not have been more exhibitions by Graeme Keith because they were always enjoyable, elegant, and educational. We are grateful to him for the organization of this presentation of Renaissance objects and accompanying catalogue which are such an appropriate conclusion to his long museum career.

Our thanks extend also to the many institutions and individuals who have contributed to the undertaking and to The Museum Society, the National Endowment for the Arts, a Federal Agency, Fidelity Savings and Loan Association, and the L.J. Skaggs and Mary C. Skaggs Foundation, whose generous grants made the exhibition possible.

Ian McKibbin White
Director of Museums

Lenders to the Exhibition

Mr. and Mrs. James W. Alsdorf, Chicago, Illinois
Ruth Blumka, New York, New York
Jerry Durham, San Francisco, California
Edward Gans, Berkeley, California
Stephen V. Grancsay, Brooklyn, New York
Cyril Humphris, London, England
Philip Kassebaum, Wichita, Kansas
Ed Nagel, San Francisco, California
Heinz Schneider, Cleveland, Ohio
The Adler Planetarium, Chicago, Illinois
The Art Institute of Chicago, Chicago, Illinois
The Cleveland Museum of Art, Cleveland, Ohio
Cooper-Hewitt Museum, The Smithsonian Institution's National Museum of Design, New York, New York
The Corning Museum of Glass, Corning Glass Center, Corning, New York
The E.B. Crocker Art Gallery, Sacramento, California
The Detroit Institute of Arts, Detroit Michigan
The Francis E. Fowler, Jr. Foundation Museum, Beverly Hills, California
The J. Paul Getty Museum, Malibu, California
Grunwald Center for the Graphic Arts, University of California, Los Angeles, California
Los Angeles County Museum of Art, Los Angeles, California
The Metropolitan Museum of Art, New York, New York
The Minneapolis Institute of Arts, Minneapolis, Minnesota
Museum of Fine Arts, Boston, Massachusetts
The Museum of Fine Arts, Houston, Texas
National Gallery of Art, Washington, D.C.
Philadelphia Museum of Art, Philadelphia, Pennsylvania
The Pierpont Morgan Library, New York, New York
The Time Museum, Rockford, Illinois
The Toledo Museum of Art, Toledo, Ohio
University Art Galleries, University of California, Santa Barbara, California
Victoria and Albert Museum, London, England
Wadsworth Atheneum, Hartford, Connecticut
Walters Art Gallery, Baltimore, Maryland
William Rockhill Nelson Gallery and Atkins Museum of Fine Arts, Kansas City, Missouri
The Wine Museum of San Francisco, San Francisco, California
The Worshipful Company of Goldsmiths, Goldsmiths' Hall, London, England
Yale University Art Gallery, New Haven, Connecticut
Anonymous Lenders (5)

Acknowledgments

We wish to express our deep gratitude to the directors and governing boards of the museums listed on the preceding page, as well as to the private collectors and dealers listed there, for their willingness to loan the delightful and sometimes fragile objects which make up this exhibition. They offer a rare opportunity for the members of the several academic communities in the San Francisco area as well as the general visitor to view and study in a single exhibition a wide variety of Renaissance decorative arts.

Special thanks go to those museum directors and curators who have personally given their time and shared with us their knowledge and advice in assembling this group of objects. While it is not possible to list everyone who helped in this undertaking, we do owe a special debt of gratitude to the following:

At the Adler Planetarium, Mr. and Mrs. R. S. Webster; at the Art Institute of Chicago, John Keefe and R. Harold Joachim; at The Cleveland Museum of Art, William D. Wixom; at the Cooper-Hewitt Museum of Design, Elaine Dee and Christian Rohlfing; at The E.B. Crocker Art Gallery, Richard V. West and Roger D. Clisby; at The Detroit Institute of Arts, Ronald L. Winoker; at The Francis E. Fowler, Jr. Foundation Museum, Basil Jenkins; at The J. Paul Getty Museum, Gillian Wilson; at the Los Angeles County Museum of Art, William E. Jones and Mary Kahlenberg; at The Metropolitan Museum of Art, Olga Raggio, Dr. Yvonne Hackenbroch, James Parker, Clare Vincent, Jessie McNab Dennis, Dr. Helmut Nickel, and Jean Maley; at the Grunwald Center for the Graphic Arts, University of California at Los Angeles, Thomas W. Travis and Phyllis Peet; at The Minneapolis Institute of Arts, Merribell Parsons and David McFadden; at The Pierpont Morgan Library, Felice Stampfle and Dr. Paul Needham; at the Museum of Fine Arts, Boston, Robert C. Moeller, Christina Corseglia, Eleanor A. Sayre and Stephanie L. Stepanek; at The Museum of Fine Arts, Houston, Kent Sobotik; at the National Gallery of Art, C. Douglas Lewis and Jack C. Spinx; at the William Rockhill Nelson Gallery and Atkins Museum of Fine Arts, Ross E. Taggart; at the Philadelphia Museum of Art, David DuBon; at The Time Museum, Seth G. Atwood and William Andrews; at The Toledo Museum of Art, William Hutton; at the University Art Galleries, Santa Barbara, David Gebhard; at the Victoria and Albert Museum, Claude Blair, Shirley Bury and Dr. Charles Avery; at the Wadsworth Atheneum, Phillip M. Johnston; at the Walters Art Gallery, Richard H. Randall; at The Wine Museum of San Francisco, Ernest G. Mittleberger; at the Yale University Art Gallery, Edmund P. Pillsbury. We would also like to acknowledge our indebtedness to the following private collectors: Mr. James W. Alsdorf, Ruth Blumka, Jerry Durham, Cyril Humphris, Philip Kassebaum and Heinz Schneider.

We particularly wish to thank Dr. Mary Louise Huntington for her research in the area of ornament prints and for undertaking the laborious task of collating the catalogue entries. Our thanks are also due to Patricia Donovan for composing interpretive labels for the exhibition, to Ursula Egli for preparing the manuscript for the typesetter, and to Renée Beller Dreyfus and Maryanne O'Malley for the composition of the exhibition brochure. David Inocencio Multivision Films produced the audio-visual program with the assistance of George Stratton and Nancy Olexo. Linnea J. West has been responsible for the design and production of the catalogue, and Michael D. Cox for the design of the exhibition and installation. We also wish to acknowledge the contribution of Edward T. Engle, Jr., who guided the catalogue through the first stages of production, and Ann Heath Karlstrom, who saw it through to completion.

D. G. K.

Introduction

D. Graeme Keith

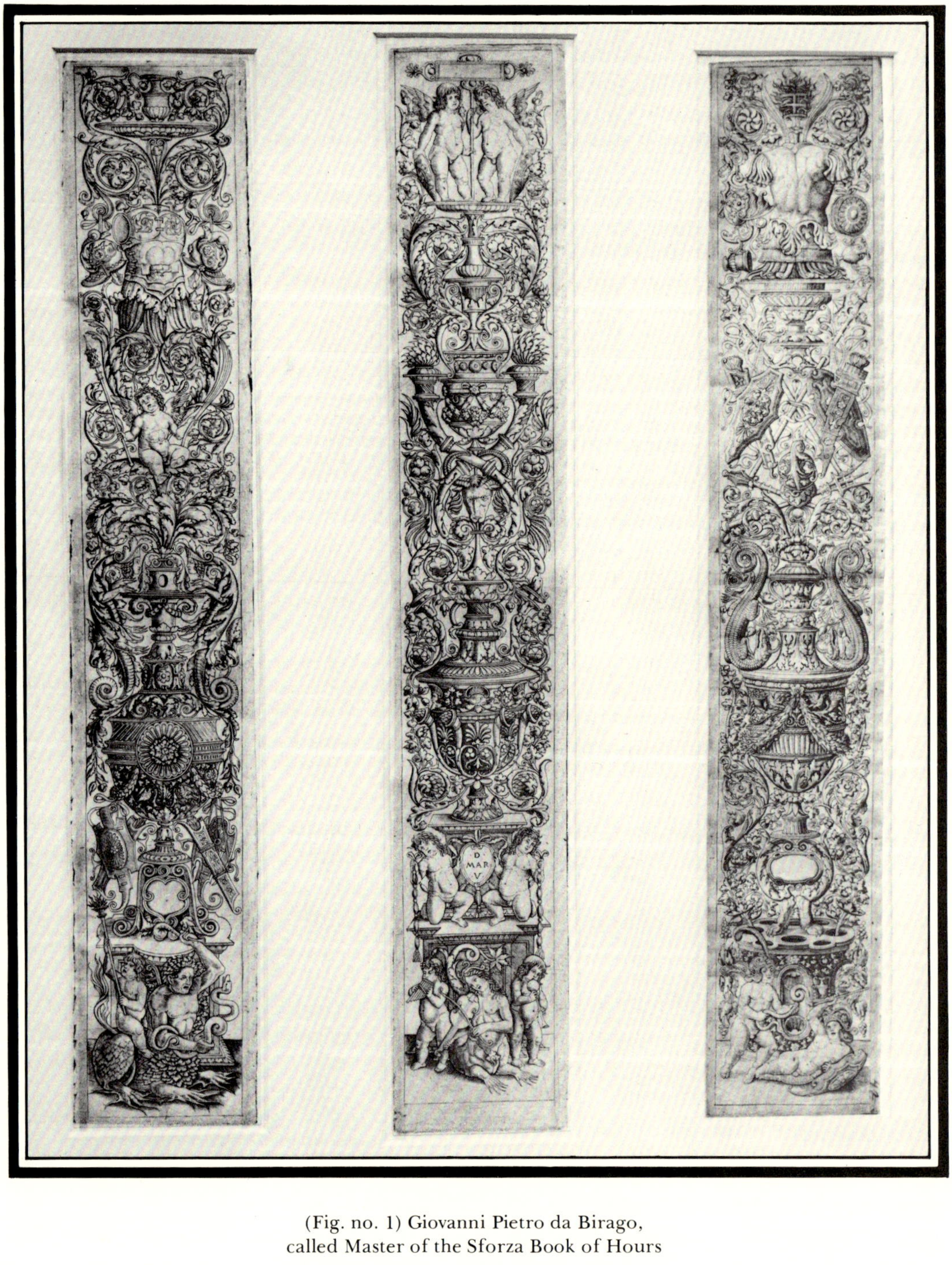

(Fig. no. 1) Giovanni Pietro da Birago,
called Master of the Sforza Book of Hours

THREE ORNAMENTAL PANELS

Lent by University of California, Los Angeles,
Grunwald Center for the Graphic Arts (Cat. no. 245).

"When evening comes, I return home and enter my study: and on the threshold I doff these everyday clothes of mine, all mud and filth, and don royal and courtly robes; and thus decently attired, I enter the ancient courts of ancient men, where, lovingly received by them, I nourish myself with the food that alone is mine and that I was born for. And I am not ashamed to talk to them and enquire after the reasons for their actions, and they, out of all humanity, answer me; and for four hours I feel no boredom, I forget every worry, I don't dread poverty, nor has death any terrors for me; I transfuse myself entirely into them."
(Quoted in translation from a letter of Niccolò Machiavelli to Francesco Vettori, December 10, 1513).

The period covered by our exhibition, from about 1425 to 1600, can be divided into three phases generally described as the Early Renaissance (ca. 1425-1480), the High Renaissance (ca. 1480-1525), and the Late Renaissance or Mannerism (ca. 1525-1600). In northern Europe the Early and High Renaissance styles occur later than in Italy and last for a much shorter time. The decorative styles characteristic of these periods developed gradually, but when they became fully crystallized, they displayed distinctive qualities. Through all three phases, however, there runs a common thread which connects them with the ancient classical world and its literature, philosophy, and art. The relationship with the literary world of the humanist is well illustrated in the eloquent passage from Machiavelli's letter of 1513 quoted above. This passage also reveals his desire — a desire shared by his contemporaries — to identify with the men of the classical past and to model his life, thinking, and moral behavior on theirs. In the exhibition and in this catalogue we seek to demonstrate the influence on the decorative arts of this renewed interest in the classics as an integral part of the broader scene of artistic achievement during the Renaissance.

Stimulated by the recovery of Greek and Latin literary masterpieces lost during the Middle Ages and by the influx of Greek scholars into Italy after the fall of Constantinople, the study of the classics, known as humanism, opened men's eyes to the impressive stature and accomplishments of the great men of the classical past. This knowledge, conveyed in poetry and prose of uncommon beauty, served to restore man's sense of dignity and self-esteem and liberated him from the spiritual confinement imposed by a church which stressed man's unworthiness, dictated a stereotyped view of the natural world, and urged him to disdain that world and its pleasures.

The Early Renaissance was a period of learning, assimilation, and codification of the principles of classical art and their application to the contemporary scene. It was a rare period of comparative intellectual tranquility during which people believed that they had rediscovered aesthetic laws that were eternally valid. They sought to create and surround themselves with works of art which would associate them with their admired ancestors in the classical world. Architects began to comb ancient Roman ruins which lay all about them, long forgotten and so little understood or appreciated during the medieval period that they were often used as stone quarries to provide materials for the construction of new buildings. They made measured drawings, sketched, studied, and absorbed the spirit and the letter of what they saw. They studied Vitruvius, the only Roman architect whose writings had survived, seeking there and in the monuments themselves the secrets of the laws of proportion in which the beauty of classical architecture seemed to lie.

The humanists who had sponsored the search for and who had themselves collected classical manuscripts were also collectors of other classical antiquities. The collections they formed included marble sculptures and reliefs, small bronzes, coins, cameos, and intaglio-cut gems. Indeed, the collecting of antiques and of contemporary bronzes in the antique manner was one of the marks of a man of culture. The demand for bronzes, which included sculptures and medals as well as utilitarian objects of contemporary use such as doorknockers, candlesticks, mortars, incense burners, and a multitude of small boxes and inkwells, was supplied by sculptors working in the studios of Florence, Mantua, Padua, Venice, Rome, and a few centers north of the Alps. As was the case with the surviving examples of Roman architecture and sculpture, the small antique objects assembled in these collections were studied by artists and craftsmen and influenced the form and design of many Renaissance objects. Besides bronzes, these included the output of the workshops of armorers, goldsmiths, jewelers, cabinetmakers, metal engravers, ceramists, enamellers, and bookbinders.

The exhibition contains a number of bronzes known to be based on objects which once belonged to Renaissance collectors. Among these is a bronze plaque (Cat. no. 10) made from a mold taken from a famous Roman cup, carved from sardonyx, which once belonged to the great Florentine humanist, Lorenzo de Medici.

The exposure of Renaissance artists and craftsmen to the literature and the artistic remnants of the classical world affected both the narrative content and the forms of the objects of utility and decoration: in content through the common use of classical subjects, and in form through a classical treatment of the human figure and the adaptation of classical shapes and ornamental devices. Even in the case of objects made for ecclesiastical use where the subjects would be Christian, the classical forms prevailed.

A wealth of classical subjects was used to decorate objects coming from workshops in every branch of the decorative arts. Examples in the exhibition include many versions of the *Labors of Hercules* (Cat. no. 12) executed in bronze and silver. Scenes from the lives of the Greek and Roman gods and heroes were commonly depicted in the engravings used by craftsmen as sources of design. They also appeared on painted majolica and enamels and were engraved, etched, and embossed on metal from the workshops of armorers and goldsmiths, in addition to being embroidered on textiles (Cat. No. 286). The Renaissance designer also drew upon a host of lesser classical figures and devices — satyrs, putti, sphinxes, masks, herms, medallions, trophies, scrolls, acanthus leaves, Roman lettering, and other motifs derived from antique sources.

These themes and motifs were assimilated by Renaissance artists and craftsmen and became a part of the vocabulary of all of the visual arts. They were portrayed in numerous engravings produced first in Italy and later in great abundance in northern Europe during the Mannerist period. The makers of these engravings reflected and, to a considerable degree, influenced the changes in style as they developed during the Renaissance. They were also important because they facilitated the dispersion of the knowledge of classical ornament throughout Europe and, through engraved versions, made many paintings by the great masters of the period widely familiar. The designers and engravers of these prints also turned to classical monuments for inspiration. But once the classical vocabulary was understood, these designers began to introduce variations of their own invention to make them entirely their own. To this early period belong the delightful "pilaster" and "trophy" ornaments by designers in the circle of Zoan Andrea (Cat. no. 245) and Nicoletto da Modena.

A Roman monument which was of special interest to the period was Nero's *Domus Aura* (Golden House) which contained in its buried rooms charming examples of Roman decorative painting; the Renaissance designs based upon them came to be known as "grotesques" (as the originals which inspired them were found in underground rooms, or grottoes). Variations of "grotesque" designs continued to come off the presses of the engravers during the Renaissance and subsequent centuries and were used as major sources of design again and again by artisans in all the decorative crafts. A particularly rich and varied output of these engraved ornament prints occurred in France and, a little later, in other countries of northern Europe. The court of Francis I at Fontainebleau, where important Italian artists including Primaticcio (1504-1570) and Rosso (1494-1541) were employed by the French king, played a leading role in the development and dissemination of the Mannerist style in both the major and minor arts. These Italian artists were engaged not only to decorate the king's palace but also to establish workshops where northern craftsmen in all branches of the decorative arts could be trained in the essentials of their craft and the principles of the new Mannerist style. Typical of these was Jacques Androuet Du Cerceau, a French Mannerist architect and engraver who produced many suites of ornamental prints. He described their intended purpose on one title page as to "serve goldsmiths, painters, stone cutters, cabinet-makers and other artisans to awaken their fantasy and apply each to his art whatever he finds appropriate."

The repertoire of Renaissance graphic design was supplied not only by architects, painters, and sculptors of the first rank, such as Donatello, Verrocchio, Mantegna, Raphael, Michelangelo, Primaticcio, Rosso, Holbein, and Dürer, but also by a host of talented and inventive followers. Several Renaissance goldsmiths, for example the great Nuremberg goldsmith Wenzel Jamnitzer (Cat. no. 264), were also active in the production of graphic designs. The exhibition includes a number of ornament prints and drawings which indicate the manner and universality of their use by craftsmen in every branch of the decorative arts.

There were other interests not connected with the classical world which had an influence on the decorative arts of the Renaissance. Among these was a fascination with the natural world, which at this time began to be seen with new eyes. Boxes, inkwells, and small sculptures in the form of crabs, frogs, and lizards appear frequently in late fifteenth-century bronzes and in goldsmith's work of the Mannerist period, as well as in the ceramics of Bernard Palissy (ca. 1510-1590) and his followers. There was also considerable influence from the arts of the Middle East, which reached Italy and other parts of Europe through Venice and Spain. The "Mauresque" or "Arabesque" was a form of Islamic ornament which appeared frequently in ornament prints and, through them, was successfully adapted and combined with classical elements by goldsmiths, armorers, bookbinders, ceramists and textile workers.

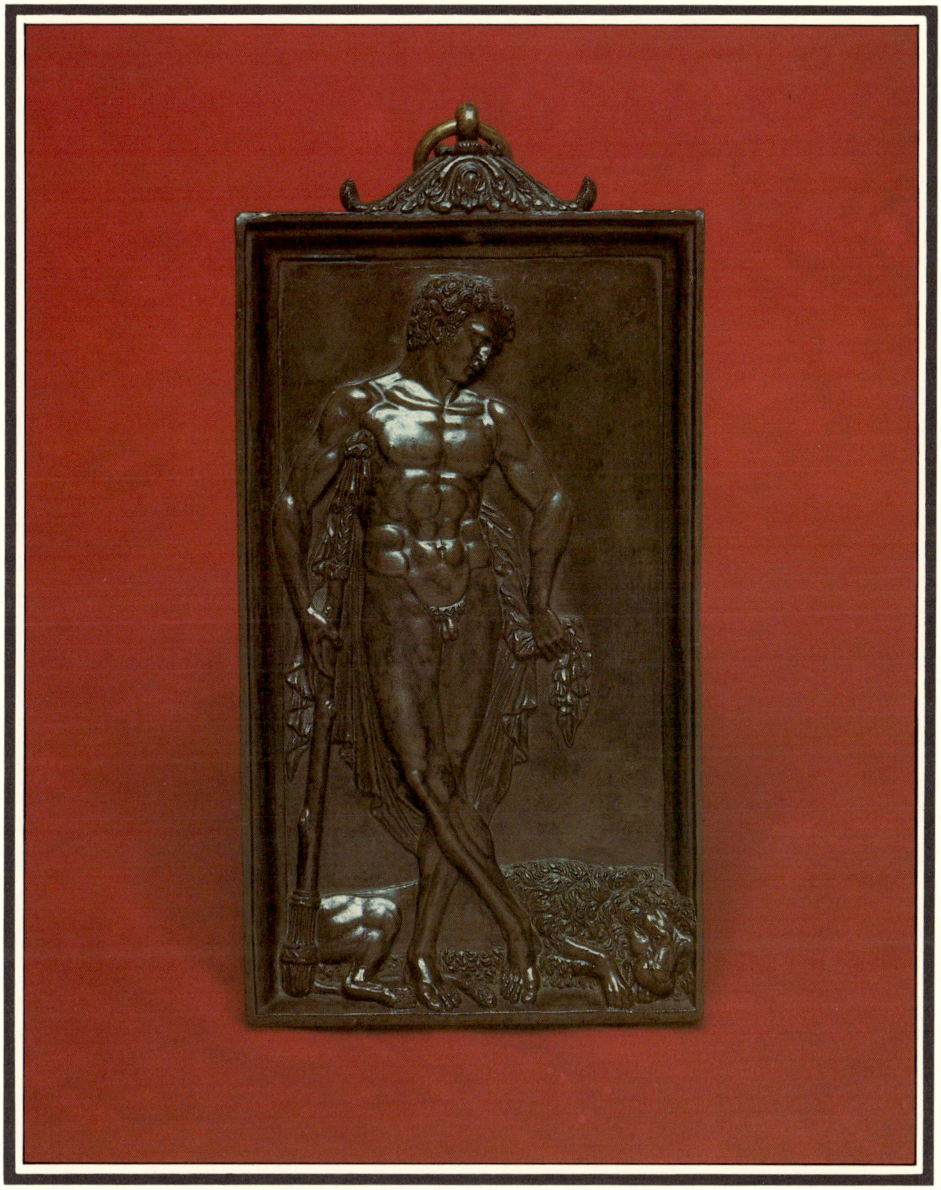

(Fig. no. 2) Pier Jacopo Alari Bonacolsi,
called L'Antico

HERCULES RESTING AFTER SLAYING
THE NEMEAN LION

Lent by The Museum of Fine Arts, Houston.
Edith A. and Percy S. Straus Collection (Cat. no. 12).

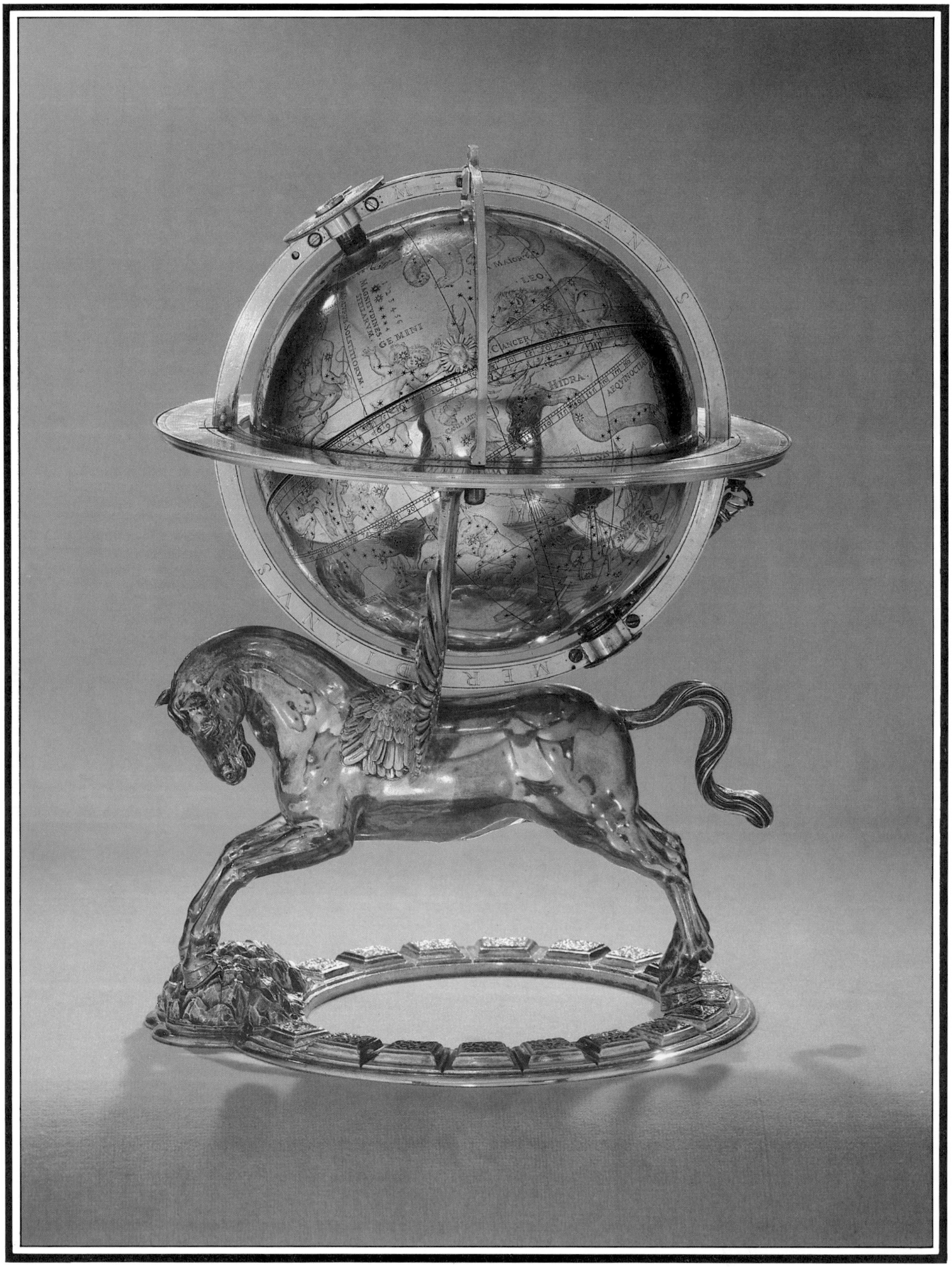

(Fig. no. 3) Gerhard Emmoser

CELESTIAL GLOBE WITH CLOCKWORKS

Lent by The Metropolitan Museum of Art, New York.
Gift of J. Pierpont Morgan, 1917 (Cat. no. 144).

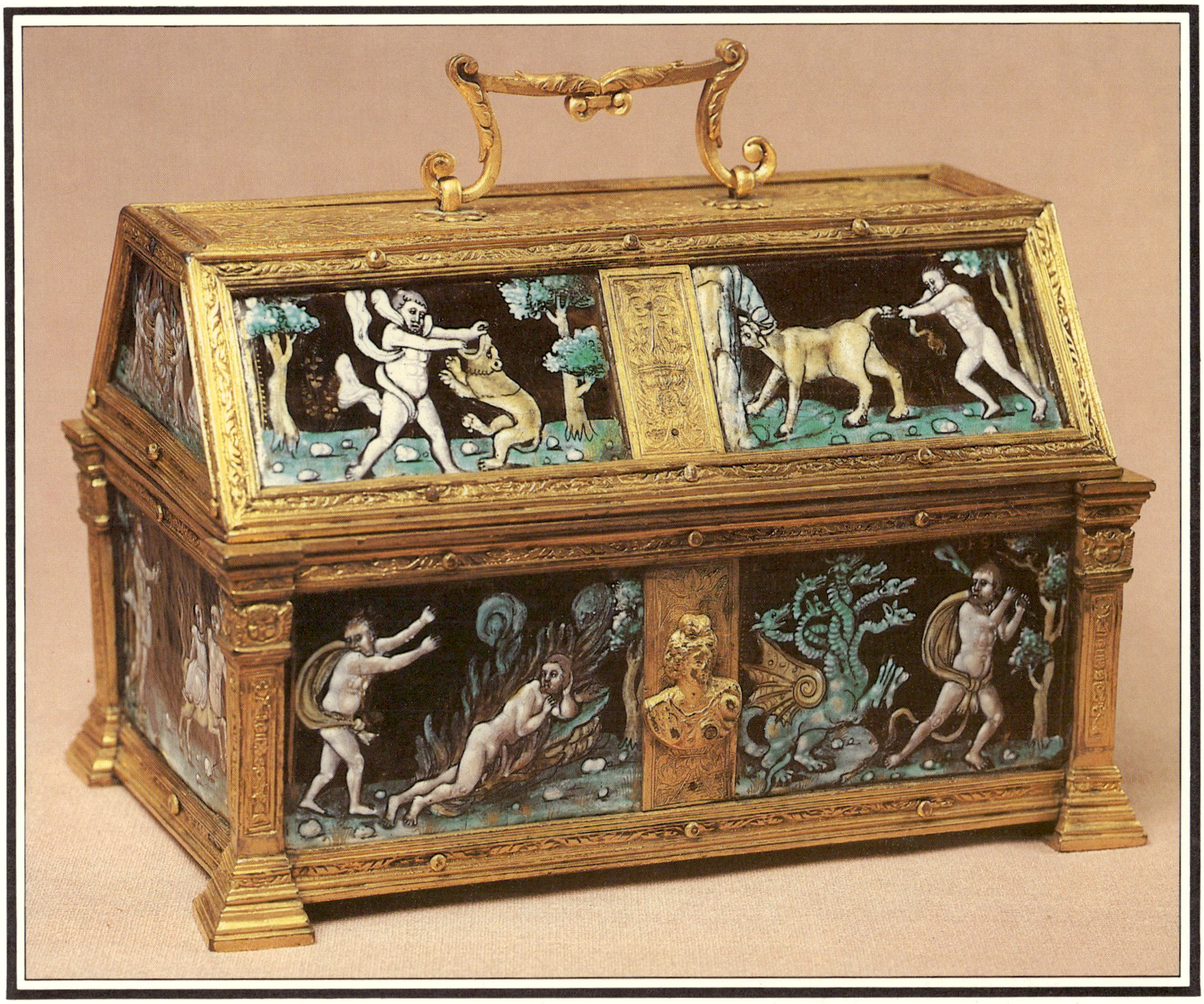

(Fig. no. 4) Couly Nouailher

HERCULES CASKET

Lent by The Walters Art Gallery, Baltimore (Cat. no. 200).

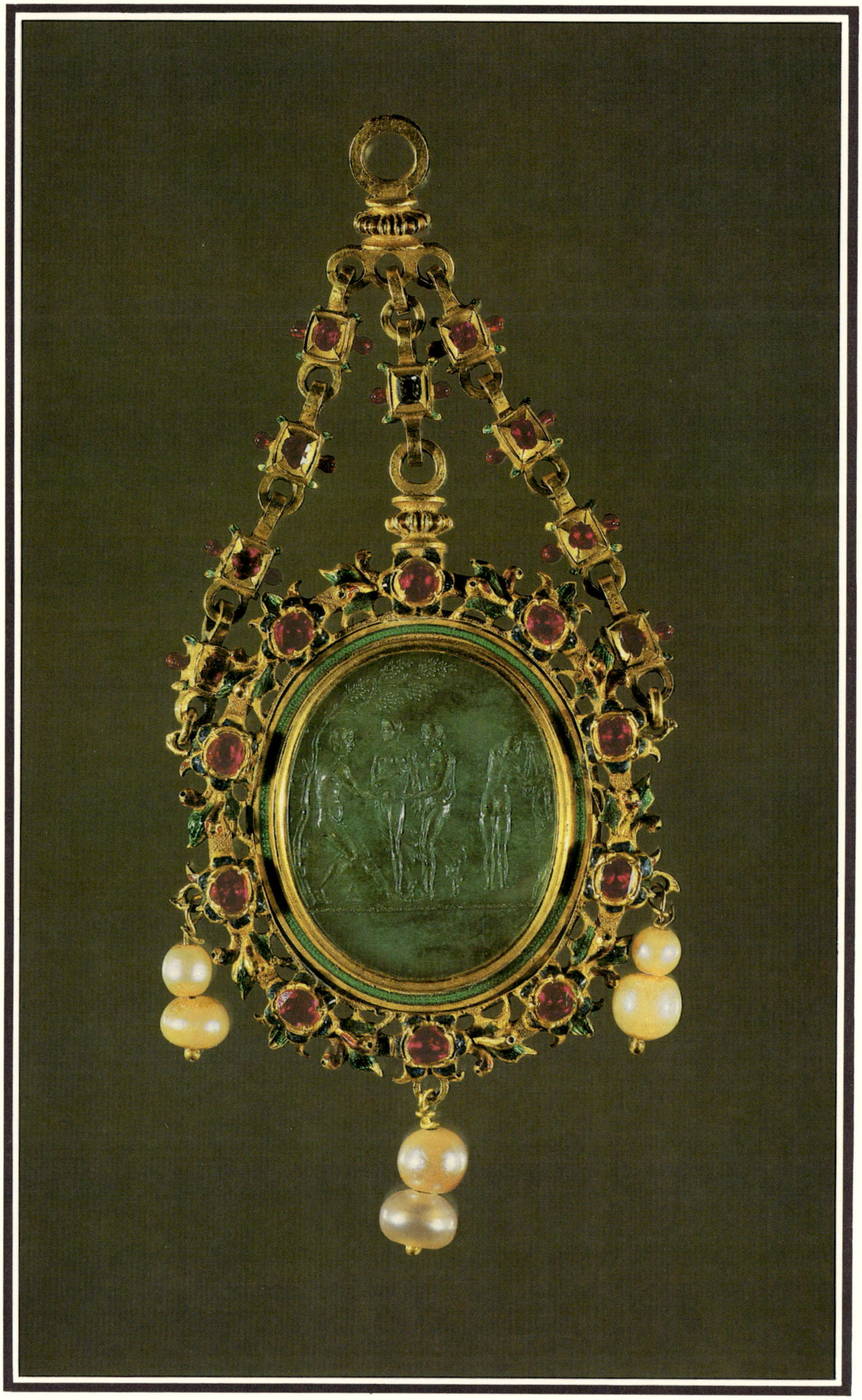

(Fig. no. 5) North Italian, second half of the 16th century

PENDANT OF "THE JUDGMENT OF PARIS"

Lent by Mr. and Mrs. James W. Alsdorf, Chicago (Cat. no. 95).

Reproduced larger than actual size.

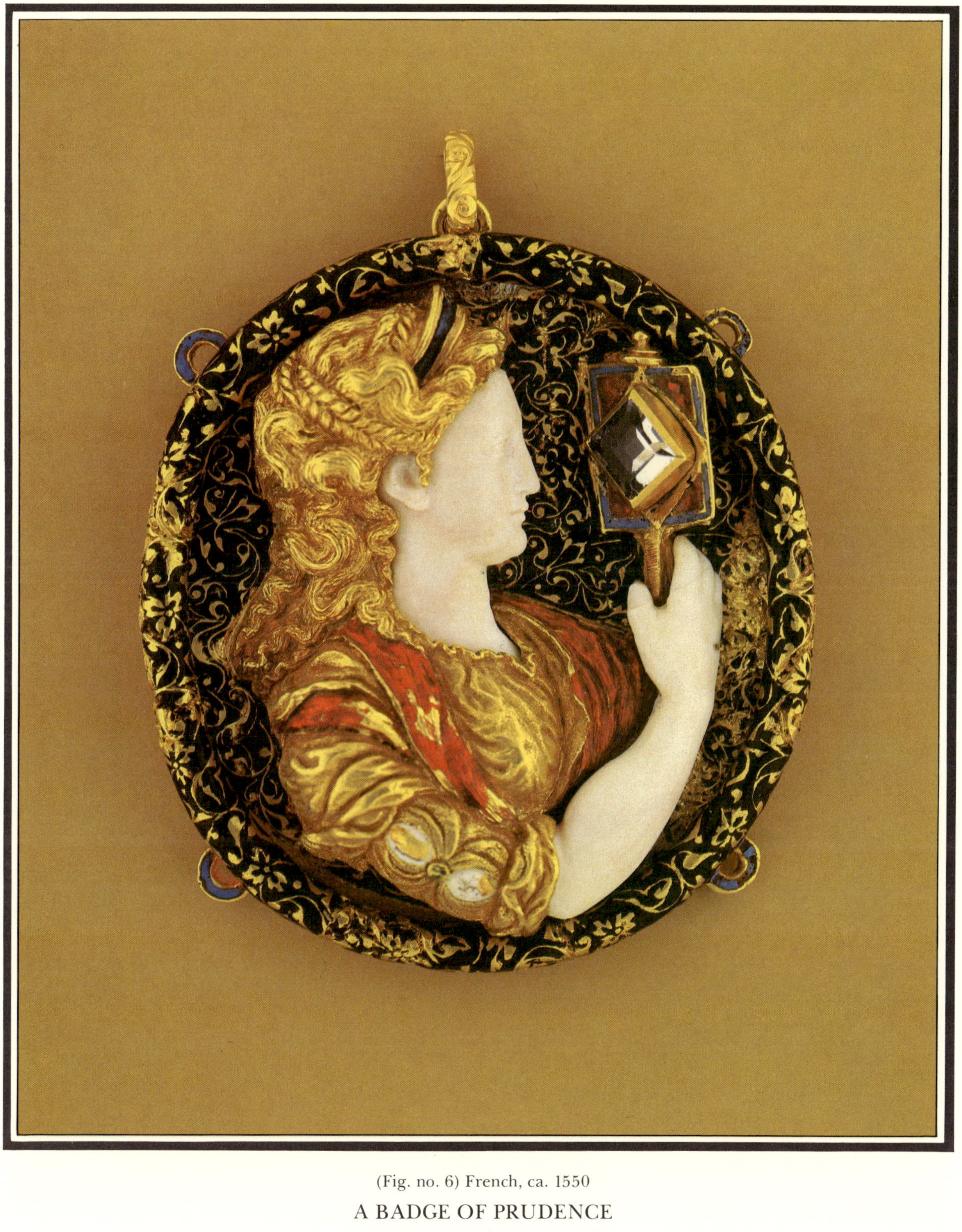

(Fig. no. 6) French, ca. 1550

A BADGE OF PRUDENCE

Lent anonymously (Cat. no. 99).

Reproduced larger than actual size.

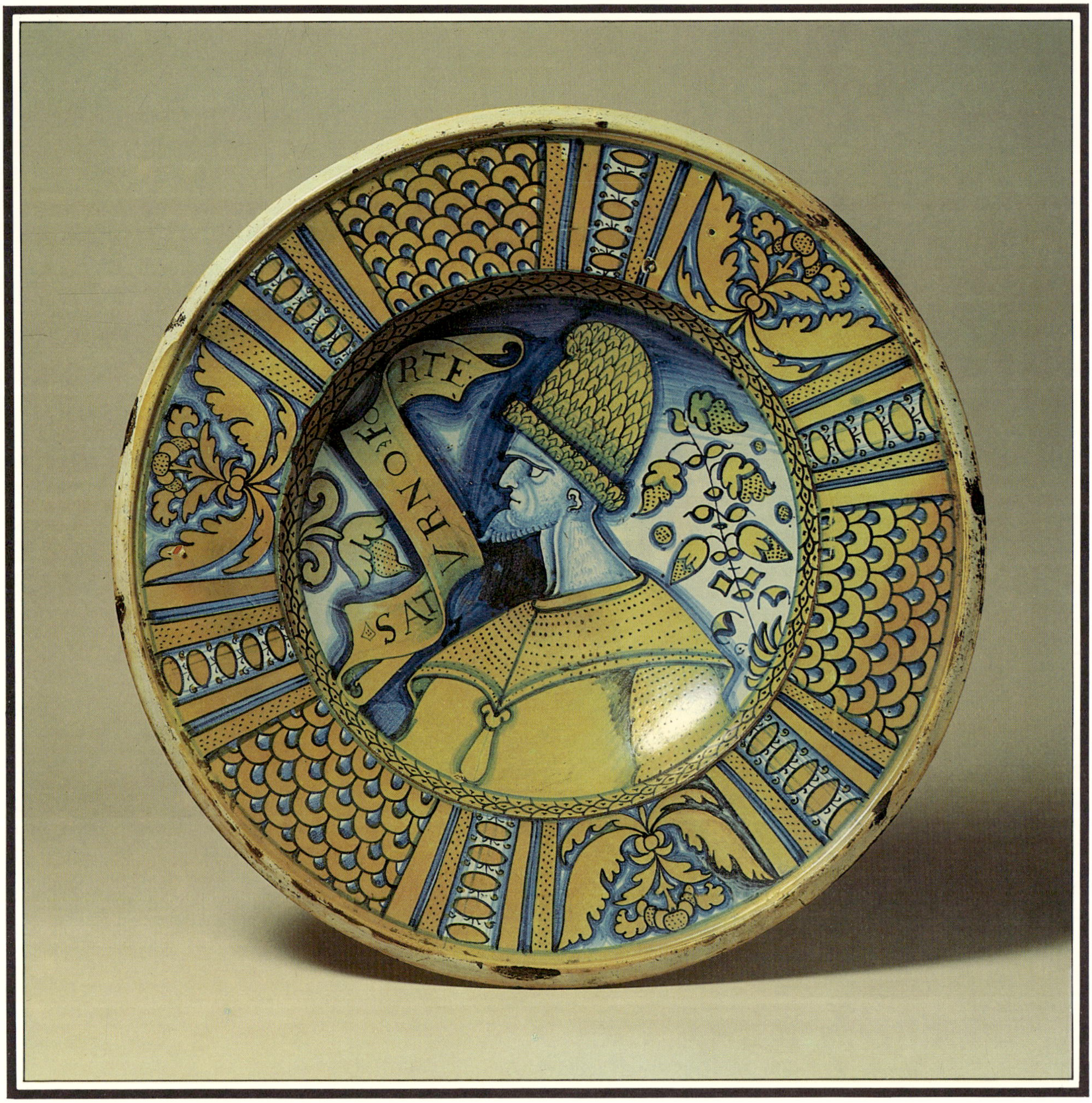

(Fig. no. 7) Italian (Deruta), ca. 1525

MAJOLICA PLATE

The Fine Arts Museums of San Francisco.
Gift of Jacob Goldschmidt (Cat. no. 185).

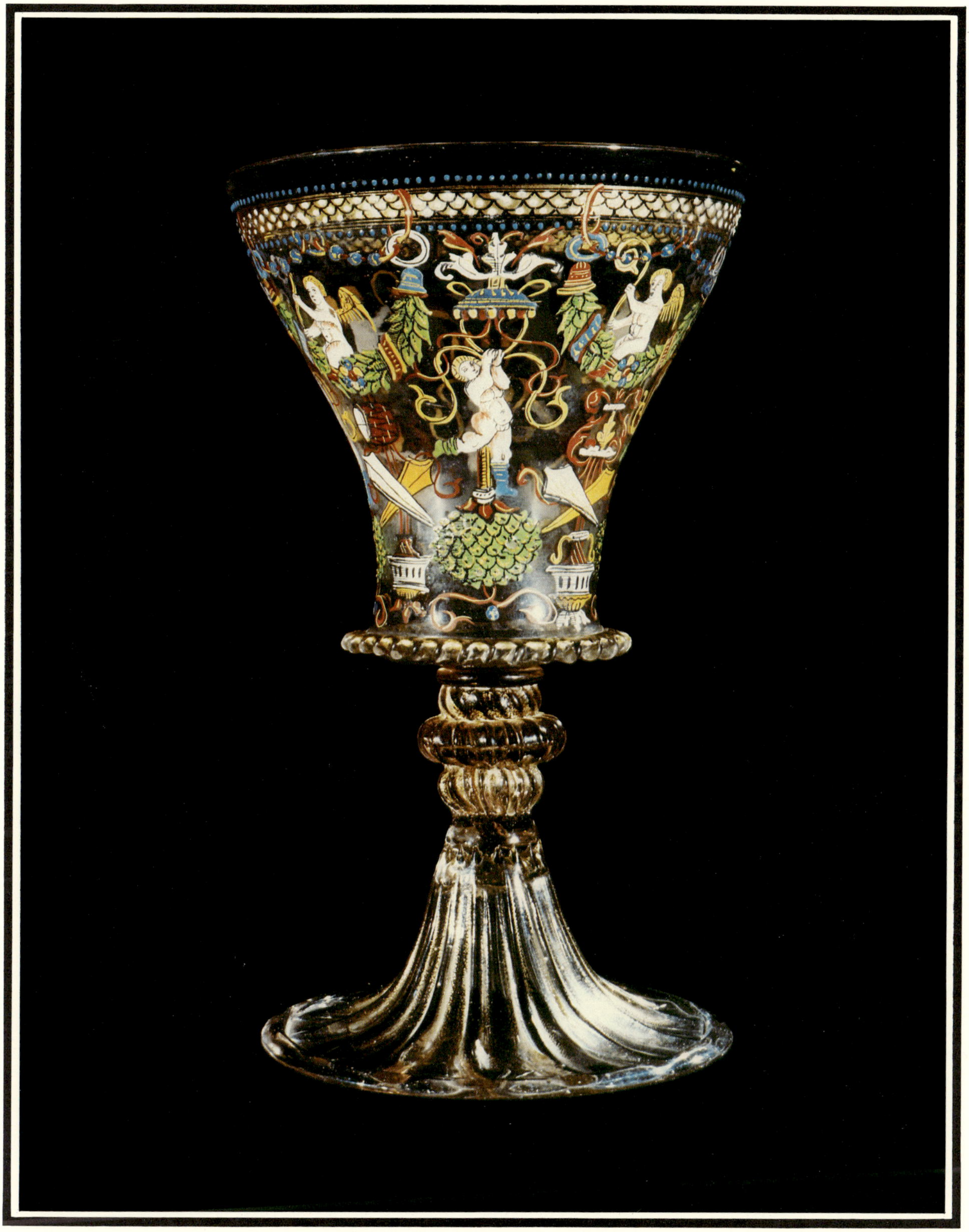

(Fig. no. 8) Italian (Venice), 1500-1525

GOBLET

Lent by The Corning Museum of Glass, Corning, New York (Cat. no. 193).

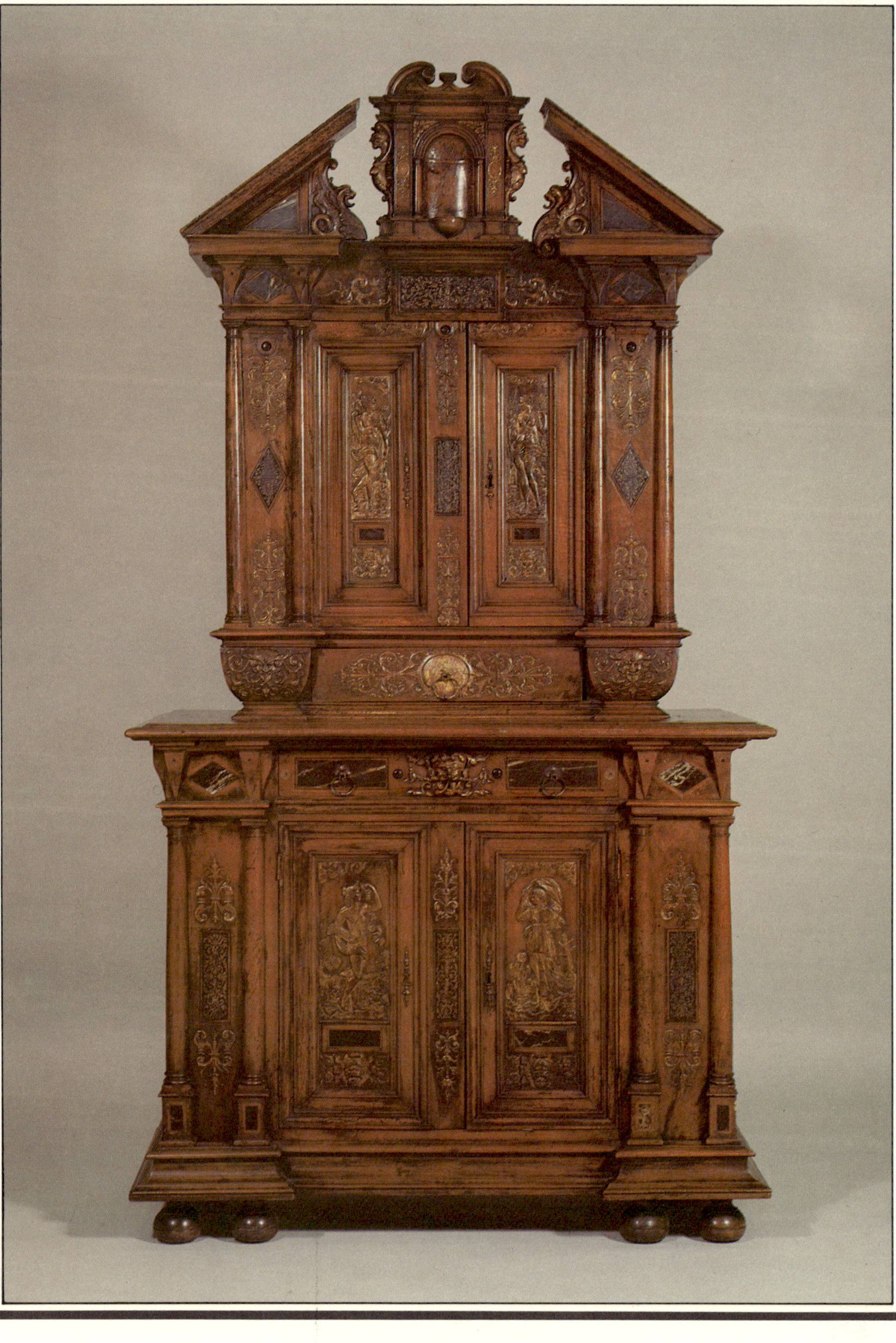

(Fig. no. 9) French, 1550-1575

CABINET

The Fine Arts Museums of San Francisco.
Gift of the Oakes Foundation, a fund within
The San Francisco Foundation (Cat. no. 217).

The Patronage of the Medici

Charles Avery

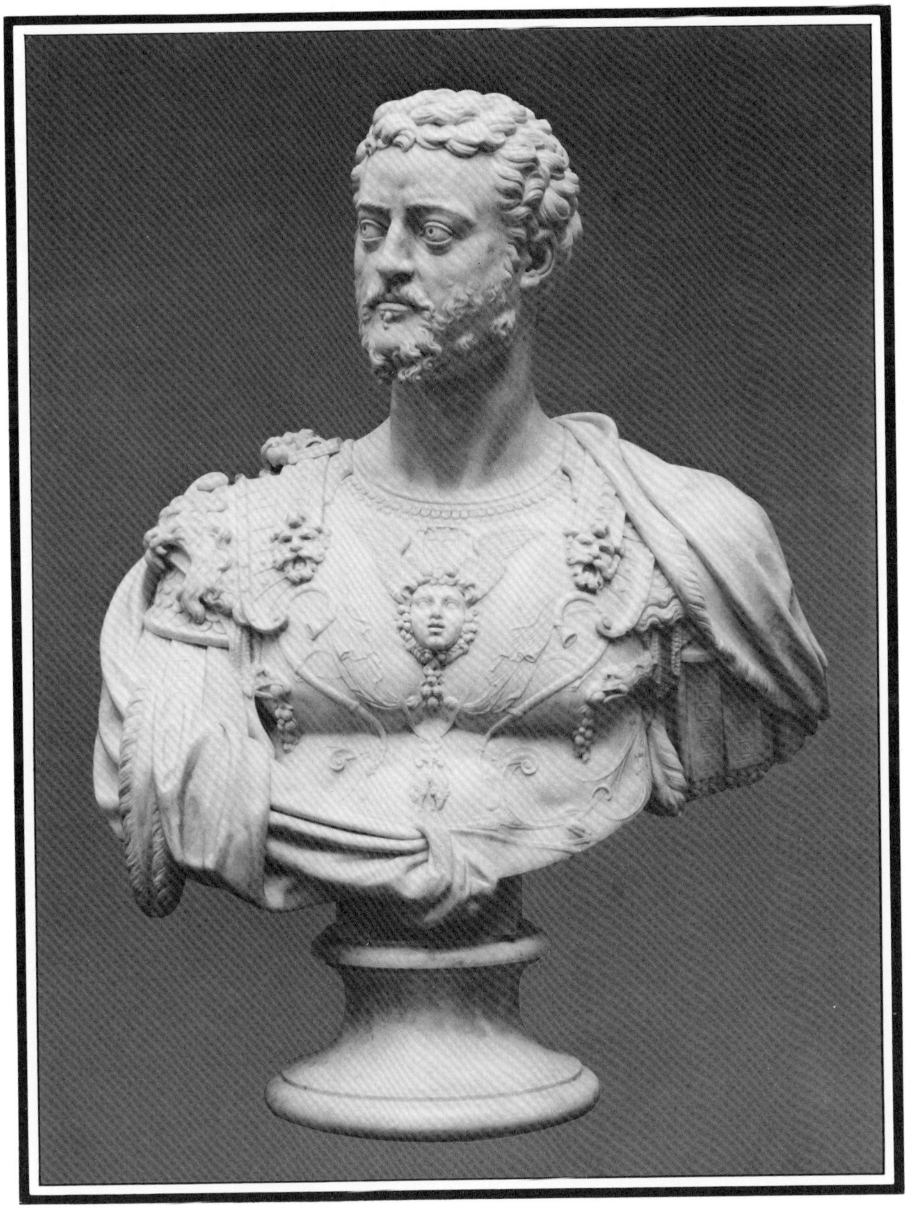

(Fig. no. 10) Attributed to Benvenuto Cellini

COSIMO I DE' MEDICI

The Fine Arts Museums of San Francisco.
Gift of the Roscoe and Margaret Oakes Foundation
(Cat. no. 1).

Prosperity and a Guilty Conscience

The Medici family was fairly prominent in Florentine politics as early as the thirteenth century, but they began to prosper conspicuously only after the foundation of their bank in 1348. Fundamental to the business of banking is the taking of interest, and in the fifteenth century this was still subject to the Biblical interdiction against usury. A means of expiating this "sin" was to devote some of one's profits to a charitable end, such as the building, repair, or decoration of a religious foundation. This was probably the motivation behind the enormous subsidies made towards the rebuilding of the parish church of the Medici — San Lorenzo — by Giovanni di Bicci and his son, Cosimo the Elder (1389-1464). This church was to be the focus of the family's patronage of religious art for over two hundred years.

Cosimo was particularly interested in architecture and had a close relationship with the architect of San Lorenzo, Brunelleschi. He was also in close contact with Michelozzo, who rebuilt, at Cosimo's expense, the monastery of San Marco with its fine cloisters and famous library. The frescoes by Fra Angelico in the cells must have received Cosimo's approval, though he did not usually condescend to deal with painting, which involved less of his money and which he normally left to his sons to supervise. His other architectural undertakings include a chapel and a cloister in Santa Croce and the Badia at Fiesole. It has been suggested that Cosimo may have drawn the plans for some of the projects himself. After salving his conscience with these religious buildings, Cosimo could turn to the needs of his family and began the Medici Palace (Fig. no. 14) whose novel architecture and courtyard decorated with reliefs of classical subjects is comparable to the contemporary palace built by Alberti for the Rucellai family.

Cosimo is recorded as a generous patron and indeed a close friend of the greatest sculptor of his day, Donatello. They were jointly involved in erecting in the Florentine Baptistry a tomb for the antipope John XXIII, whom Giovanni di Bicci had financed and harbored in Florence. Donatello executed all the narrative relief decoration in Brunelleschi's Old Sacristy at San Lorenzo and later modeled a pair of bronze pulpits for the church. In a different vein, a famous and enigmatic bronze *David,* the first life-sized nude statue of the Renaissance, was a product of their mutual interest in classical art. It seems to have been designed to stand in the middle of the courtyard of the Palace. We are told that Cosimo also patronized Desiderio da Settignano, the brilliant but short-lived marble sculptor, many of whose ideas derived from Donatello.

The most complete biography of Cosimo has been left us by the bookseller Vespasiano da Bisticci, who testifies to his patron's intense interest in the new learning and his amazing generosity in financing the search for ancient manuscripts and the making of copies from existing rare works. He took great pains to stock the library that he had founded at San Marco and also began to build up the one at San Lorenzo. Vespasiano provides eloquent testimony of Cosimo's contributions to the practical side of Renaissance humanism.

Nostalgia for Antiquity

Cosimo's son Piero the Gouty (1416-1469), who inherited the bank on Cosimo's death in 1464, had very different interests. Perhaps to compensate for his crippling affliction, he concentrated less on architecture, which had been his father's preserve, than on more sedentary pursuits such as collecting, reading, and the appreciation of paintings. Such was his nostalgia for life in the manner of the ancients that he had built for himself a special study to house his collection of Graeco-Roman gems and cameos, coins, and statuettes (Cat. no. 10). The most significant remnants of Piero's rich collections are the illuminated manuscripts now in the Laurentian Library; they show his taste for opulent ornament. He also revived a characteristic Roman type of sculpture, the portrait bust. Mino da Fiesole's portrait of Piero dating from 1453 is the earliest of this type in the Renaissance and was set, as in a Roman house, over the entrance to his apartments. Piero's prominence was relatively short, for he outlived Cosimo by only five years; but he was undoubtedly active as a patron of the arts in his own right long before he became the head of the Medici family in 1464. As early as the year 1438 he had been in a position of sufficient influence to have been solicited for an important commission by the painter Domenico Veneziano.

Piero and his younger brother Giovanni were delegated the responsibility of dealing with painters during their father's lifetime. It was to Piero that artists like Filippo Lippi and Matteo de' Pasti addressed their pleas for work or funds. A letter of Benozzo Gozzoli from 1459 shows how closely the artist had to follow Piero's instructions in every detail of his famous frescoes in the chapel of the Medici Palace. Gozzoli's highly ornamental style may be seen as harking back to the International Gothic style that had been favored by aristocratic patrons of an earlier generation. Similar characteristics in Uccello's series of enormous panels showing the *Battle of San Romano* (National Gallery, London; Louvre, Paris; Uffizi, Florence), commissioned for the walls of a room in the palace, display a toy-soldier quality reminiscent of late Gothic tapestries. The *Labors of Hercules* by Antonio Pollaiuolo, now known only from engravings and tiny painted reproductions, were also hung in the palace. These were avant-garde in the extreme realism of the nudes in action and the classical subjects, a quality also to be seen in Pollaiuolo's bronze statuette of *Hercules and Antaeus* in the Bargello.

Piero supervised completion of the work at the Badia of Fiesole, employed Verrocchio (Fig. no. 12) in the Old Sacristy at San Lorenzo, and commissioned Michelozzo to work on tabernacles in San Miniato al Monte and in Santissima Annunziata. All were marked as Medicean commissions by prominent coats of arms or other heraldic devices.

An Arbiter of Taste

With Piero's death in 1469, his son Lorenzo, dubbed "the Magnificent," (1449-1492) came to power (Fig. no. 13). Lorenzo exemplifies the Renaissance ideal of the Universal Man—one who could turn his hand with equal facility to all the most important activities in life. He played a leading role in Florentine politics and international diplomacy and was a good businessman, although the profits of the bank were being reduced by external economic pressures. His popularity, however, like that of his handsome brother Giuliano, was due to his capacity as a sportsman and reveler. He was also a dedicated humanist and collector, as is indicated by the rare series of ancient vases made of semi-precious stone and bearing his initials that are still to be seen in Florence. Antique cameos bearing his mark are to be found scattered throughout great collections. The enormous cost of this kind of collecting and the reduced profits of the bank prevented him from sponsoring artistic undertakings on the same lavish scale as his father or grandfather, but his household provided ample employment for the studios of Verrocchio and the Pollaiuolo brothers. Sculpture, bronze-founding, painting, and a multitude of minor decorative tasks were occasioned by Lorenzo's love of spectacle and display. Verrocchio produced portrait-busts of both brothers (National Gallery of Art, Washington, D.C.), a monumental tomb in San Lorenzo for their father and their uncle, the celebrated bronze *David* that so patently emulates Donatello's earlier statue for their grandfather, the *Boy with a Dolphin* for a fountain at their country villa of Careggi, and much other work. This impressive list may suggest that Lorenzo, like Cosimo, favored sculpture as an art, perhaps because of its durability; but it must be admitted that our knowledge of his patronage of painting is severely limited by the destruction of two great fresco cycles on which he employed painters of the caliber of Filippo Lippi, Domenico Ghirlandaio, and Sandro Botticelli.

Lorenzo (Cat. no. 161) seems to have been considered an arbiter of taste by his contemporaries. His opinion was sought on a wide variety of artistic topics, ranging from the merits of two rival models for a funeral monument to the design of a new palace proposed by his great rival, Filippo Strozzi. Lorenzo also inherited his grandfather's talent for architecture and submitted, along with the professionals, an entry in the competition for the design of a new façade for the cathedral in Florence.

The sculptor most intimately associated with Lorenzo was Bertoldo, a pupil of Donatello who continued to specialize in bronze casting and who lived in the Medici Palace, devoting himself to small reliefs (Cat. no. 20) and statuettes in the nature of collector's pieces. To him was entrusted the execution of a medal to mark the assassination of Giuliano and the escape of Lorenzo during the Pazzi conspiracy of 1478. His most famous relief, showing a battle between horsemen, was designed to go over a fireplace in the Palace; this masterpiece was based on a ruined Roman sarcophagus. It had a profound effect on a young sculptor, Michelangelo, whose talent had been remarked by Lorenzo shortly before his death in 1492. It is to Lorenzo's eternal credit as a patron of the arts that from 1489 to 1492 he entertained Michelangelo in the Palace and thus gave him an unrivaled opportunity to learn from the greatest minds of the day, who were assembled under the same roof.

Lorenzo's son, Piero the Unfortunate, was permitted to maintain control of Florence for only two years. The exile to which the family was condemned as Savonarola rose to power marks the only serious gap in their patronage of the arts. The High Renaissance at Florence took place without their participation, and it was not until the election of a member of the family to the Papacy in 1513 that they were able to reassert themselves in the role of patrons.

Medici Popes and High Renaissance

In the first decade of the sixteenth century, the center of the art world had shifted from Florence to Rome, under the lavish and intelligent patronage of Pope Julius II della Rovere. Painters, architects, and sculptors were gathered from Florence and elsewhere by the promise of ambitious projects and handsome rewards. Bramante, Raphael, and Michelangelo all obeyed the summons.

In 1513 Lorenzo the Magnificent's second son, Giovanni (1498-1526), was elected to the papacy as Leo X; this signaled the Medici's achievement of the highest ambition of any Renaissance family. The event found its natural expression in renewed patronage of the arts. Among the greatest projects of Leo's predecessor had been the frescoing of the Sistine Chapel ceiling by Michelangelo and the decoration of the first of the *stanze* in the Vatican by Raphael. The Medici pope retained Raphael to decorate the next two *stanze* in the suite of papal offices and to design full-scale cartoons (now in the Victoria and Albert Museum) for the tapestries with which Leo wished to hang the lower parts of the walls of the Sistine Chapel. This project, dating from about 1515, gave Raphael an opportunity to compete with the ceiling of his rival Michelangelo, a supreme challenge which he met with characteristic equanimity. Raphael also painted the Pope's portrait, catching the psychology of his patron with miraculous ease.

The open rivalry between Raphael and Michelangelo, which Leo somewhat unscrupulously exploited to his own ends, came to a head with an informal competition that he arranged over a colossal painted altarpiece. Michelangelo was represented by his Venetian protégé, Sebastiano del Piombo, who painted the huge *Raising of Lazarus* (National Gallery, London) using the master's sketches. Raphael executed the *Transfiguration* (Vatican Museum), adding the finishing touches from his deathbed. It represents the greatest expression of Raphael's art, moving beyond the aesthetic principles of the High Renaissance in the direction of the succeeding style — Mannerism. The *Raising of Lazarus* is less successful, probably because Sebastiano, not Michelangelo, was the artist. It is nevertheless a masterpiece and represents a great achievement in terms of patronage. Leo X died soon after its completion.

During the whole of Leo's papacy, there had been much artistic activity in Florence, beginning with the festive decorations for an official visit paid by the pope to his native city in 1515. These were of an elaboration to suit the occasion, and every artist in the city was employed in making some part of the temporary decorations — triumphal arches, floats, false façades, etc. This seems to have reminded Leo that the Medici parish church of San Lorenzo still lacked a proper façade (as it does yet today), for he commissioned Michelangelo to design one. Ultimately, however, he preferred to channel available funds into the building of a new sacristy, Michelangelo's Medici Chapel (Fig. no. 11), to house tombs of all the recently deceased members of the family, including his father, Lorenzo the Magnificent. At much the same date, Michelangelo was also commissioned to build a great new library in the cloisters to house the phenomenal collection of manuscripts and printed books that had by now ac-

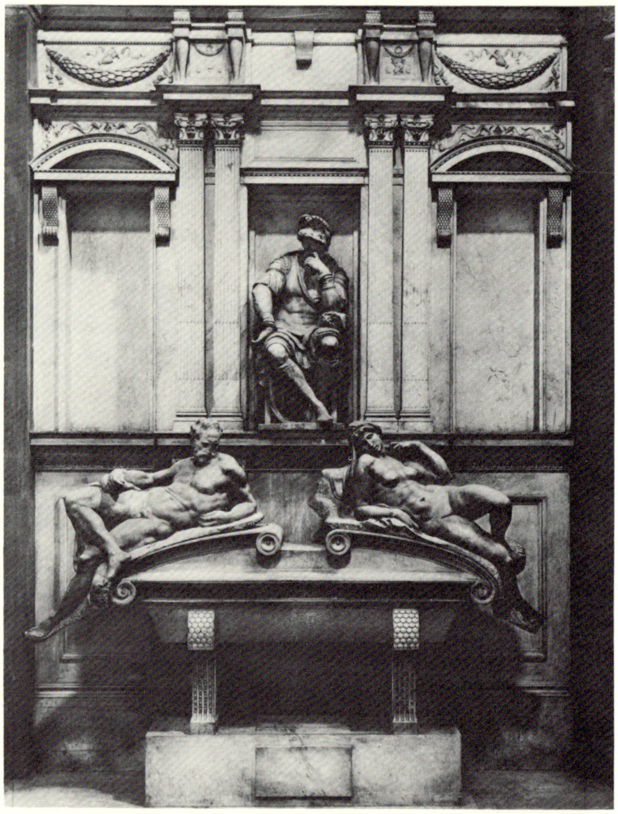

(Fig. no. 11) Michelangelo Buonarroti (1475-1564)

TOMB OF GIULIANO, DUKE OF NEMOURS

New Sacristy (Medici Chapel), San Lorenzo, Florence
(Ed.ne Alinari)

(Fig. no. 12) Andrea Verrocchio

TOMB OF PIERO AND GIOVANNI DE' MEDICI (Detail)

Old Sacristy, San Lorenzo, Florence.
(Photograph, courtesy of the author)

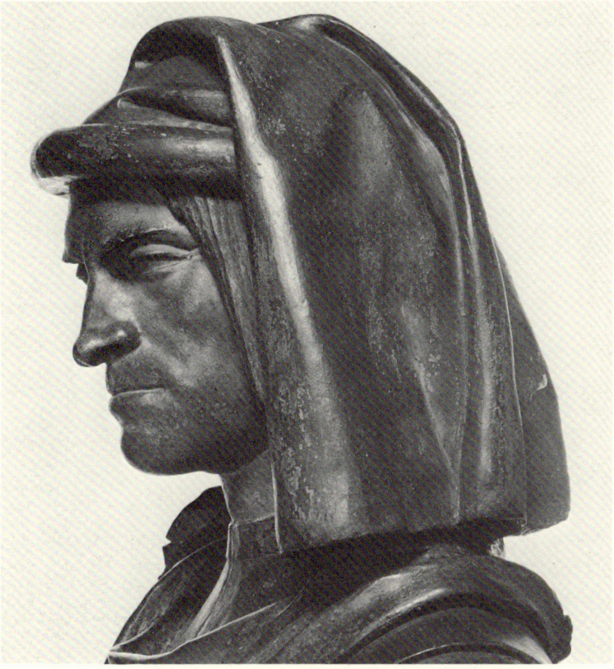

(Fig. no. 13) Andrea Verrocchio (1436-1488)

LORENZO THE MAGNIFICENT

National Gallery of Art. Samuel H. Kress Collection, 1943

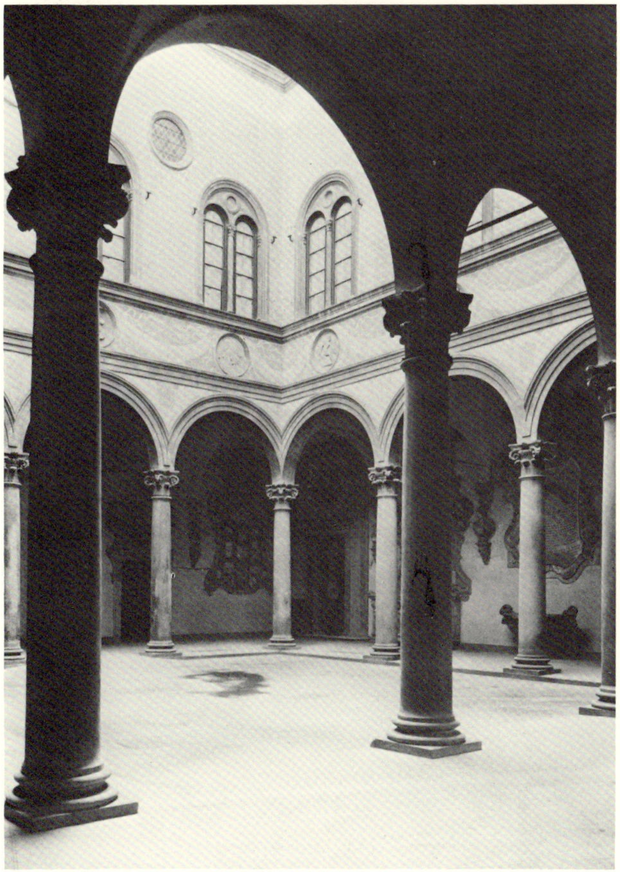

(Fig. no. 14) Bartolommeo di Michelozzo (1396-1472)

COURTYARD, MEDICI PALACE

Florence (Ed.ne. Alinari)

cumulated. No doubt Leo intended these two great schemes to recall the achievements of his ancestor, Cosimo, in Brunelleschi's Old Sacristy and Michelozzo's Library in San Marco.

In 1523 another Medici, Giulio (1509-1535), was elected Pope Clement VII. His reign was overshadowed by political difficulties which resulted in the Sack of Rome by the German emperor in 1527 and a revolt in Florence in favor of a republican government, which Clement had to crush. He was responsible for continuing pressure on Michelangelo to complete the two schemes in San Lorenzo. In Rome, he employed Sebastiano del Piombo as official portrait painter and was the earliest patron of Benvenuto Cellini, who designed his coinage, commemorative medals, papal seals, and jewelry. Clement showed a percipience common to his family in spotting the talent of Cellini, who was to be one of the principal sculptors and goldsmiths of the century and was later patronized by the Medici duke, Cosimo I, in the 1540's.

Propaganda and Mannerism

Pope Clement VII (Cat. no.44) regained control of Florence from the short-lived republican government by laying siege to the city in 1529 with the troops of the German emperor, Charles V. An illegitimate Medici cousin, Alessandro (1511-1537), was installed as governor with the title of duke, which was henceforth to be hereditary. Alessandro turned into the worst sort of tyrant, unscrupulous and debauched; he was murdered in 1537 by Lorenzino, a distant cousin, and a new duke, Cosimo I (1519-1574), was chosen by Emperor Charles V.

During this first troubled decade of Medici rule in Florence little attention could be paid to the arts. One or two commissions for frescoes in Medici villas were given to the Mannerist painter Pontormo, and he and Vasari (Cat. no.252) painted a number of strikingly original portraits of past and present members of the family. The sculptor Bandinelli finished his group of *Hercules and Cacus* in 1534, but it was immediately unpopular because of its symbolic connection with the Medicean tyranny. He also received commissions for a pair of monumental tombs for the Medici popes, Leo X and Clement VIII, in Rome (Santa Maria sopra Minerva).

Cosimo I (Cat. no. 1) came to the throne in the midst of a conspiracy — a last manifestation of the republican spirit in Florence — which he crushed with ruthless violence; thereafter, however, he managed to establish a stable and peaceful, though despotic, regime. By 1540 he was in a position to commence a program of rebuilding and redecorating and to dispense new artistic commissions. Henceforth, art in Florence was to be in the service of the ruler and a close circle of courtiers. In an age that lacked the mass media we know today, works of art played an important role in the communication between ruler and subject. The demand for art as political propaganda and the glorification of the regime was the primary factor in the continuation of artistic traditions in Florence for the next two centuries. With this change in the patrons' motivation went a change in the character of art produced in the city. Florentine art became "court art." Intellectual and emotional intensity that made demands on the spectator was replaced by the detachment and virtuosity of Mannerism. The emphasis on precious materials, luxurious superficialities, and sheer feats of craftsmanship was exemplified by the works and writing of Benvenuto Cellini. By the middle of the century, the same aims were apparent in a salt-cellar of precious metals (or in a piece of jewelry) as in a major public statue or painting. The art of Cellini, or of the painters Bronzino and Vasari, is characteristic of this era of patronage. Practically speaking, all of their output was for Cosimo and his son Francesco.

An interest in elegantly landscaped gardens outside the palaces and villas of the Medici led to an emphasis on garden sculpture, frequently of a humorous kind: fountain figures piped to spout water at every angle and evocative, naturalistic grottoes with trick waterworks, peopled with animals or birds, occupied the attention of all the top sculptors. A whole new range of ideas and imaginative possibilities was thus opened, to a great extent replacing the typical Early Renaissance concentration on tomb sculpture. The Medici set a fashion which spread to many other parts of Europe by the end of the sixteenth century.

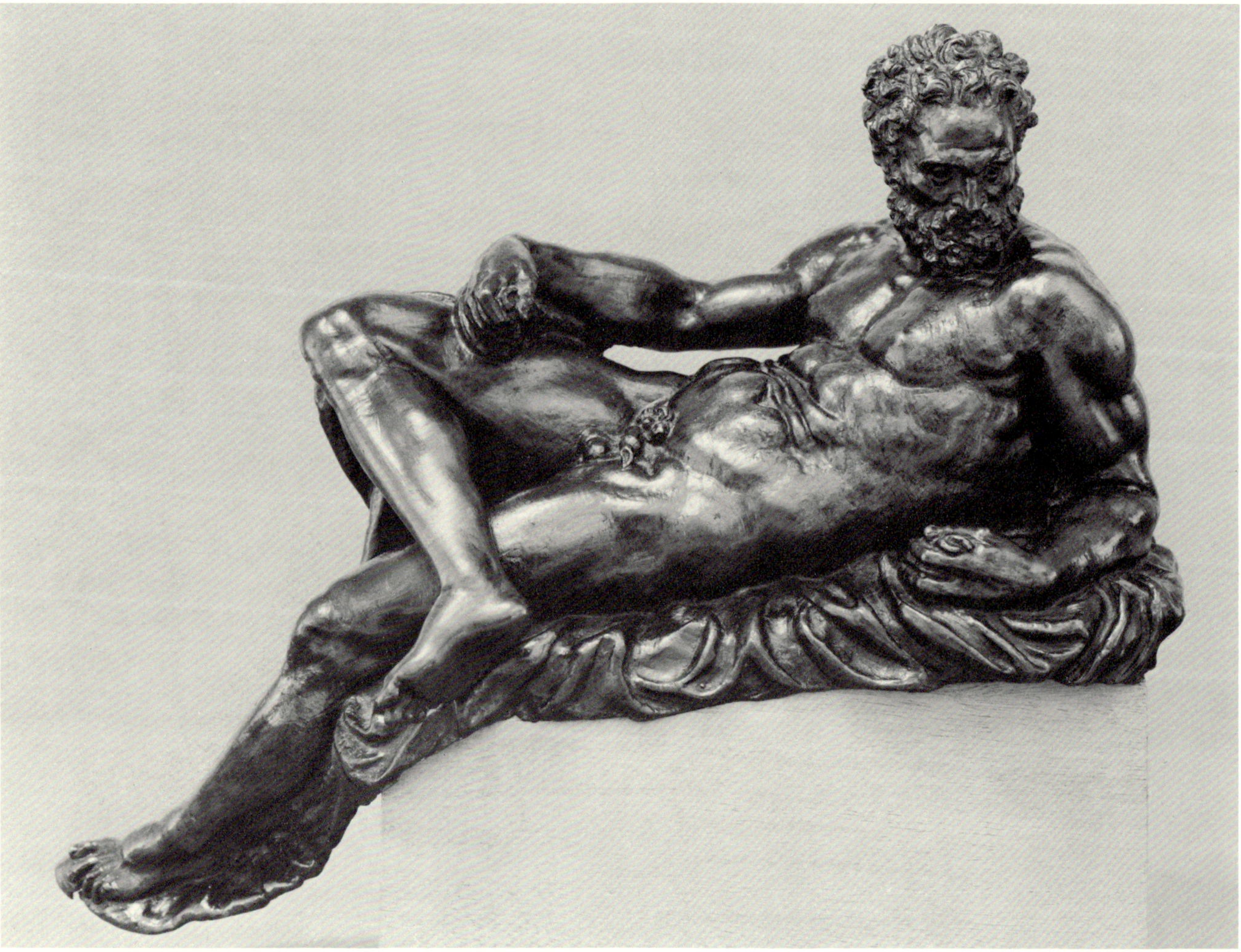

(Fig. no. 15a) Italian (Florence), 1550-1575

EVENING

Lent anonymously (Cat. no. 7).

The most important architectural schemes were the building of the Ducal Offices (Uffizi) by Vasari and the adaptation by Ammanati of the old Pitti Palace to accommodate Cosimo and his family. Painting and sculpture transformed the inside of the Palazzo Vecchio into a fitting seat of government; the choir of the Cathedral was redesigned with sculpture by Bandinelli. A tapestry manufactory was established, with the best Flemish weavers who could be hired, to produce the necessary wall-hangings from cartoons by leading artists. Painting and sculpture were otherwise focused particularly on portraiture of the ruling family and their courtiers, as exemplified by the work of Bronzino.

The Collector's Cabinet

Although Cosimo I did not die until 1574, he retired from the active management of family affairs in 1565. This responsibility he delegated to his son Francesco (1541-1587). Francesco, however, was uninterested in the affairs of Tuscany, and the central government rapidly deteriorated. His interests lay elsewhere. He was fascinated by the natural sciences and conducted many of the affairs of state from the laboratory bench, unwilling to interrupt his experiments. Some of these were relevant to the decorative arts. For example, he discovered how to melt rock crystal to permit the easy molding of *objets d'art* (instead of the laborious process of carving crystal in its natural state) and how to reproduce porcelain imported from China (Cat. no.179). Nearby, in the newly-constructed Uffizi, he installed a number of artists in fully-equipped studios to supply the needs of his court; goldsmiths' work was probably the most significant product here, and in this capacity Cellini was employed by Francesco. These studios continued in production with successive generations of craftsmen recruited from all over Europe, drawn by

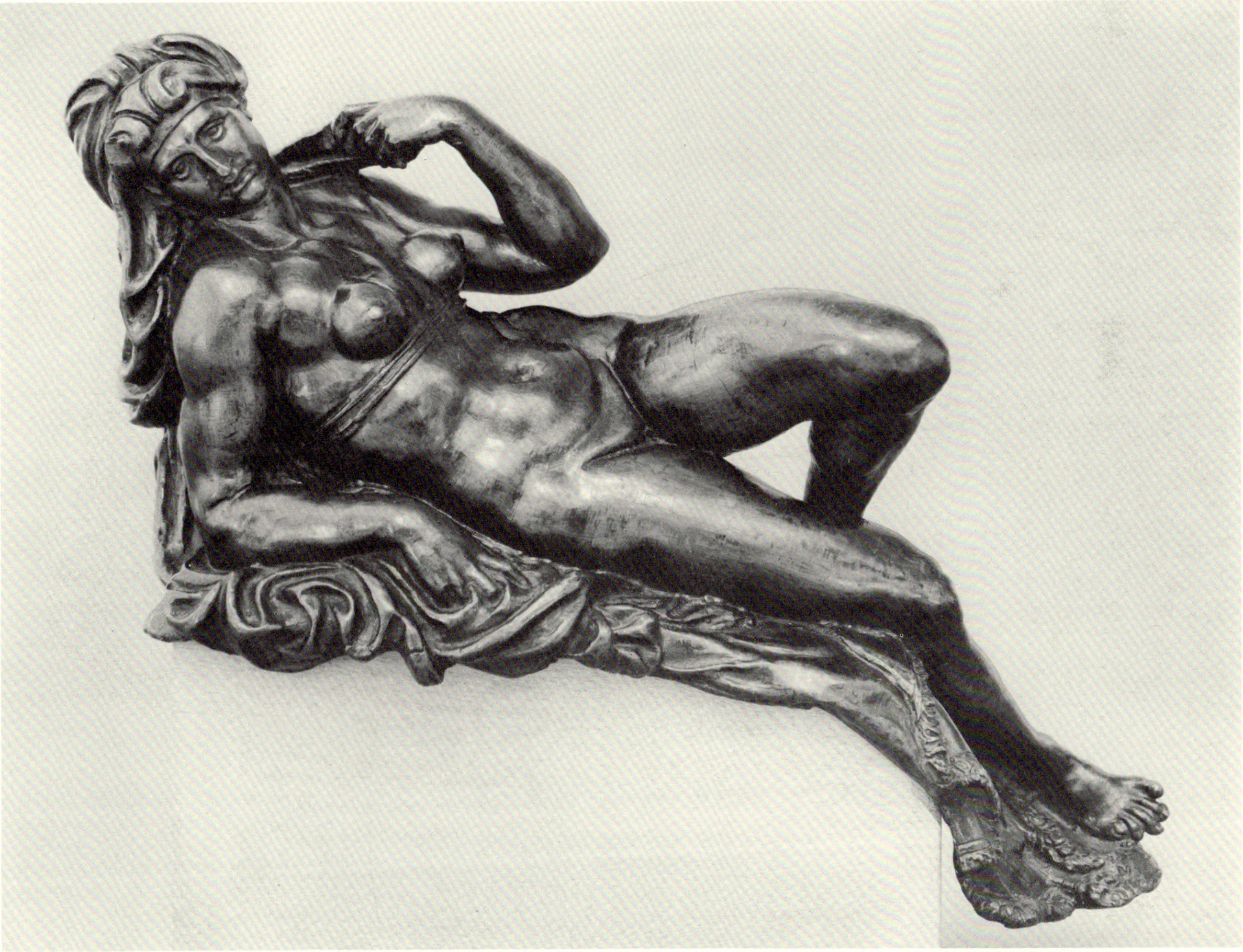

(Fig. no. 15b) Italian (Florence), 1550-1575 period of Cosimo I

DAWN

Lent anonymously (Cat. no. 7).

Michaelangelo died 1564

the rich rewards and exciting opportunities that the Medici could offer.

After Francesco's marriage and assumption of power he lived in the Palazzo Vecchio (Cosimo having retired to the Pitti Palace.) Here he built for his personal enjoyment a collector's cabinet that was probably modeled on the study of Piero the Gouty in the old Medici Palace. A series of exquisite, late-Mannerist paintings depicting the arts and sciences decorate the doors of the wooden cupboards lining the walls of this *studiolo,* while its corners contain niches for eight handsome bronze statuettes. They were commissioned from separate artists, probably to expedite production, and constitute an invaluable cross-section of painting and sculpture in Florence about 1570. In the cupboards of the *studiolo* was stored a private museum of natural curiosities and artifacts in precious materials for the delectation of Francesco and his intimates.

Not all Francesco's funds and energies were absorbed by the decorative arts on a small scale. As fate would have it, he was the patron who presided over a complete revival of the art of sculpture in Florence (indeed in all of Italy and ultimately throughout Europe) in the person of Giovanni Bologna. This immigrant from Flanders rapidly proved himself to be capable of all but rivaling the great Michelangelo. By 1565 he was in a position to model his first masterpiece, the world-famous *Mercury,* as a diplomatic gift for use in the negotiations of Francesco's marriage. Then, in quick succession, he produced a brilliant group as a pendant to Michelangelo's own *Victory* for display at the wedding celebrations, *Samson* and a *Philistine* (Victoria and Albert Museum) for a Medicean fountain, and the *Rape of the Sabine Women* for the Piazza. Between them, the artist and his patron wrought a greater change in the outward appearance of the city than anyone since the days of Donatello and Cosimo the Elder. Other sculptors such as Ammanti, Danti, Bandini, and Poggini also enjoyed Francesco's favor. He must be accounted one of the greatest patrons of this art that Florence had ever seen.

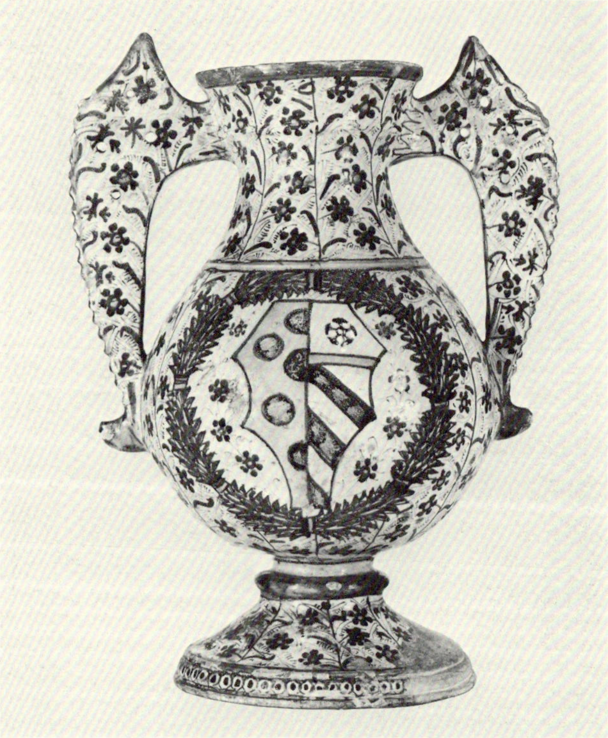

(Fig. no. 16) Italian (Florence), ca. 1470

MAJOLICA VASE WITH THE MEDICI/ORSINI ARMS

Lent by The Detroit Institute of Arts. Presented to Russel A. Alger House by the Women's Committee (Cat. no. 161).

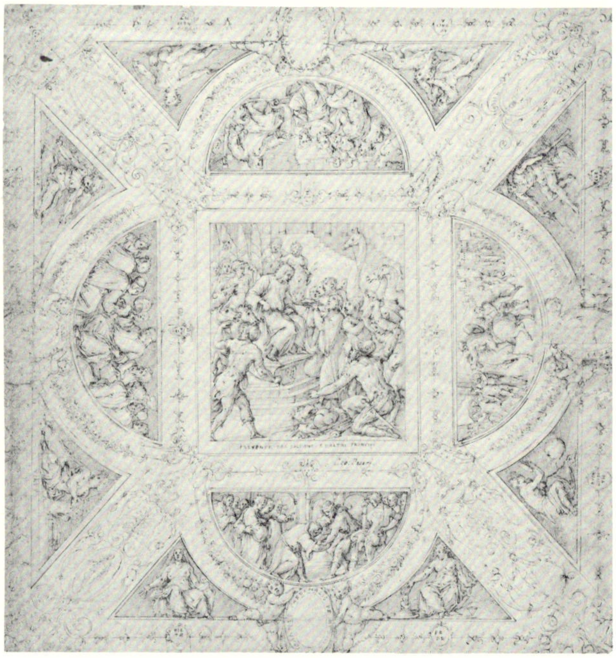

(Fig. no. 17) Giorgio Vasari

CEILING DESIGN FOR THE SALA DI LORENZO IL MAGNIFICO

Lent by The Pierpont Morgan Library, New York (Cat. no. 252).

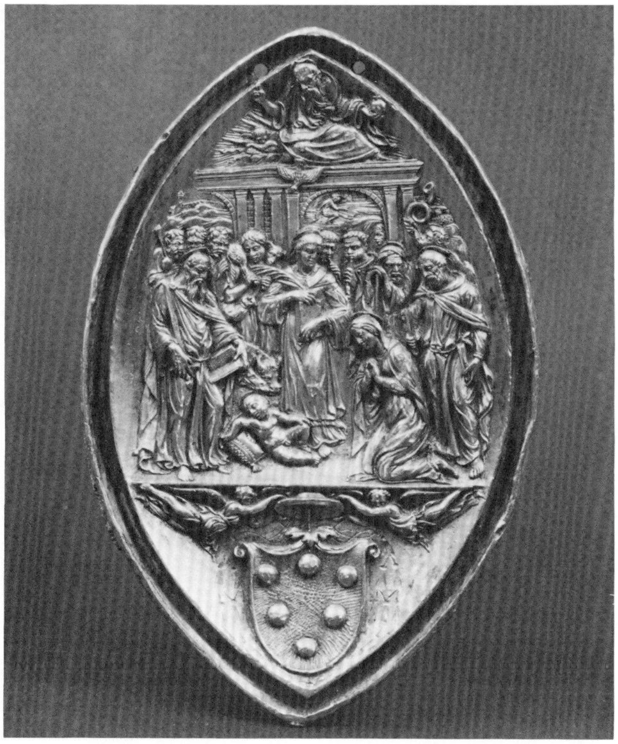

(Fig. no. 18) Attributed to Lautizio da Perugia

PRESENTATION MODEL FOR THE SEAL OF CARDINAL GIULIO DE' MEDICI (1478-1534)

Lent by Heinz Schneider, Cleveland, Ohio (Cat. no. 44).

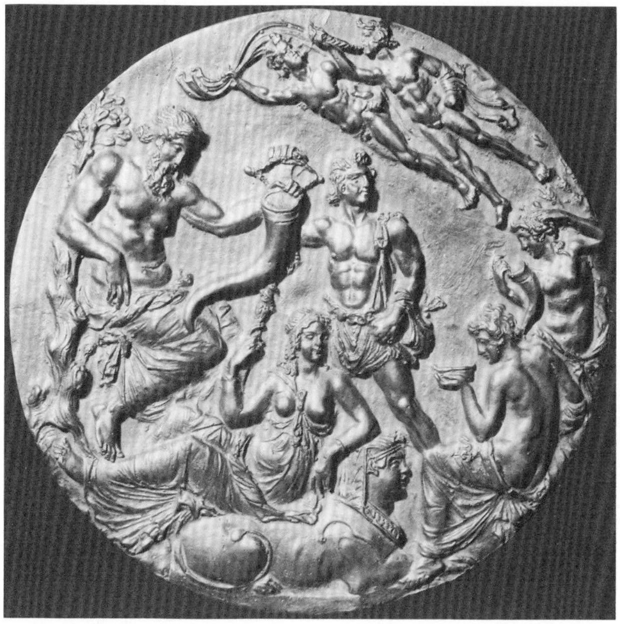

(Fig. no. 20) Italian (Florence), 15th century

TAZZA FARNESE

Lent by University Art Galleries, University of California, Santa Barbara. The Morgenroth Collection (Cat. no. 10).

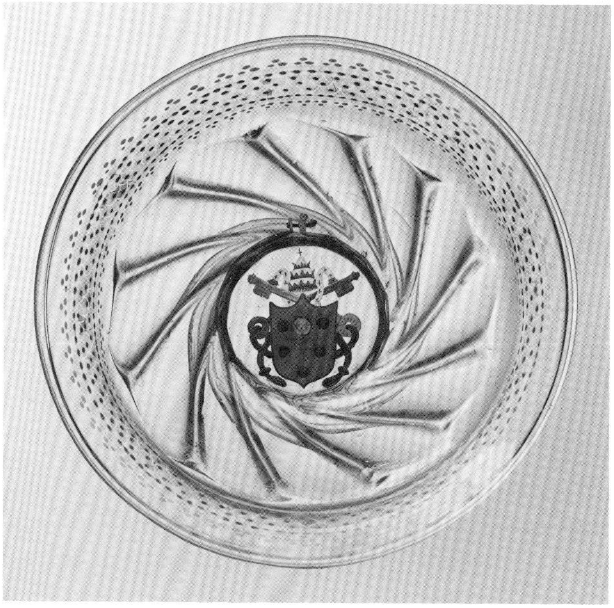

(Fig. no. 19) Italian (Venice), early 16th century

TAZZA

Lent by The Metropolitan Museum of Art, New York. Gift of J. Pierpont Morgan, 1917, (Cat. no. 194).

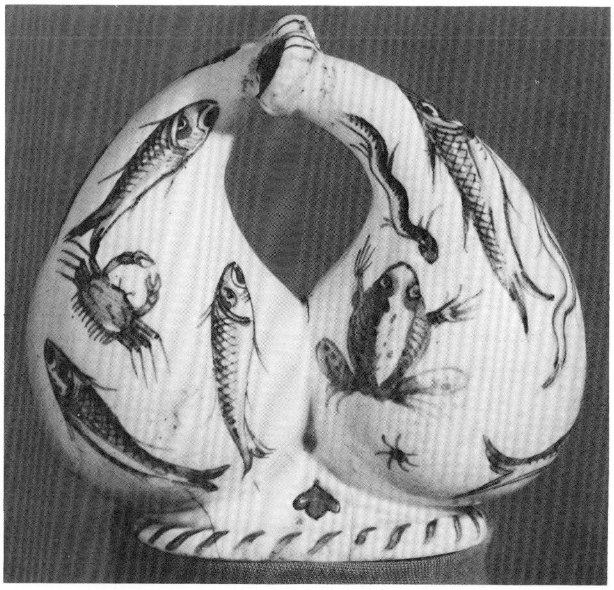

(Fig. no. 21) Italian (Florence), ca. 1575

"MEDICI" PORCELAIN CRUET

Courtesy, Museum of Fine Arts, Boston. Gift from the Estate of Professor Henry Williamson Haynes, through Miss Sarah H. Blanchard (Cat. no. 179).

Small Bronzes

William D. Wixom

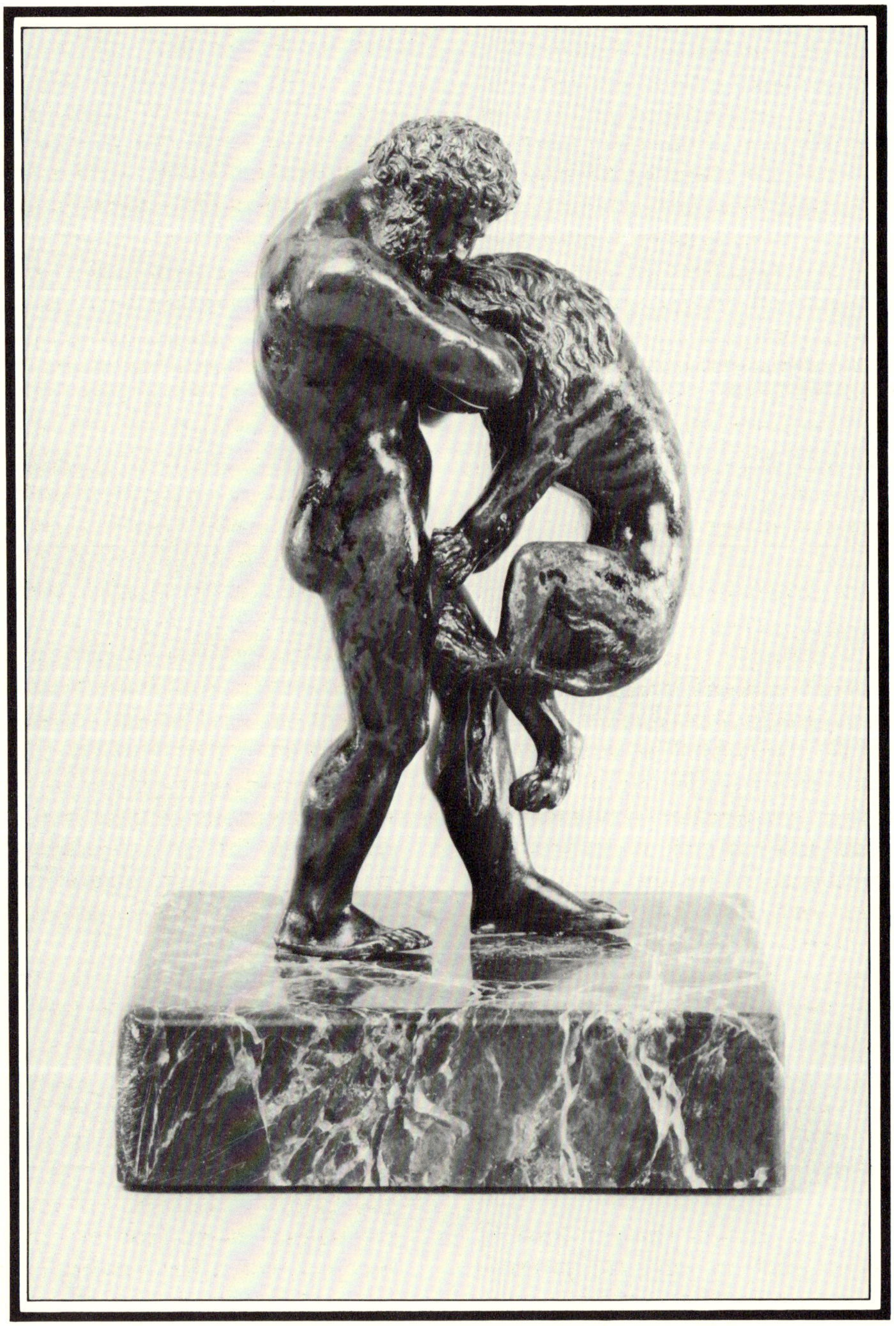

(Fig. no. 22) Attributed to Camelio
(Vettor di Antonio Gambello)

HERCULES AND THE NEMEAN LION

Lent by The Cleveland Museum of Art.
Gift of Dr. and Mrs. Sherman Lee in Memory of Paul Mallon
(Cat. no. 5).

A delight and pleasure of a cultivated Renaissance man — whether prince, churchman, scholar, or humbler lay-connoisseur — derived from the ownership and contemplation of bronze portrait medals, statuettes, small reliefs, and related objects. This taste had its basis in a revived interest in classical antiquity which began with collection of ancient bronzes and which led in some instances to collections which combined both ancient and Renaissance bronzes. This potential juxtaposition, together with a growing admiration for newly discovered ancient sculptures, was important for Renaissance artists, who, along with the humanist scholars, were eager to recreate ancient forms, however selected and adapted. Indeed, many Renaissance bronzes were purposefully evocative of visual, literary, and philosophical elements perceived from the rediscovered remains of the earlier period. Sometimes this eclecticism was so subtle that Renaissance works were later regarded as ancient. However, intentional deception was rare, and reduced replicas of ancient monumental works such as the Flora Farnese (Cat. no. 8) were barely more frequent; antiquity was generally a source for inspiration rather than imitation.

Bronze, an alloy chiefly of copper and tin, is easily cast in either simple or elaborate shapes. Hard and durable once the casting has cooled, it preserves much of the subtlety of the model. Renaissance casting techniques were already described in the sixteenth century by Gauricus, Cellini, and Vasari. Both solid and hollow casts were produced through the "lost wax" method in which a mold was formed around a wax model and the melted-out wax was replaced by molten bronze. If the cast was hollow, a clay core with a thin layer of wax was used. Hollow casts not only conserved an expensive metal but also avoided some of the technical problems of solid casts. The use of the piece mold presumably began in the late fifteenth century. The evolution of this technique, with all its details and subtleties, was complex, but it was significant because it made possible the preservation of the model which, as a result, could be rendered in other materials, including wood.

Bronze reliefs were usually the products of similar casting techniques, as were the portrait medals. The wax originals of the medals were mounted on slate or wood disks; the obverse and reverse sides, being separate, allowed the production of separate molds of fine ash or gesso mixed in water. When hardened, these molds were lifted away from the models and then joined to receive the molten bronze.

Frequently a particular composition, whether a statuette, relief, or medal, occurs in a series of examples, sometimes referred to as variants. In rare cases, a common original model is reflected in these multiple casts, presupposing in some cases the use of piece molds. For reliefs and medals, casts were often made in molds taken from earlier castings. The further removed a cast was from the original or first model, the more diffuse the details and the smaller the cast, resulting from the shrinkage of the cooling bronze. In all categories, many details distinguish an early cast from a late one, including nuances of modeling, surface imperfections in casting, repairs and fills, use of bases, width of borders, and thickness of casts.

Two of the most important aspects in the creation of Renaissance bronzes were those of finish and patina. The bronze fresh from casting was cleaned and cleared of ducts and air vents; flaws were plugged, rough surfaces smoothed, textural distinctions heightened, and details sharpened through sensitive tooling. Then the surfaces were treated, changing the medium brilliance of the raw bronze to a color desired by both the artist and his patron. To accomplish this the bronze was either fire-gilded (mercury gilded) or darkened with a patina applied chemically, with lacquer, or through natural corrosion and dulling of the surfaces. Some of the patinas must have been initially inspired by ancient bronzes. No Renaissance bronze was intentionally left unpatinated.

The independent bronze statuette of the Renaissance developed first in Florence in the latter part of the fifteenth century, although its origins can be traced in the statuettes made by Ghiberti (1378-1455) and Donatello (ca. 1386-1466) as portions or details of their larger works. In the next generation of Florentine sculptors, Pollaiuolo (ca. 1432-1498) and Bertoldo (ca. 1420/30-1491) were essentially responsible for the revival of this ancient art form (Cat. no. 20).

A charming example of an independent bronze statuette in the humanist taste is the diminutive *Dancing Boy* of ca. 1500 (Cat. no. 3). Though at first glance it could be taken as ancient, it in fact combines elements from several ancient prototypes together with a Renaissance simplification, exquisite surface texture, and enriched dark brown lacquer. This bronze, indeed nearly all the other statuettes in the exhibition, could easily have found honored places in a Renaissance collection of small ancient bronzes such as existed in Padua, Venice, Mantua, or Florence.

Certainly the *Warrior on Horseback* of ca. 1510 (Cat. no. 4) is such a work; it could have been directly inspired by an ancient bronze or by a group from an ancient battle sarcophagus. Yet the character of the modeling, the details, the surfaces, and the black lacquer patina underscore its Renaissance Paduan authorship. Among a total of eight variants, this group is unique in retaining its original rider (these were always cast separately). The perfection of modeling, the proportions, the expressive movement, and the fine patina represent a high and sustained level of quality that would have made this example eminently suitable for the finest humanistic collection.

Some Renaissance bronzes were inspired by ancient coins. The Cleveland *Hercules and the Nemean Lion* (Cat. no. 5) derives from the composition of a Greek coin of Heraclea. The attribution to Camelio (ca. 1455/60-1537), based on stylistic similarities with documented or accepted works by this Venetian sculptor, is not surprising because Camelio was also a goldsmith and medalist as well as Master of Dies in Venice. What a contrast to the Hellenistic contortion of a contemporary group of the same subject lent from Houston (Cat. no. 26). This expressive work, deriving inspiration from another aspect of antiquity and variously attributed to northern Italy and to Florence, is admirable for its three-dimensional composition, for the richness of its gilt surfaces, and for the vivid contrasts of textures.

Several of the later statuettes in the exhibition dating from the second half of the sixteenth century demonstrate a continued inspiration from the ancient world. Yet major stylistic alterations are evident. One key change is seen in the sensuous three-dimensional diagonal movement given to figurative sculptures, the result called *figura serpentinata*. The bronze statuette (Cat. no. 6) after a marble *Ganymede* by Cellini (1500-1571) in the Bargello in Florence is a good example. Cellini reused an ancient marble fragment acquired by Cosimo de' Medici in 1548, adding a head, arms, feet, and a spread-winged eagle to complete the group. In its new context, the ancient work is caught up in a new curvilinear movement in space, suggesting that ancient sources were subject to a subtle assimilation, therefore making detection of ancient models more difficult. This is especially clear in those statuettes which reflect the genius of two of the most inventive Florentine sculptors of the High Renaissance, Michelangelo (1475-1564) and Giovanni Bologna (1529-1608).

Closely related to the statuettes are those bronze objects which often contain figural elements while at the same time having some useful or decorative function. This group includes mortars (Cat. no. 42), palace doorknockers (Cat. no. 40), papal bells (Cat. no. 47), incense burners (Cat. no. 37), altar candlesticks (Cat. no. 35), and various types of containers for the scholar's desk such as inkwells, sandboxes, and writing caskets (Cat. nos. 24, 25). Many of the ornamental motifs on these objects are classically derived. Included in this repertoire are acanthus and laurel leaves, swags with fruit, bucranes, lions' paws, palmettes, shells, and dolphins, as well as such fantastic creatures as centaurs, satyrs, sphinxes, tritons, dragons, marine monsters, and Gorgon or Medusa heads. Some of these classical forms found their way into German and French bronzes as the Renaissance spread northward. The interest of the humanist and his perception of the classical world included also some of the lowliest creatures of nature. The direct casts from nature and those objects closely modeled on nature (Cat. no. 29) are fine examples in Paduan taste with useful functions for the scholar's study.

The earliest category of small and independent Renaissance bronzes to develop was the Italian portrait medal. With sources in ancient Roman imperial medallions, in the small medal of Francesco Carrara of ca. 1390, and in the medallions of ca. 1400 produced for the duke of Berry, Pisanello (ca. 1395-1455) was able to design and model from 1438 to ca. 1449 a series of portrait medals of such outstanding beauty that they set the standard and the conventions for all subsequent medalists. The purpose of making such an object was to commemorate and aggrandize a particular personality by rendering his portrait on the obverse. The reverse usually bore an emblem of the person, an equestrian portrait of him, or a symbolic image referring to his life or aspirations. Two medals, depicting Niccolò Piccinino, condottiere of Perugia, and Leonello d'Este, marquis of Ferrara, are good illustrations of the designs for which Pisanello was noted (Cat. nos. 16, 17). Matteo de' Pasti (active from 1441-1467/8), Sperando of Mantua (ca. 1431-1504), and Bertoldo are represented by medals which continue this tradition.

Allied technically to the medals are the small one-sided reliefs, known as plaquettes. These have connections with some medallic reverses and with some statuettes in their classical origins of subject matter and meaning. Rich in mythology and visual metaphors, the plaquettes were often intended for decoration on inkstands, sandboxes, writing caskets, bases of incense burners, and other modest but useful objects. However, Eric Maclagen suggested caution in assuming all plaquettes had utilitarian purposes. Some of them, he insisted, must have been intended simply as works of art like engravings that were "bought by the humbler amateur who could not afford sculpture or paintings, and were kept and handled and enjoyed for their own sake, in the fifteenth and sixteenth centuries no less than at the present day...."

Several of the earliest bronzes in this category are in fact casts after ancient hardstone carvings. The interior relief of a sardonyx cup from 200-100 B.C., known as the *Tazza Farnese,* was reproduced in a fine Early Renaissance bronze cast made in Florence when the cup was in the collection of Lorenzo de' Medici (Cat. no. 10).

Occasionally a Renaissance print was the transmitter of a classical subject or composition. Of the two circular reliefs related to or from the workshop of the Venetian goldsmith and relief artist Alessandro Leopardi (active after 1482-1522/3), one is of special interest in that it derives its composition and style from an engraving by Mantegna (1431-1506) (Cat. no. 14). The source for the stylistically related *Triumph of Neptune* (Cat. no. 13), not identified in prints, may eventually be found in the world of ancient intaglios.

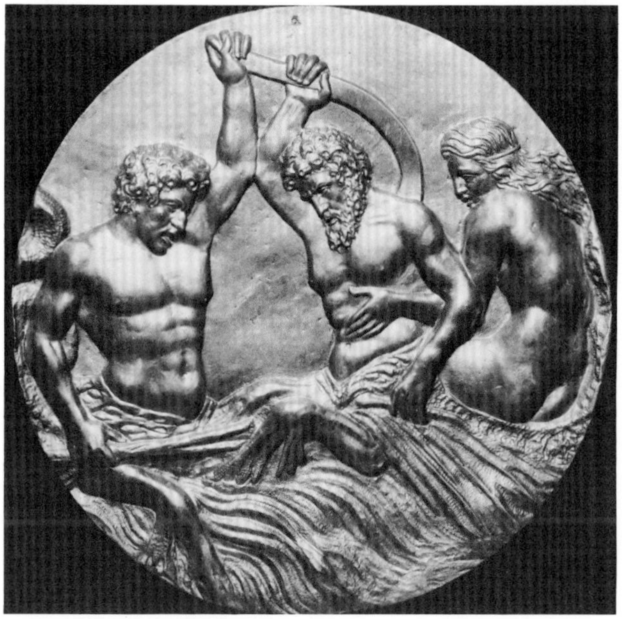

(Fig. no. 23) Italian (Padua), early 16th century

COMBAT OF TRITONS

Lent by University Art Galleries, University of California, Santa Barbara.
The Morgenroth Collection (Cat. no. 14).

Two reliefs reflect the intense humanistic interest of the Gonzaga Court in Mantua. The first is the superb classicistic relief of *Hercules Resting* (Cat. no. 12), attributed to Antico (ca. 1460-1528) on the strength of stylistic similarities with his roundels depicting the *Labors of Hercules.* The second Mantuan work (Cat. no. 11), whose earlier attribution to Donatello has been long abandoned, is the Morgenroth replica of the famous *Martelli Mirror* in London. The composition is notable for its combination of motifs derived from antique gems. The style is that of an artist working in the circle of Antico.

Jennifer Montagu has recently pointed out that humanists, with their keenness for classical texts, were "aware of the veneration which small bronzes had received in ancient times." She quotes Statius (ca. 45-96 A.D.) from his *Silvae* speaking about a small seated Hercules: "I fell deeply in love, nor, though long I gazed, were my eyes sated with it; such dignity had the work, such majesty, despite its narrow limits. A god was he!...Small to the eye, yet a giant to the mind....What preciseness of touch, what daring imagination the cunning master had, at once to model an ornament for the table and to conceive in his mind mighty colossal forms!"

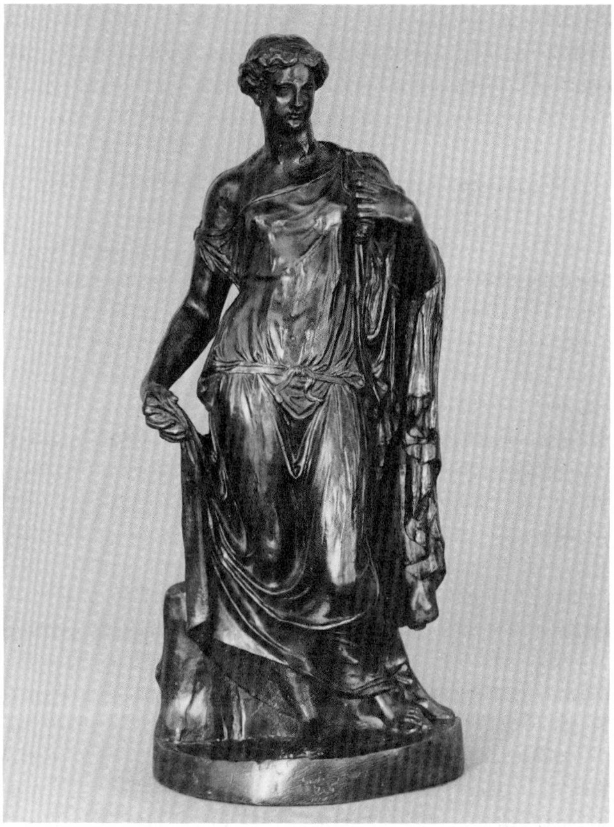

(Fig. no. 24) Italian (Florence), second half of 16th century

FLORA FARNESE

Lent from a private collection (Cat. no. 8).

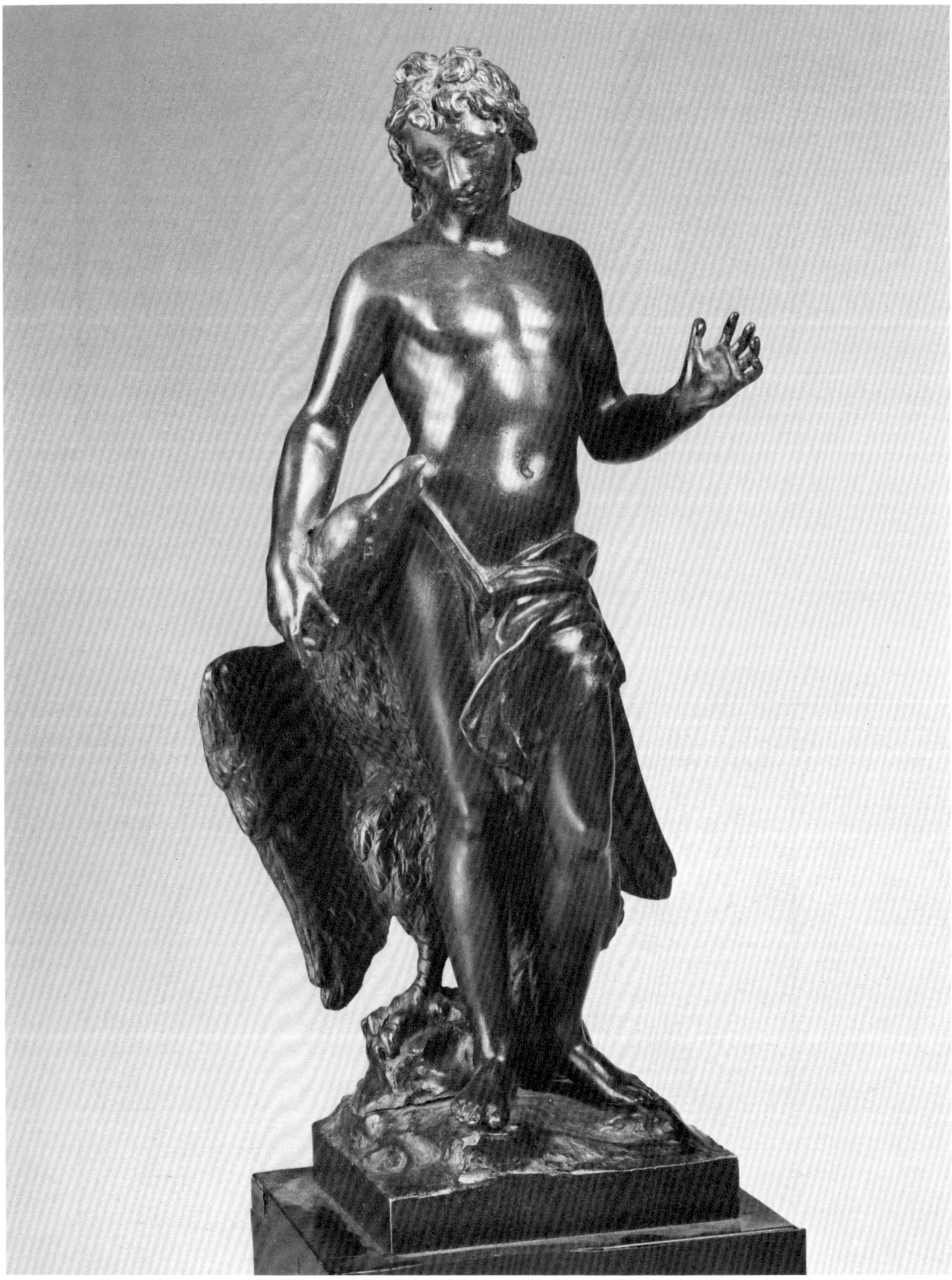

(Fig. no. 25) Italian (Florence), 16th century

GANYMEDE

The Fine Arts Museums of San Francisco.
Gift of E. John and Rose Magnin (Cat. no. 6).

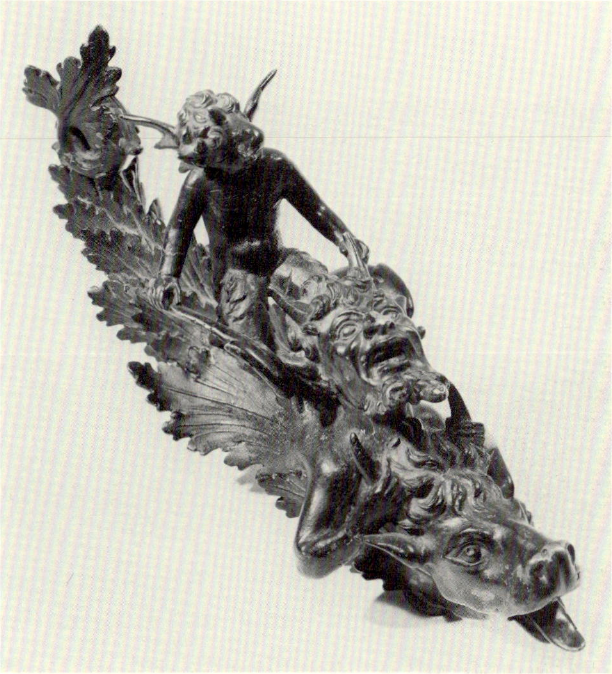

(Fig. no. 26) Andrea Briosco, called Riccio

DOORKNOCKER

Lent by The Cleveland Museum of Art.
Gift of Mr. and Mrs. Severance A. Millikin (Cat. no. 39).

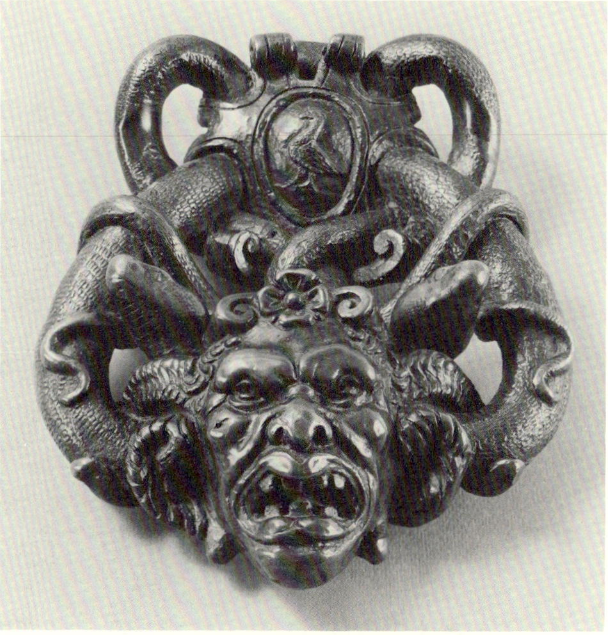

(Fig. no. 27) Italian (Venice), mid-16th century

DOORKNOCKER

Lent by The Cleveland Museum of Art.
Purchase from the J. H. Wade Fund (Cat. no. 40).

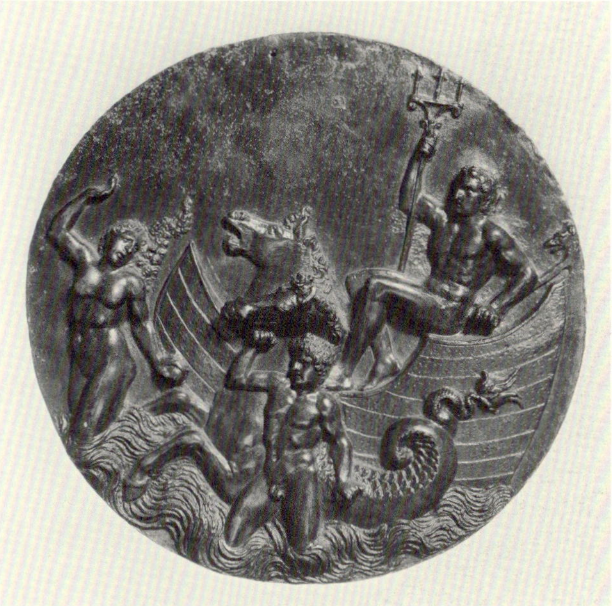

(Fig. no. 28) Italian (Venice), ca. 1500

THE TRIUMPH OF NEPTUNE

Lent by National Gallery of Art, Washington, D.C.
Samuel H. Kress Collection, 1957 (Cat. no. 13).

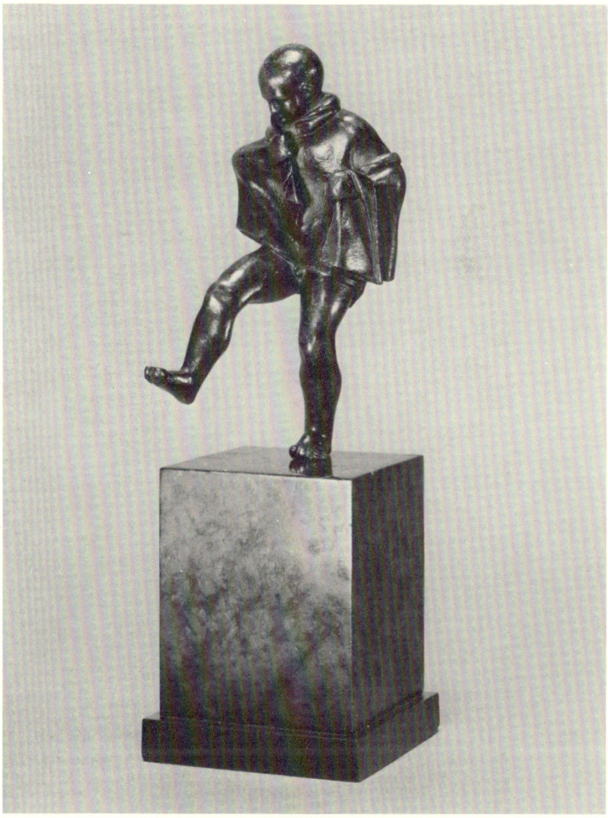

(Fig. no. 29) North Italian, ca. 1500

DANCING BOY

Lent by The Cleveland Museum of Art.
The Severance and Greta Millikin Purchase Fund (Cat. no. 3).

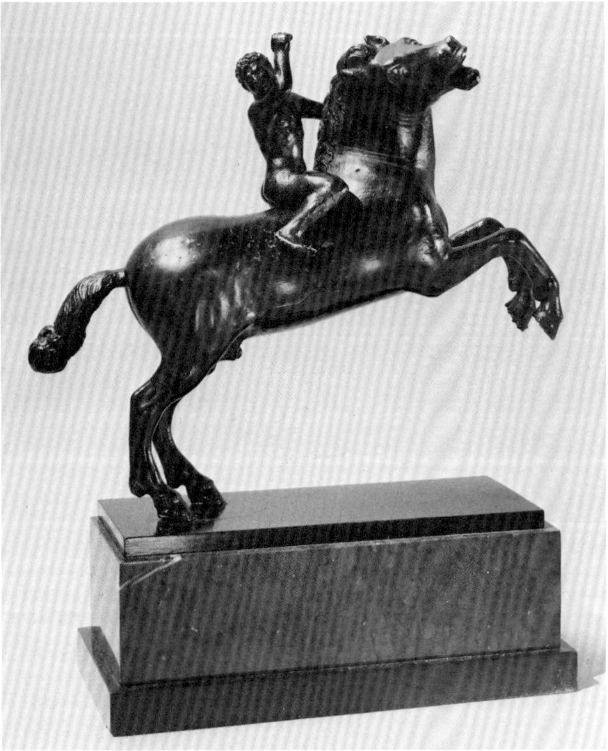

(Fig. no. 30) Italian (Padua), ca. 1510

WARRIOR ON HORSEBACK

Lent by Heinz Schneider, Cleveland, Ohio (Cat. no. 4)

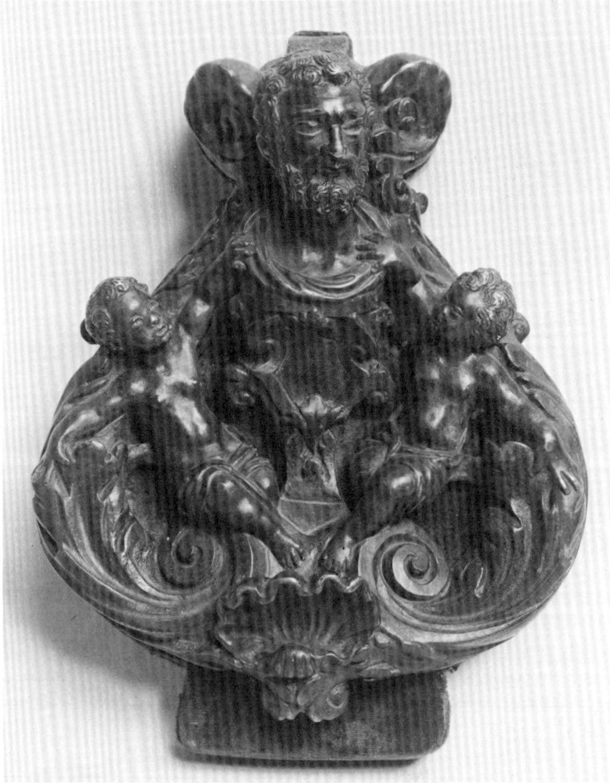

(Fig. no. 31) Italian (Venice), late 16th century

DOORKNOCKER

The Fine Arts Museums of San Francisco.
Gift of Mr. Castillan, Paris (Cat. no. 41).

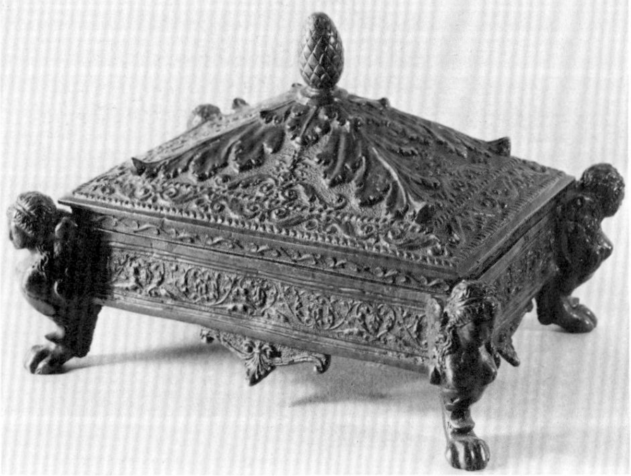

(Fig. no. 32) Attributed to Severo da Ravenna

WRITING CASKET

Lent by The Cleveland Museum of Art.
Purchase from the J. H. Wade Fund (Cat. no. 24).

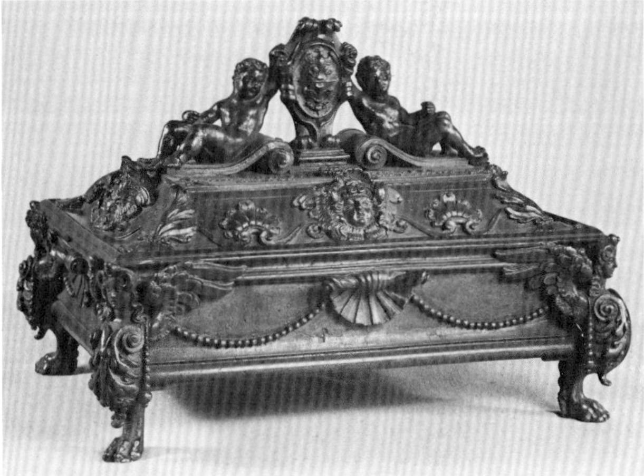

(Fig. no. 33) South Italian, ca. 1570

INKSTAND

Lent by Victoria and Albert Museum, London (Cat. no. 32).

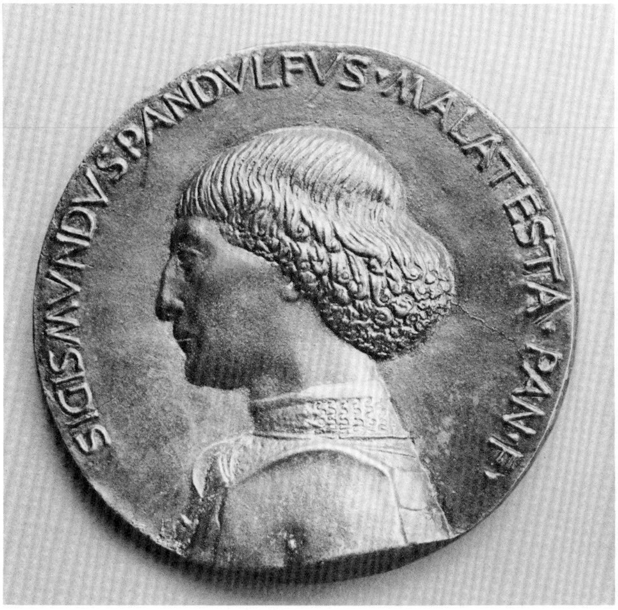

(Fig. no. 34) Matteo de' Pasti

DOUBLE-FACED MEDAL OF SIGISMONDO PANDOLFO MALATESTA

Lent by William Rockhill Nelson Gallery and Atkins Museum of Fine Arts, Kansas City. Nelson Fund (Cat. no. 18).

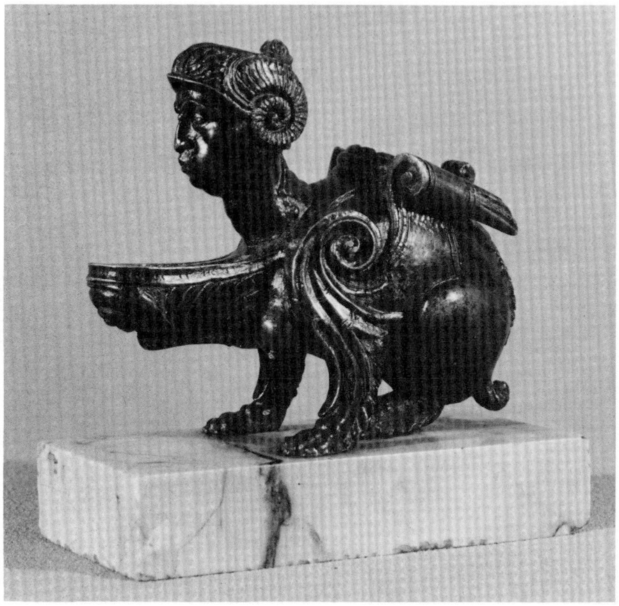

(Fig. no. 36) Attributed to Andrea Briosco, called Riccio

OIL LAMP IN THE FORM OF A SPHINX

Lent by Cyril Humphris, London (Cat. no. 34).

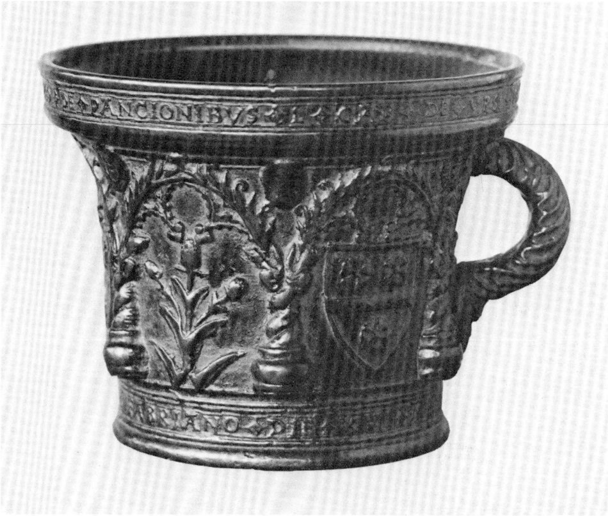

(Fig. no. 35) Italian (Fabriano), dated 1465

MORTAR

Lent by Victoria and Albert Museum, London (Cat. no. 42).

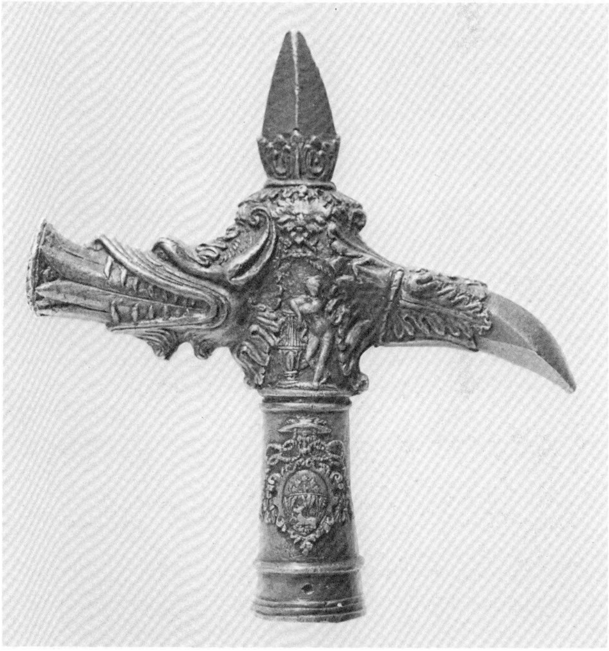

(Fig. no. 37) Italian (Rome), mid-16th century

JUBILEE HAMMER

Lent anonymously. (Cat. no. 48).

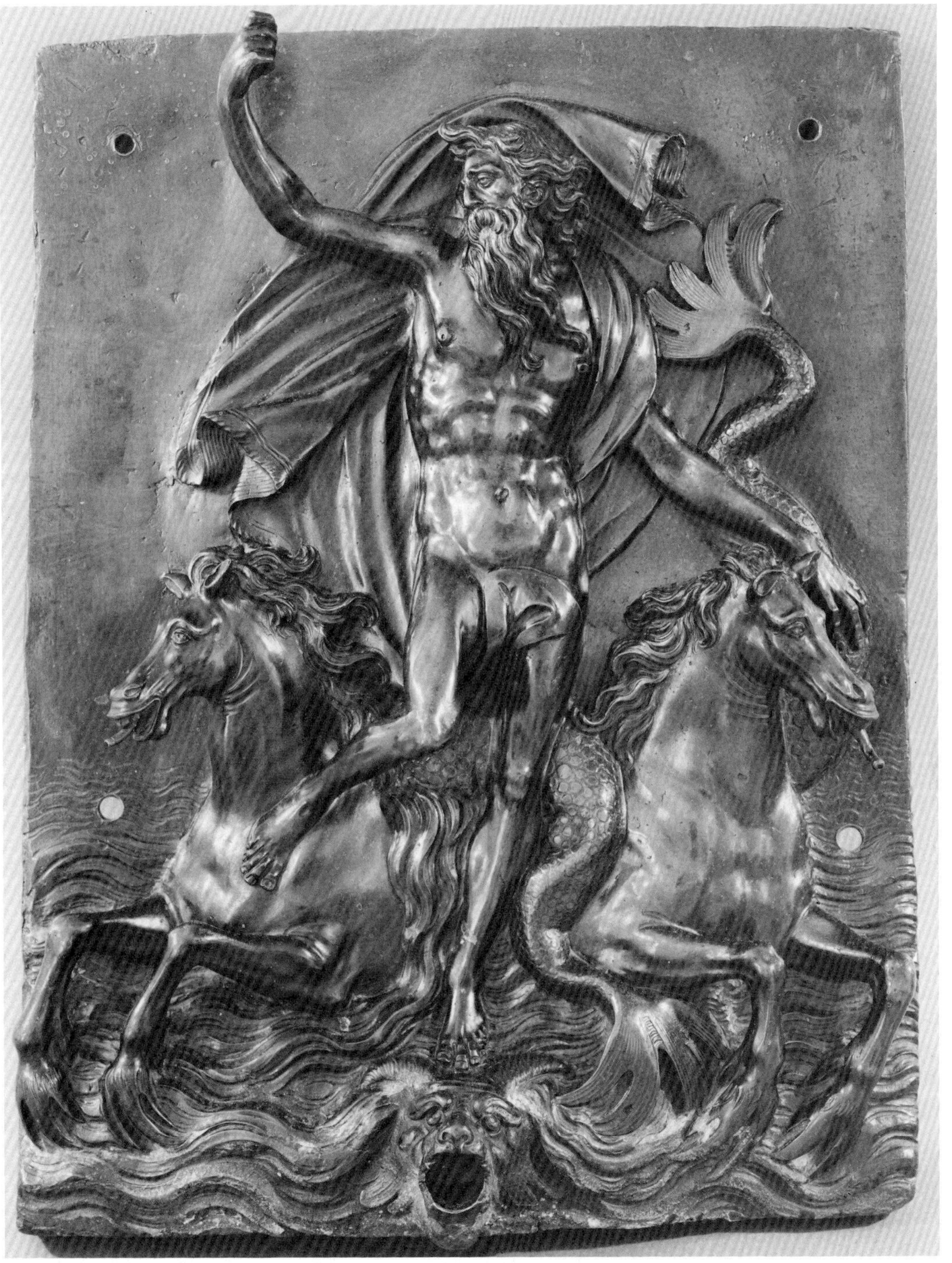

(Fig. no. 38) Italian (Florence), 1560-1570

WALL FOUNTAIN: NEPTUNE

Lent by The Toledo Museum of Art.
Gift of Edward Drummond Libbey (Cat. no. 49).

Goldsmiths' Work and Jewelry

Yvonne Hackenbroch

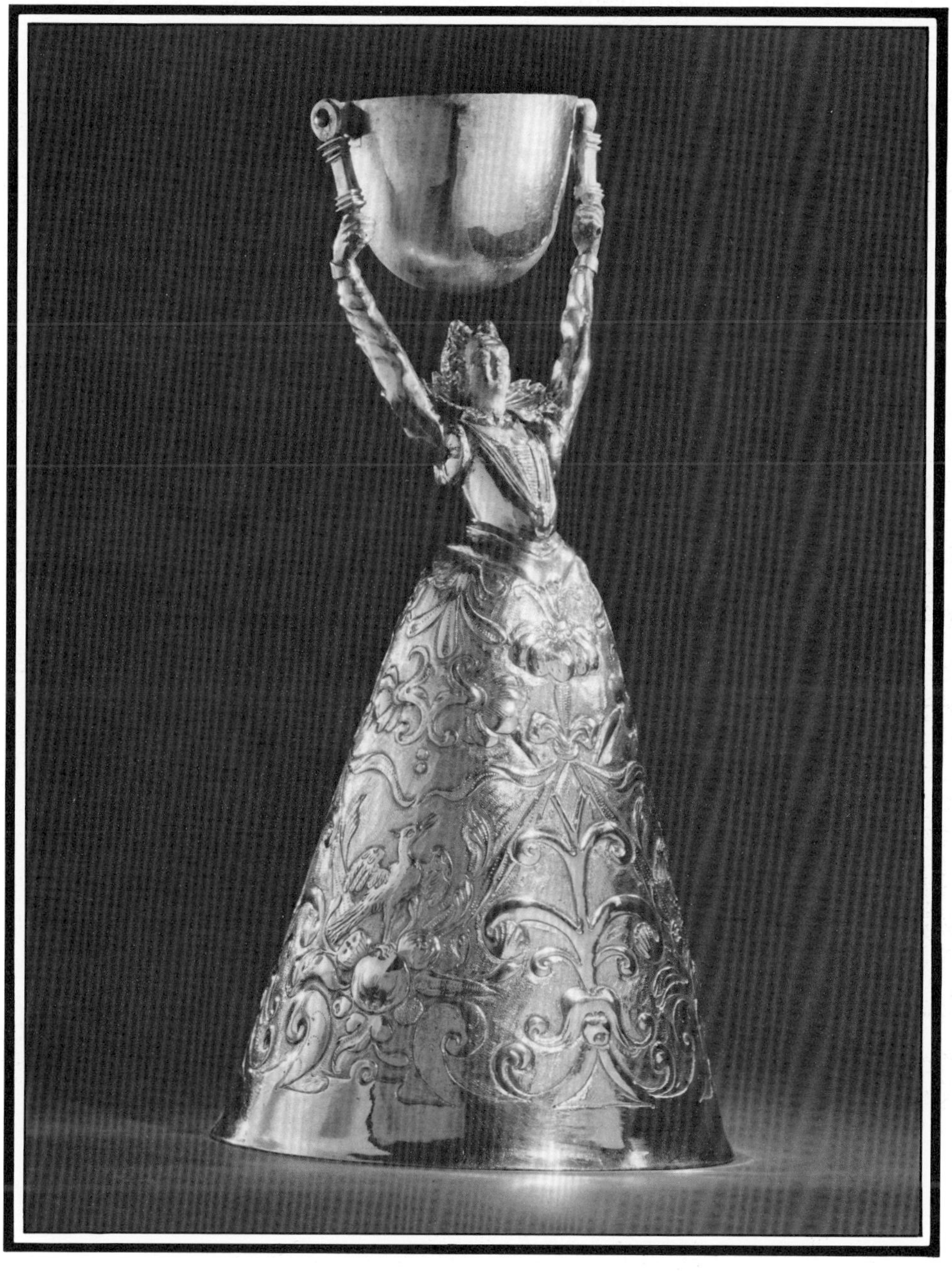

(Fig. no. 39) German (Augsburg), ca. 1600

WAGER CUP

Lent by The Metropolitan Museum of Art, New York.
Gift of J. Pierpont Morgan, 1917 (Cat. no. 65).

The goldsmith occupied a leading position among artists of the Renaissance period because of his extremely varied activities. These included the training of future painters, sculptors, and even architects, many of whom would spend some of their formative years in his workshop. This practice linked the various arts more closely together at this time than during any other period and placed the goldsmith at the center of most artistic enterprises. With the dawning of a new age, the goldsmith changed patrons. He no longer filled the needs of church and clergy primarily but was drawn into the recently formed circles of humanist collectors, patrician families, and merchant bankers. The sudden influx of gold, silver, and precious stones from the New World brought further changes. This new bounty, unloaded in the ports of Spain, contributed in no small measure to the increasing sophistication of the goldsmith's art. Thereafter he was frequently called upon to contribute objects that would enhance the life-style of a client, or reflect personal taste or ambition. Although the works of art assembled in this exhibition cannot be wholly representative of the period, they nevertheless indicate basic trends. The hazards of survival were great, for this period included such catastrophes as the Sack of Rome in 1527, the Massacre of the St. Bartholomew Night in Paris in 1572, and the Sack of Antwerp in 1576 — events that were followed by wholesale looting and destruction.

Our brief review of goldsmiths' work begins with a silver-gilt dish of Spanish early sixteenth century origin (Cat. no. 72). The generous use of silver was typical in a country where its supply was plentiful, and the Moorish influence, as seen in the embossed ornament, was frequently present on the Iberian peninsula. Also from Spain comes a chalice with a bell-shaped bowl set in an open-work calyx above a hexagonal stem and knot, originating about 1540 in Castille or Aragon (Cat. no. 52). Liturgical silver harking back to Gothic prototypes was evidently far more traditional in form and decoration than secular objects, although some of the conventional foliage was treated with a new boldness.

In Germany, the great center for work in gold was Nuremberg where the painter Albrecht Dürer, himself the son of a goldsmith, executed some of the most admirable drawings available for use by these artists. Few such drawings survived the rough handling in busy workshops, but those which did are of rare sensitivity. The following generation knew how to give more permanence to their inventions. Initially making woodcut engravings, they soon changed to the more precise copper engravings published in Nuremberg that enjoyed a wide circulation among practicing goldsmiths. A few such engravings are shown, including one by Wenzel Jamnitzer, who may be considered the most prominent among the German masters (Cat. no. 264). Jamnitzer, born in Vienna in 1508, came to Nuremberg before 1534 where he established a flourishing workshop, assisted by members of his large family.

His engraved designs introduced late Renaissance form and ornament to southern Germany. Jamnitzer developed a special taste for making casts of reptiles and insects. Although a first impetus might have been similar work cast in bronze by Riccio in Padua, Jamnitzer concerned himself with smaller forms and creatures better suited for casting in silver. He introduced this *style rustique* to the goldsmith and produced such well-known objects as the table bell at the British Museum, once owned by Horace Walpole at Strawberry Hill. After 1548, German guild laws required that plate be stamped with a maker's mark, usually in combination with the assay mark of the town. These regulations render it possible to separate Jamnitzer's own work from that of other masters who used his inventions as points of departure for their own creations. The maker's mark of W. Jamnitzer appears on a silver-gilt frame that might originally have formed part of one of those complex coffrets that had been made for members of noble families (Cat. no. 89).The female allegories, rendered in low relief, are named ARITHMETICA, GEOMETRIA, PERSPECTIVA, ARCHITECTVRA. They appear amidst intricate cartouche work forming a profuse, though well-organized, background.

Also from Nuremberg is a wager cup of about 1600 by an unidentified maker (Cat. no. 65). Such drinking vessels, formed by the voluminous skirt of a lady who is holding a second, smaller cup in her raised hands, were used to amuse dinner guests who were expected to drink out of both cups without spilling the wine.

One of the original set of twelve silver-gilt dishes of about 1570, known as the Aldobrandini Tazzas, is included in the present exhibition (Cat. no. 70). Each one shows the figure of an emperor, in this case Augustus, standing above the dish on which the high points of his reign are chased in four crowded scenes separated by fluted columns. Similar flutings appear again on the high foot, which was altered on six of the other known examples but remains untouched on this one. Beneath each dish, the arms of Cardinal Ippolito Aldobrandini are lightly pricked in, more like an afterthought than a sign of original ownership. They refer nevertheless to one of the earliest owners, elected pope under the name Clement VIII in 1592. The tazzas are of imposing character and size and must have fitted very appropriately in a Roman palazzo. They illustrate the international phase of late sixteenth-century art, when goldsmiths traveled widely and their work lost some of its local characteristics. In the absence of hallmarks, one can only speculate that the set was executed by a group of artists, probably from Augsburg, who were also well acquainted with decorative engravings from France and Italy.

A rare exhibit of French origin is the bronze frame of a purse (Cat. no. 91). The ornamental vocabulary closely resembles that seen on engraved title pages and goldsmiths' designs by Pierre Woeiriot (1532-ca. 1596). As most of Woeiriot's (Cat. no. 269) work was published in Lyons, we are tempted to consider this purse as a work from provincial France, made during the third quarter of the sixteenth century.

Also from provincial France come the painted Limoges enamels. It is interesting to note that during the fifteenth century the themes of such enamels had been predominantly liturgical. But during the sixteenth century an increasing interest in humanist themes manifested itself, stimulated through the writings and teachings of great humanists like Guillaume Budé and through the productions of the printing presses of Paris and Lyons. Woodcut illustrations contributed essentially to introduce themes of Greek mythology and Roman history to these enamel painters, who also excelled in portraiture. They painted on copper in grisaille or in colors, usually on a dark ground, and occasionally heightened with gilding. Typical of this popular art from Renaissance France is the casket showing the Labors of Hercules mounted within gilt metal (Cat. no. 200). The enamels are attributable to a member of the Nouailher family of painters, active about the middle of the sixteenth century. Typical of the style of Pierre Reymond, on the other hand, is the pair of circular salts with mythological hunting scenes that include the tragic death of Actaeon (Cat. no. 201).

Among the works combining several materials is an agate cup on baluster stem with silver-gilt mounts (Cat. no. 59). The goldsmith, Jörg Ruel of Nuremberg, active after 1598, may have availed himself of carved agate from the workshop of a Hapsburg court artist in Prague. Ruel added at one end of the bowl a cast silver-gilt figure of a double-tailed mermaid resting on two dolphins, at the opposite end a horned animal's head. Another more modest combination is a carved coconut converted into a tankard by means of silver-gilt mounts that a Bamberg goldsmith added about the turn of the century (Cat. no. 62).

The combination of different materials was certainly not confined to Germany alone. Such preferences reflect the broadening horizons that had been stimulated by a taste for rare substances, natural or artificial, precious or semi-precious. Among these were Chinese Ming porcelains (Cat. no. 67), nautilus shells from the Pacific Ocean, mother-of-pearl and baroque pearls, foreign or local pottery (Cat no. 64), amber, particular stones, and Venetian or domestic glass. These combinations manifest the new trend of collectors in the later sixteenth century, a period when several famous *Kunst-* and *Wunderkammern* were founded by heads of state. Two objects originating from Elizabethan England show that this fashion for combining the rare with the familiar found an equally enthusiastic response there. One example is a pillar salt (Cat. no. 77) made of crystal and silver-gilt, with London maker's marks, 1577: a bird in a shaped shield. Even rarer is a tall, cylindrical flagon of speckled marble complete with a marble cover, in unmarked silver-gilt mounts of about 1580 (Cat. no. 63). These mounts comprise a domed base, encircling bands with embossed strapwork, a bold tapering handle ascending from a smaller scroll, a cast thumb-piece, and a cast spherical finial.

Also from Elizabethan England comes a large rosewater dish of 1599 with the Cholmondeley arms centered and executed in translucent enamel (Cat. no. 75). The allover design alternates chased and embossed decoration. Repeated on the border and central boss are oval reserves with dolphins in rippling water, a motif characteristic of a sea-faring nation. Tudor roses on scrolling stems are flat-chased with an astonishing freedom of movement that recalls a pattern seen in Elizabethan embroideries.

Most of the jewels included are pendants, and some of these come from Spain. We are relatively well-informed concerning Spanish jewelry designs, particularly those from Barcelona. This is due to the survival of the *Libres de Passanties* of the Barcelona guild of goldsmiths. These drawings, most of which are signed and dated, originated with apprentices who submitted them to gain their freedom as members of the guild. They allow us to date Spanish pendants, and occasionally rings as well, with a certain measure of accuracy. The pendants in the form of an eagle (Cat. no. 102) and a dolphin (Cat. no. 103) fit within the stylistic range of drawings dating from the last quarter of the century. They show once again the generous weight of Spanish goldsmith's work and the lavish use of emeralds and other precious stones, usually in cabochon form.

Far more ambitious, in both design and execution, is the nef-shaped pendant of a three-masted carrack (Cat. no. 104). Each mast has a white sail, the hull is made of crystal backed by mottled brown varnish, and a sea serpent forms the keel. The three voyaging sailors are attired in contemporary costumes of brightly colored enamel. Small rubies and pearls add a touch of romance to this nef, the design of which is based on a type similar to that of Christopher Columbus's flagship, the *Santa Maria.* Such nef pendants were often intended as *ex-voto* offerings, to assure the safe return of a passenger from a perilous sea voyage.

Typical of the Mannerist period in Germany is a pendant centering Diana accompanied by one of her hounds (Cat. no. 97). The tiny group, executed in enameled gold, is placed before a niche or tabernacle supported by columns and surrounded by openwork scrolls hung with pearls. The general design follows those seen in engraved pattern books (Cat. no. 271) which circulated from workshop to workshop. They enabled the jeweler to prepare pendants and hold them in semi-readiness until a client would decide upon the particular figure he wished to have displayed on the platform at the center.

These few remarks, intended to tie together objects from different backgrounds and countries, can do no more than indicate the contribution of the goldsmith to the artistic scene of the sixteenth century. We have observed the versatility of his technique and his receptiveness to the changing demands which affected the form and decoration of objects that were to enhance the life-style of a new society.

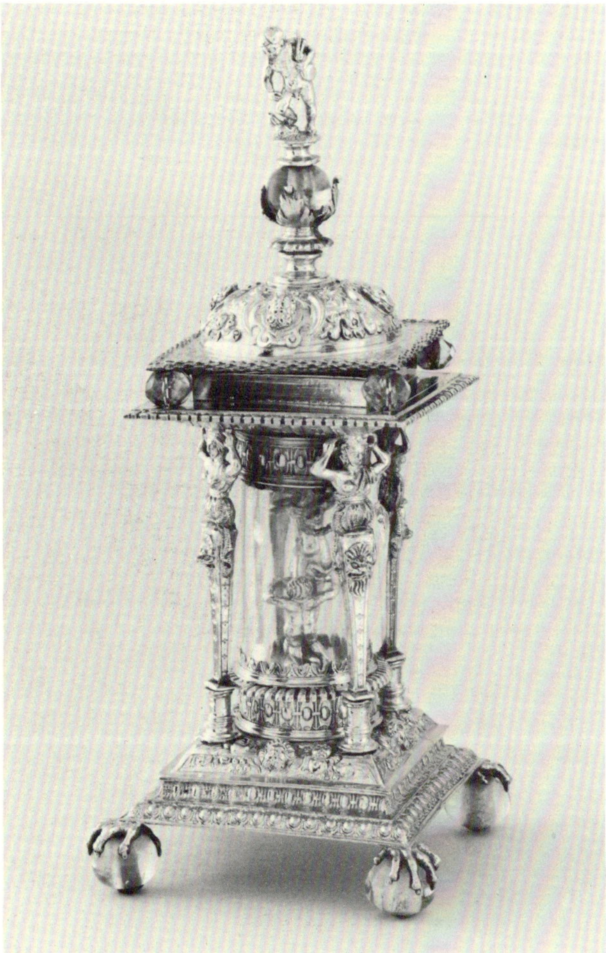

(Fig. no. 40) English (London), 1577-1578

PEDESTAL SALT WITH COVER

Courtesy, Museum of Fine Arts, Boston. Theodora Wilbour Fund No. 2, in memory of Charlotte Beebe Wilbour (Cat. no. 77).

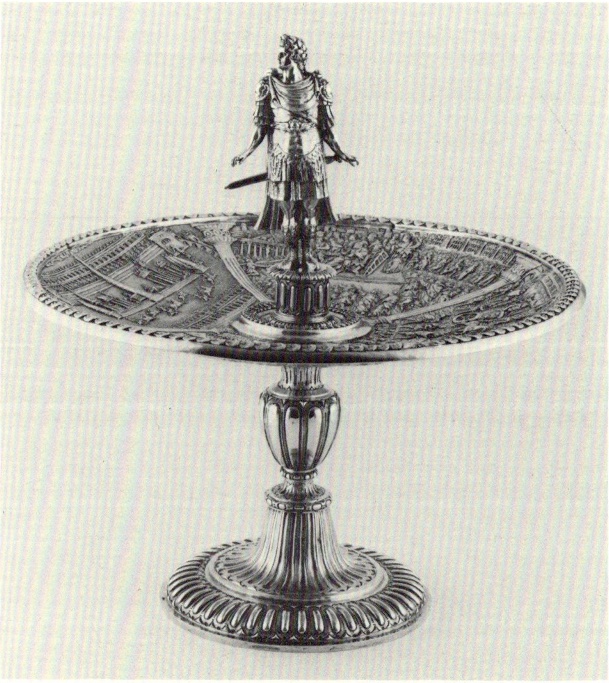

(Fig. no. 41) Italo-German, ca. 1575

TAZZA

Lent by The Minneapolis Institute of Arts. The James Ford Bell Family Foundation Fund, the M. R. Schweitzer Fund, and The Christina N. and Swan J. Turnblad Memorial Fund (Cat. no. 70).

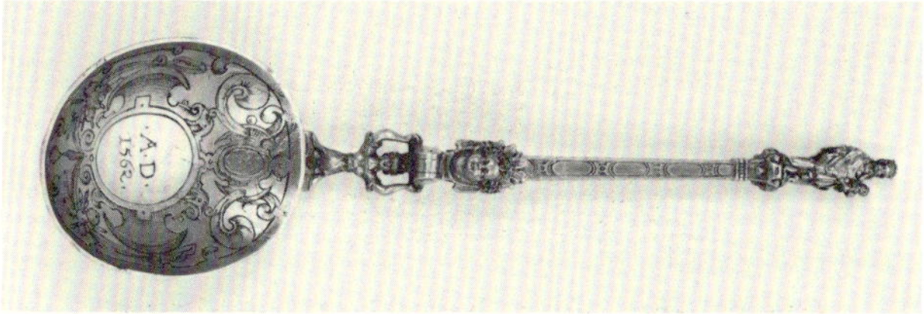

(Fig. no. 42) Flemish (Tournai), dated 1562

COMBINED FOLDING SPOON WITH FORK AND TOOTHPICK

Lent by Victoria and Albert Museum, London (Cat. no. 82).

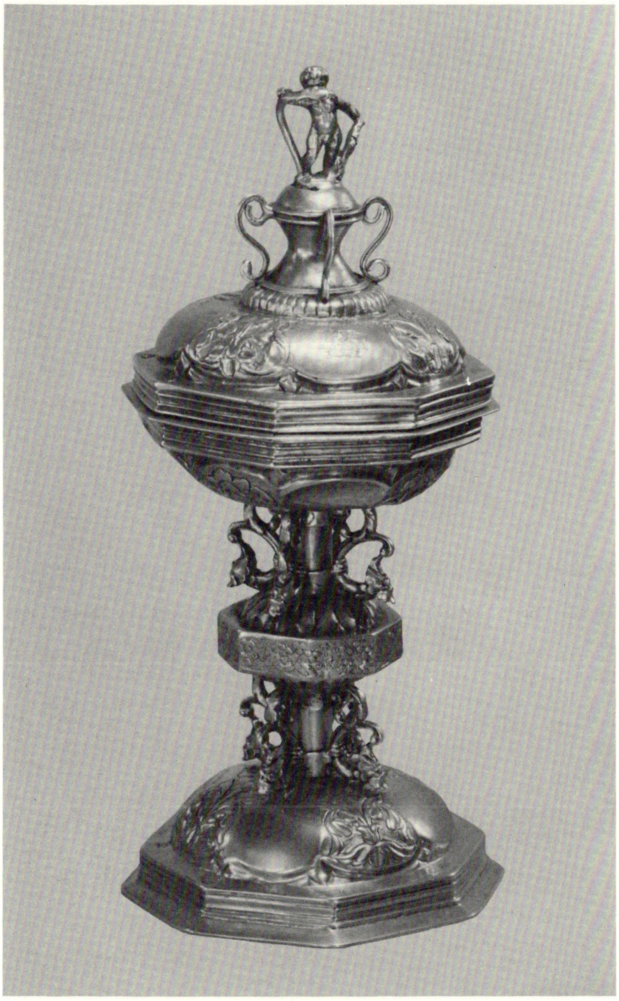

(Fig. no. 43) English (London), 1542

HENRY VIII SALT

Lent by The Worshipful Company of Goldsmiths, Goldsmiths' Hall, London (Cat. no. 76).

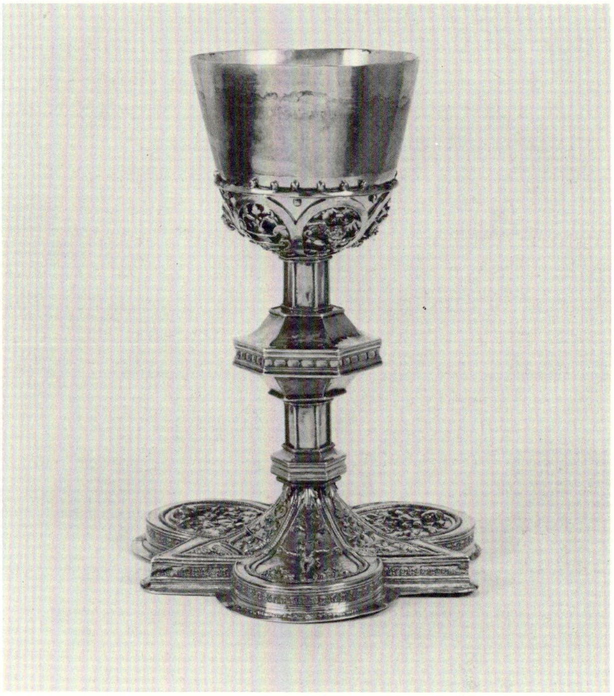

(Fig. no. 44) Spanish, ca. 1540

CHALICE

Lent by Victoria and Albert Museum, London (Cat. no. 52).

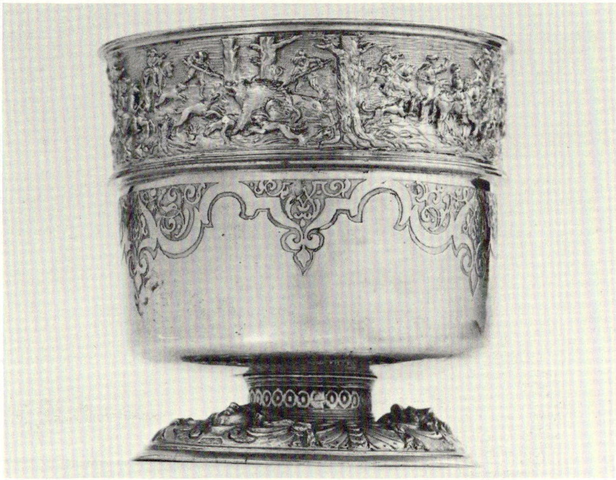

(Fig. no. 45) German (Nuremberg), mid-16th century

FOOTED CUP

Lent anonymously (Cat. no. 58).

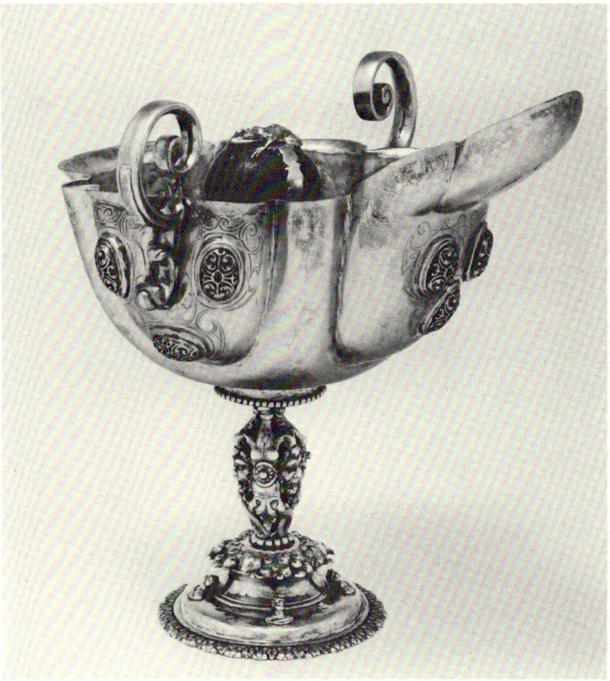

(Fig. no. 46) M. Urbiola

POISON CUP

Lent by The Art Institute of Chicago. Gift of Mrs. Chauncey McCormick. (Cat. no. 68).

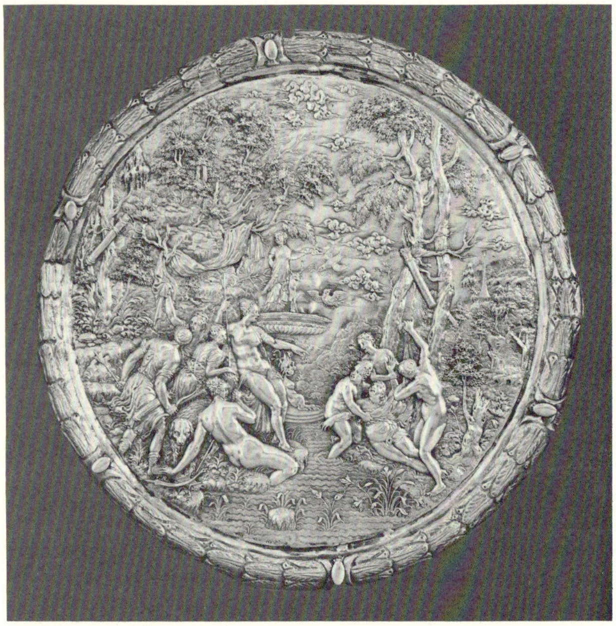

(Fig. no. 47) Attributed to Hans Jamnitzer

EMBOSSED PLAQUE FROM A TAZZA

Lent by Victoria and Albert Museum, London (Cat. no. 69).

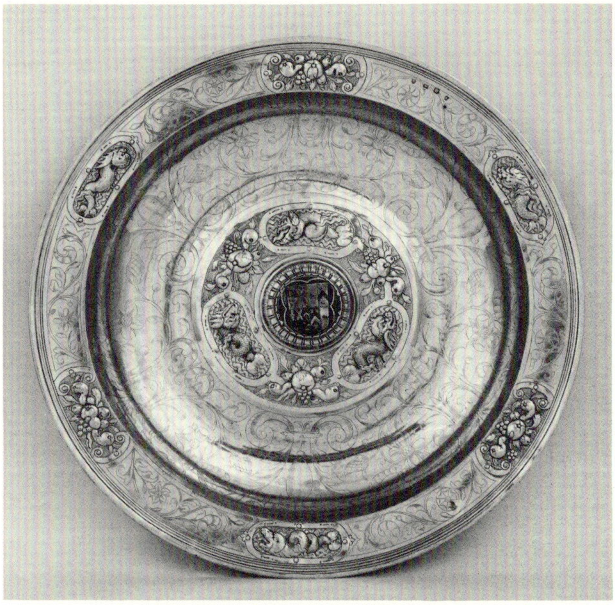

(Fig. no. 48) English (London), 1599

ROSEWATER DISH

Courtesy, Museum of Fine Arts, Boston.
Gift of Richard C. Paine (Cat. no. 75).

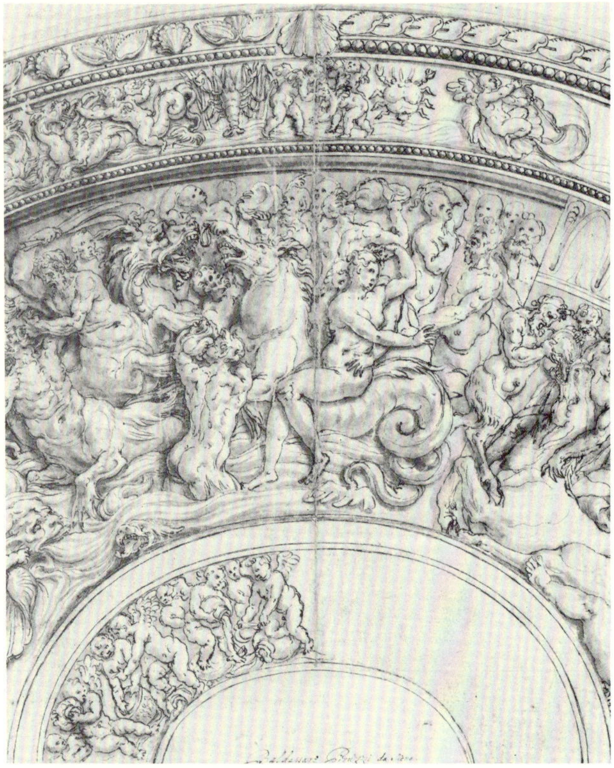

(Fig. no. 49) Italian, 16th century

TWO DESIGNS FOR A DISH

Lent by The Pierpont Morgan Library, New York
(Cat. no. 251).

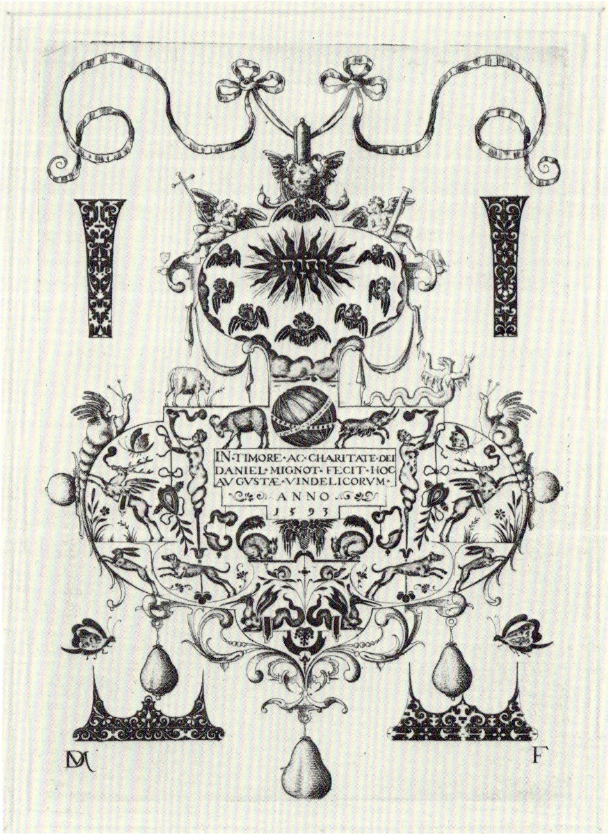

(Fig. no. 50) Daniel Mignot

DESIGN FOR A PENDANT

Courtesy, Museum of Fine Arts, Boston.
George Nixon Black Fund (Cat. no. 271).

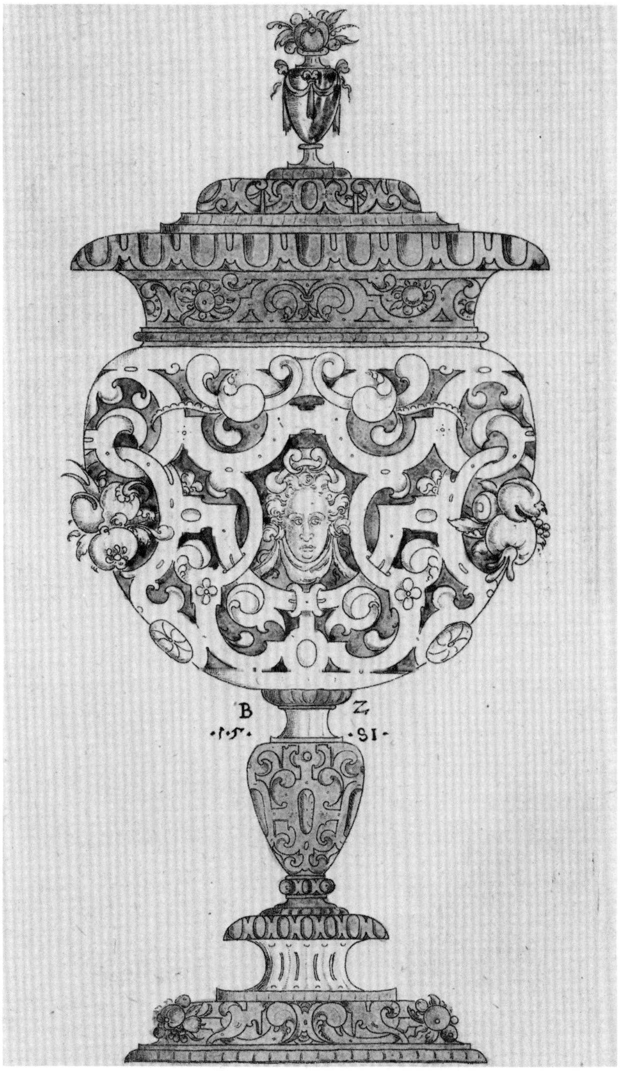

(Fig. no. 51) Bernhard Zan

DESIGN FOR A COVERED GOBLET

Courtesy, Museum of Fine Arts, Boston.
Horatio Greenough Fund (Cat. no. 265).

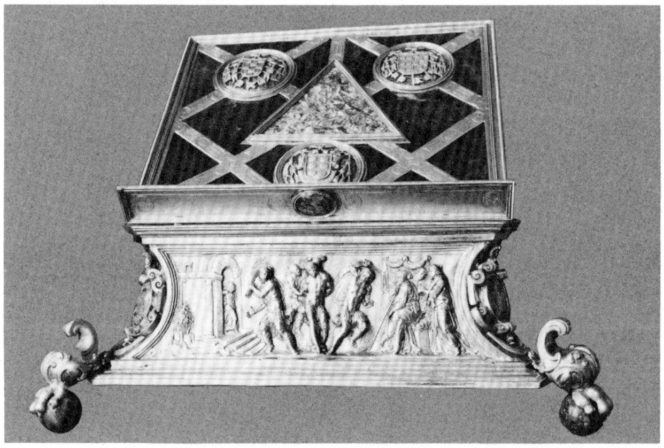

(Fig. no. 53) Spanish, 16th century

LECTERN

Lent by The Walters Art Gallery, Baltimore (Cat. no. 90).

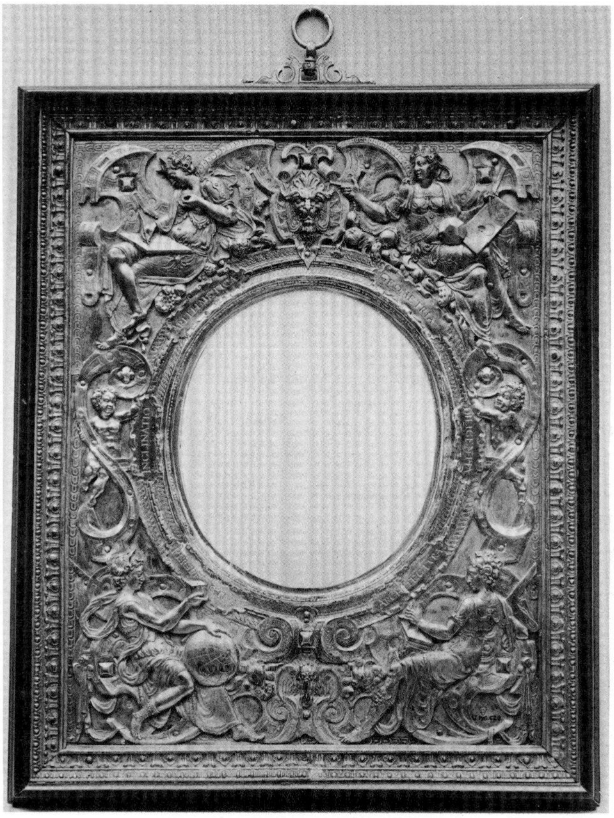

(Fig. no. 52) Wenzel Jamnitzer

MIRROR FRAME

Lent by The Metropolitan Museum of Art, New York.
Gift of J. Pierpont Morgan, 1917 (Cat. no. 89).

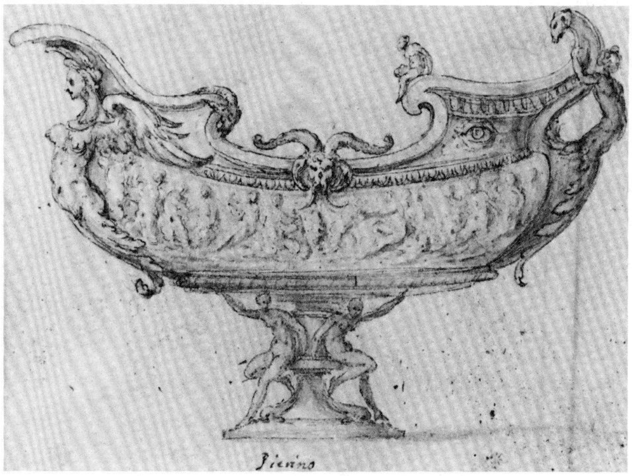

(Fig. no. 54) Perino del Vaga

DESIGN FOR A BOAT-SHAPED EWER

Lent by Cooper-Hewitt Museum, The Smithsonian Institution's National Museum of Design, New York (Cat. no. 249).

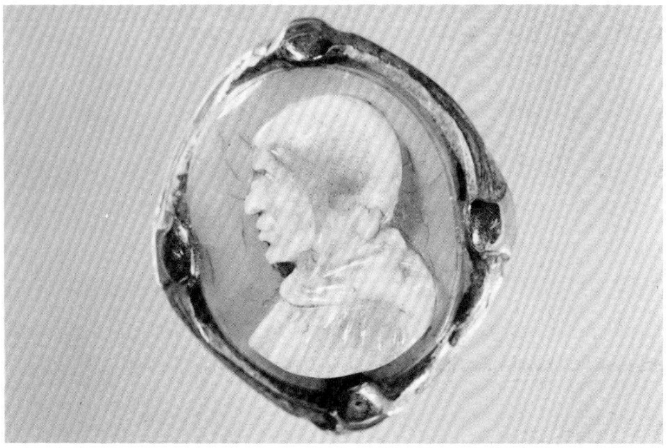

(Fig. no. 55) Italian, early 16th century

RING WITH A PORTRAIT OF SAVONAROLA

Lent by Mr. and Mrs. James W. Alsdorf, Chicago (Cat. no. 92).
Reproduced larger than actual size.

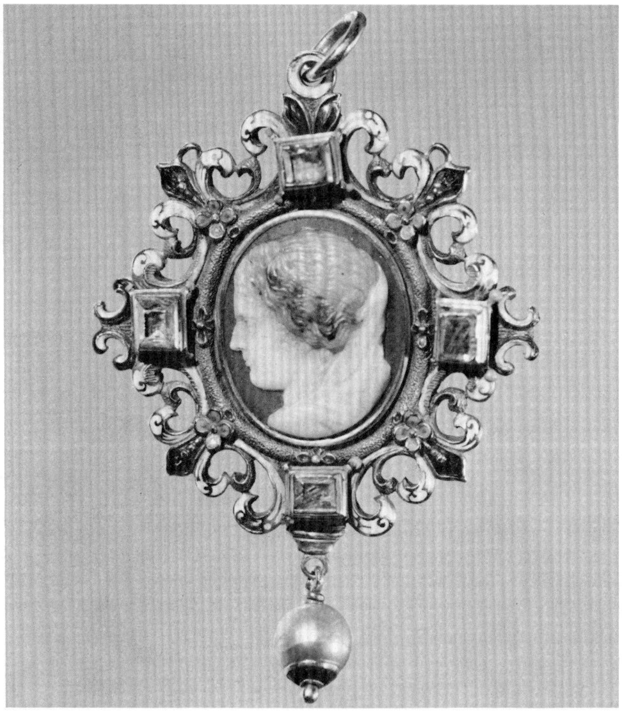

(Fig. no. 56) French, late 16th century

CAMEO PENDANT OF JUNO AND MINERVA

Lent by Mr. and Mrs. James W. Alsdorf, Chicago
(Cat. no. 100). Reproduced larger than actual size.

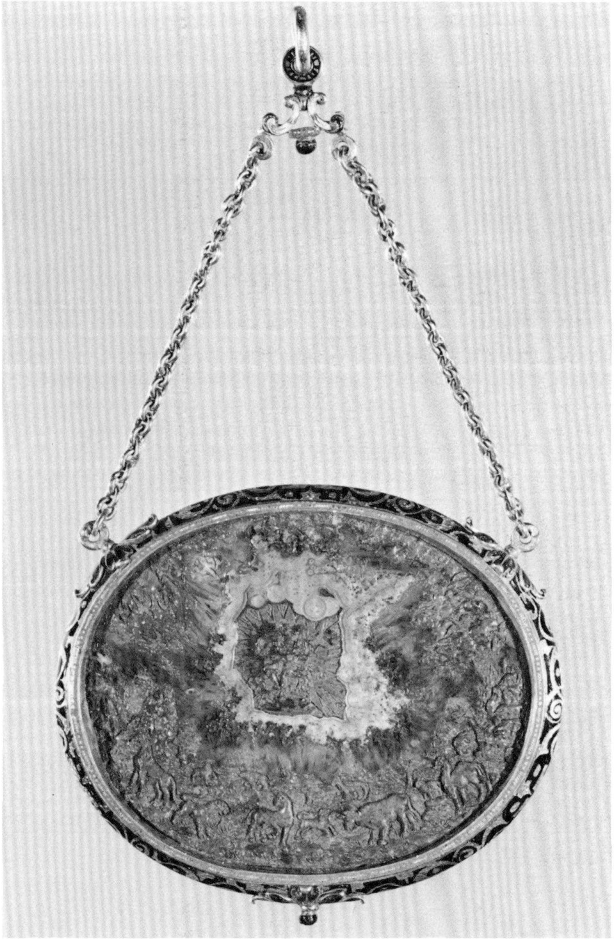

(Fig. no. 57) Manner of Alessandro Masnago

PENDANT OF ORPHEUS AND THE ANIMALS

Lent by Mr. and Mrs. James W. Alsdorf, Chicago (Cat. no. 96).
Reproduced larger than actual size.

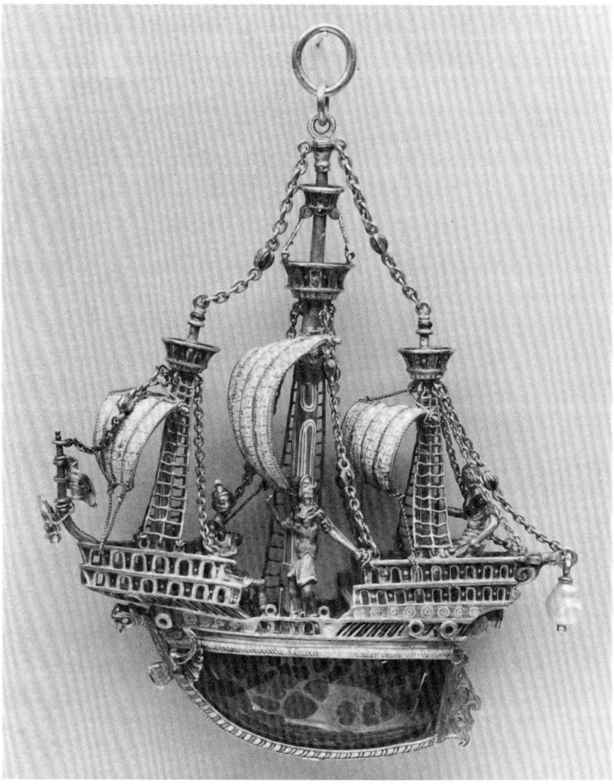

(Fig. no. 58) Spanish, late 16th century

NEF PENDANT

Lent by The Metropolitan Museum of Art, New York.
Gift of The Michael Friedsam Collection, 1931 (Cat. no. 104).

Renaissance Arms and Armor

Stephen V. Grancsay

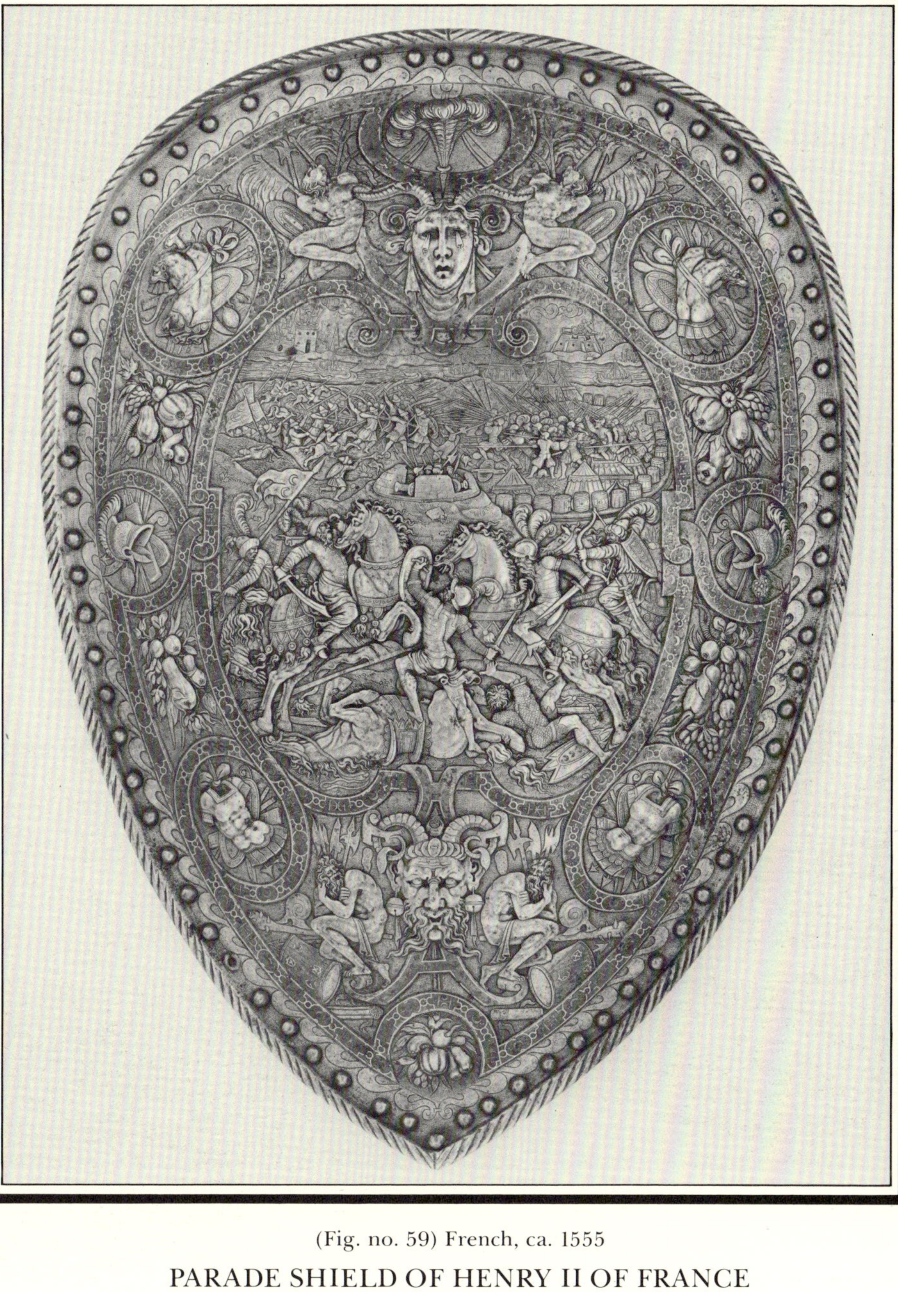

(Fig. no. 59) French, ca. 1555

PARADE SHIELD OF HENRY II OF FRANCE

Lent by The Metropolitan Museum of Art, New York.
Harris Brisbane Dick Fund, 1934 (Cat. no. 113).

The inspiration of the Renaissance was the study of classical antiquity, its literature and its art. These studies led to a different outlook on life, from the medieval religious attitude of self sacrifice and plans for a good life in the future, to the attitude of taking advantage of the good things of life here and now. The ideal was to forget the horrible realities and to indulge in a sort of poet's martial heaven where men fight in glittering armor and hunt all day long.

There was an unbroken continuity in the making and wearing of personal body armor from early times. Since warfare was one of the principal activities of the Renaissance, the deeds of the classical warriors were imitated, and classical legends, military activities, works of art, and historical events were used as ornamental motifs on the armor. There was a gradual transition from the use of religious subjects to the use of classical themes, and often a combination of both religious and secular subjects appeared on the same objects. An exchange helmet in the Metropolitan Museum that belongs to the armor of Philip II of Spain in the Royal Armory in Madrid is embossed with more than fifty mythological and historical figures.

The metalsmiths' shops were the training schools for many of the great artists of the Renaissance. Brunelleschi, Verrocchio, Ghiberti, Pollaiuolo, and Luca della Robbia all were trained as metalsmiths before they embarked upon the higher arts. The ornamental motifs for arms and armor were sometimes especially designed and they were often taken from contemporary engravings, as we shall presently see. Many engravers were trained as gold and silversmiths, hence they were familiar with the practical application of their ornament. When designs were prepared especially for armor they were shaped to conform to the curved surfaces of the elements to be decorated. A close relationship existed between painter, sculptor, goldsmith, and armorer. The same man who painted the king's banners, his shields, horse trappings, and his devotional pictures, also created the designs for his helmets and body armor. The carver who worked at the architectural details of his chapel could, in addition, fashion a crest for his helmet, and the artist who etched armor and weapons busied himself as well with etching plates for reproducing prints on paper.

The subject of historical arms and armor like those in this exhibition is more a part of art history than of military history. Emperors, kings, and princes were the patrons of armorers, and many of the giants in art collaborated with armorers by making designs for armor and its accessories. Among these artists were Leonardo da Vinci, Cellini, Pollaiuolo, Dürer, the Burgkmairs and Hopfer. Giorgio Vasari, in whose work on the eminent artists of his time we find so much valuable information, wrote at length of a shield which Leonardo painted. Cellini in his autobiography wrote, "I had a straight fowling-piece made by my own hands; and (so bright was it) both within and without there was never seen a mirror like it." Antonio Pollaiuolo, in addition to painting, ran a thriving establishment in Florence that produced prints and metalwork of various kinds. It is recorded that the Florentines presented Duke Federigo de Montefeltro, on his triumphal entry into the city after his successful campaign of 1472, with "a silver helmet studded with jewels and chased in gold by the masterly hand of Pollaiuolo."

The Helmschmieds of Augsburg collaborated with some of the ablest artists of their time. Among them were Albrecht Dürer and both Hans Burgkmairs, father and son. These artists worked for the Emperor Maximilian I and, as a part of their duties, designed and decorated his armor. Maximilian commissioned Dürer and the elder Burgkmair (1473-1531) to make the drawings for a two-part project, a triumphal procession and a triumphal arch through which the procession would be imagined to pass. The procession had been the prerogative of victorious generals in the ancient Roman republic, and an arch had commemorated the martial successes of such Roman emperors as Titus and Constantine. Dürer also made the designs (six of which are known) for the silver armor that Maximilian ordered in 1516 from his court armorer Koloman Helmschmied (1476-1532). Dürer's original design for the saddle of this armor is in the Morgan Library. The six drawings are actual patterns of the plates to be decorated. Twice on Dürer's Triumphal Arch appears the chain of vases and lilies which is the Collar of the Order of Temperance of which Maximilian was a member; this motif reappears in Dürer's design in the Albertina for the visor of the helmet. Koloman Helmschmied also made the trellised targe in the Royal Armory in Madrid that was etched by Daniel Hopfer and that bears his signature and the date 1536. As Hopfer was Koloman Helmschmied's son-in-law, one may safely assume that many more of the productions of the famous Helmschmied family were etched by Hopfer. To bring his activities nearer home, Hopfer is believed to have etched the backplate in the Metropolitan Museum with figures of Saint Sebastian that were taken directly from Hans Baldung Grien's single sheet woodcut made about 1505.

The armor and weapons in this exhibition are evidence of the splendor of a great age of art. The earliest element is a Milanese helmet known as a barbute, made about 1450 (Cat. no. 105), which in contour resembles the Corinthian helmet. In this type of headpiece, the Greek ideal of purity and simplicity of form was admirably re-created by the Renaissance armorers. Our barbute is a masterpiece of metalwork, a fine example of formal beauty resulting from functional efficiency. Its shape is singularly graceful and elegant, showing the intrinsic beauty of the plain surface of skilfully modeled metal. The pure silhouette of the piece is only a part of the original decorative scheme. Italian armorers of the fifteenth century had learned to combine simplicity of line with protective features that could hardly be improved upon; hence the energies of artists were increasingly expended upon ornamentation and enrichment. A barbute with its rich velvet covering, gilded bronze borders, and personal crest formed an ensemble of great elegance. Excellent examples may be seen in contemporary representations, such as Pisanello's sketch dated 1448 for the medal of Alfonso of Aragon in the Louvre and in the Metropolitan Museum's intarsia-paneled study from the Ducal Palace at Gubbio, which was designed about 1480 by the Sienese Francesco di Giorgio for the celebrated humanist and condottiere Federigo da Montefeltro. Among the weapons and armor shown in Duke Federigo's *trompe l'oeil* closet is a barbute surmounted by the crowned Montefeltro eagle.

Three other decorative helmets are in the exhibition. The triple-crested burgonet of the State Guard of Emperor Charles V, made in Augsburg about 1530, is of great technical and historical interest (Cat. no. 106). The skull with three combs, each with engrailed border, is wrought in one piece, with a peaked umbril on which is stamped the pine cone of Augsburg and the mark of the imperial armorer Koloman Helmschmied. At the base of the skull on each side is a keyhole perforation for securing a colorful fabric covering (the artist who decorated armor sometimes copied or adapted the design of a fabric). The third headpiece is a close helmet of Innsbruck workmanship that was made about 1525 to be worn in a pageant. Its skull is conspicuously ovoid, with the median ridge embossed as the comb of a cock. The cock's crest, plumage, and wattles are skillfully represented. The crest of the cock was worn upon the headgear of ancient Greek heroes, and in the days of chivalry it gave its name to the heraldic figure or device worn upon the helmet of a knight.

In contrast to the German-made helmets is a headpiece that was made for Claude Gouffier, marquis of Boisy, Grand Equerry of France (Cat. no. 108). The Boisy helmet is of typical French form, as may be seen by comparing it with the helmets of the French royal harnesses in the Musée de l'Armée in Paris. The Château of Oiron (Deux Sèvres) in Touraine was built by Claude Gouffier conjointly with his mother, Hélène Hangest-Genlis, to whom the arts are indebted for that mysterious ware, called "Faïence d'Oiron," fabricated under her direction. Hélène was the governess of the dauphin Henri d'Orléans, later Henry II (1547-1559). It is of interest to note that much of the enriched armor of the time of Henry II is decorated with interlaced strapwork similar to that which decorates some of the faïence d'Oiron. An excellent example of this interlaced strapwork pattern is etched on the Boisy helmet. In addition to an etched Latin motto, the initials C and F (for Claude and his wife Françoise) appear as a monogram in its Greek form, interlaced Phi and Chi. With the growth of Hellenism, there was a fashion for Greek initials. This monogram, or its Latin equivalent (C and F), appears frequently in the interior decoration of certain parts of the Château d'Oiron. The same monogram appears at the bottom of several miniatures from a book of hours that was painted by Jean Cousin for Claude Gouffier. In the writer's collection is an embossed knee cop which is engraved with Claude's monogram. Embossed motifs and a repeated trefoil motif that appear on the knee cop also appear on the armor worn by Henry II in his portrait by Primaticcio in the Musée Condé, Chantilly. After Claude's death it was necessary to sell his collection to pay his debts. The Florentine Seigneur d'Adjacet (D'Adjouto) purchased "ung harnois d'homme d'armes compleat, gravé et dorré à moresque," decoration which could describe that on our Boisy helmet.

The art of embossing was fully developed five thousand years ago; however skill in this technique was raised to new standards by Renaissance metalworkers. It was natural that, as the art of armor developed from the shaping of contour to the embellishment of surface, the functions of armorer and goldsmith should blend. The new style required a new kind of craftsmanship in which the talents of several artisans were required: the armorer to fashion the contours of the piece, the ornament designer to plan the pattern of decoration, and the goldsmith to execute the design. A splendid example of a highly ornamented "dress" or "parade" harness is the embossed armor of the duke of Alba (Cat. no. 114). It was made by Lucio Piccinino of Milan and represents the ornate

Milanese style at its best. Every element is decorated with luxuriant designs in relief, drawn from the classical repertory. These feature Medusas, satyrs, sphinxes, putti, bound captives, anthropomorphic lion masks, and figures of Mars and Victory — all derived, or rather adapted, from antique art. The organization of these decorations is for the most part in symmetrical, vertical bands, joined by festoons of fruit or by strap-work from which masks and bunches of fruit are suspended. The Alba motifs and their systematic arrangement are similar to the ornamentation on the Farnese armor in the Waffensammlung in Vienna. The family resemblance becomes particularly clear when one compares an arm defense and pauldron of the Alba armor with original drawings for the same elements of the Farnese armor, which are also in the Kunsthistorisches Museum in Vienna.

Another historical example of embossed armor is the right pauldron (Cat. no.109) of a magnificent pageant armor of pseudo-Roman style made by Bartolomeo Campi, goldsmith, engraver, and armorer of Pesaro for Guidobaldo II of Rovere-Montefeltro, duke of Urbino (1514-1574). The Medici inherited the armory of the dukes of Urbino in 1631, and the mate of our pauldron and the breastplate *en suite* are still in the Medici collection in the Bargello in Florence. The Medici pauldron appears in Titian's portrait of D. Claudius Caesar, one of twelve portraits of Roman emperors that Federigo Gonzaga commissioned Titian to paint in 1536 to decorate a gallery of the castle at Mantua. In a Florentine manuscript of 1642 (of which the Metropolitan Museum has a copy), Antonio Petrini gives an accurate description of Guidobaldo's harness as it was then shown to visitors to the Grand Ducal Armory, but he says it belonged to Hannibal the Carthaginian!

Several remarkable examples of French royal embossed armor are exhibited in the Metropolitan Museum. The embossed parade shield was made for Henry II (Cat. no. 113) after the original design in the Staatliche Graphische Sammlung in Munich. Companion shields are in the Musée du Louvre: one in steel, also made for Henry II, and the other in gold and enamel made for Charles IX. Pierre Verlet, *Conservateur en Chef* of the Louvre Museum, has identified the maker of the Louvre gold shield as the Paris goldsmith Pierre Redon. Also belonging to Henry II is a mace (Cat. no. 121) signed DIDACVS . DE . CAIAS . FACIEBAD, which was damascened by Diego de Cayas, who worked for Francis I and his son. The design shows a scene from the life of Saint Hubert, oriental figures, and two inscriptions besides the signature: DECVS . ET . TVTAMEN . IN . ARMIS (Virgil *Aeneid* v. 262 — "a glory and defense in battle") and DONEC . TOTVM.IMPLEAT.ORBEM ("Until he fill the earth [with his glory]"), a motto used by Henry II with his device of interlaced crescents.

The Milanese armorer who made the embossed shield of Charles V (Cat. no. 112) emulated the sculptors and goldsmiths of the period by creating pictures in a most difficult medium. The central scene represents the surrender of John Frederick, Elector of Saxony, to Charles V after the battle of Mühlberg in 1547. The design is copied after a drawing by Marten van Heemskerck, signed and dated 1554, in the British Museum. It is one of twelve drawings representing the chief victories of the emperor Charles V. The border of our shield is made up of trophies of arms and armor, allegorical figures of the four seasons, and heads of Roman emperors wearing golden laurel wreaths. The decoration of the shield is embossed, gilded, and silvered, with details in delicate damascene work. Another element associated with Charles V is one of a pair of tassets that belonged to a harness made for the emperor by the Augsburg armorer Matthäus Frauenpreis (Cat. no. 111). It is embossed, etched and gilded, displaying a griffin segreant and the column of Hercules surmounted by emblems of the

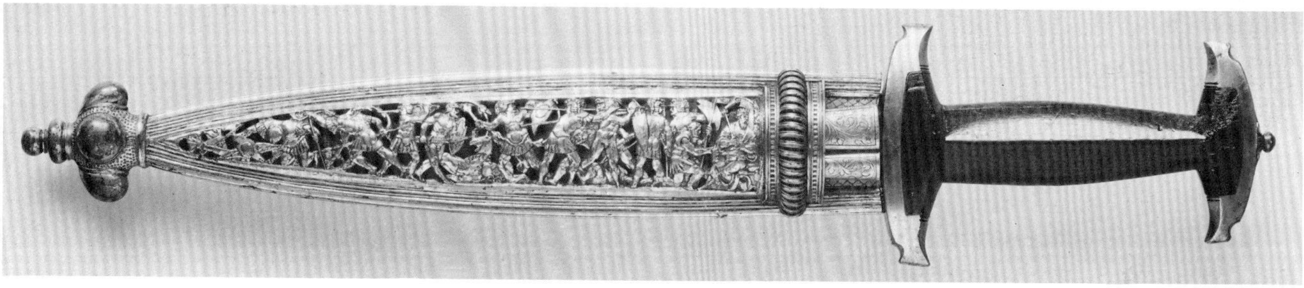

(Fig. no. 60) Swiss, dated 1567

DAGGER WITH SHEATH

Lent by The Metropolitan Museum of Art, New York.
Gift of Jean Jacques Reubell, 1926, in memory of his mother,
Julia C. Coster, and his wife, Adeline E. Post,
both of New York City (Cat. no. 119).

Order of the Golden Fleece. The griffin is associated with the imperial arms, as may be seen in the drawings by Albrecht Dürer of Maximilian's Triumphal Arch. The column of Hercules may be considered an allusion to the extension of Spanish dominion to America (transplanting the column of Hercules) where the emperor's conquistadors were active.

The earliest etched armor in the exhibition is a Milanese breastplate (Cat. no. 110) that was made about 1500. A wide horizontal band is etched in the early manner with cross-hatched background; in the center is the Christ Child flanked by St. Christopher and St. Sebastian. The same shaded backgrounds of close-set diagonal lines are found in the prints of the artist-goldsmiths of north Italy at this date, as for instance in *The Battle of Naked Men* by Pollaiuolo (1432-1498) and in the engravings of Mantegna.

During the sixteenth century, enriched side arms were worn as dress weapons rather than for military use. The Italian (Brescia) falchion (Cat. no. 115) of the early sixteenth century which was exhibited in the Madrid Exposition of 1892 is believed to have belonged to Francis I of France, whose emblem was the salamander which forms a prominent motif of the guard. A rare type of civilian weapon of slightly later date (1525-1550) is a cinquedea (Cat. no. 117), a large dagger or short sword. Cinquedea blades were often richly gilded and etched with Renaissance borders and compositions of figures chosen from the Bible and classical mythology. The basal region of the blade of our cinquedea is damascened in gold, on one side picturing Charon and on the other Neptune. Of the same period as the cinquedea is an Italian dagger with hilt of gilded bronze whose rich decoration in flowers, scrolls, and masks suggest the work of the medallist. A specialized form of dagger with sheath, dated 1567, is typical of daggers worn by Swiss officers of high rank (Cat. no. 119). Its sheath is of gilt bronze, pierced with a battle scene showing warriors in classical armor. Such daggers have been named in modern times "Holbein" daggers because a design of the Dance of Death often found on these sheaths is derived from a drawing by Holbein himself. The swept hilt rapier and dagger *en suite* have hilts of steel, filed spirally with great precision and completely mercury gilded (Cat. no. 120). They came from the Dresden Historical Museum and origi-

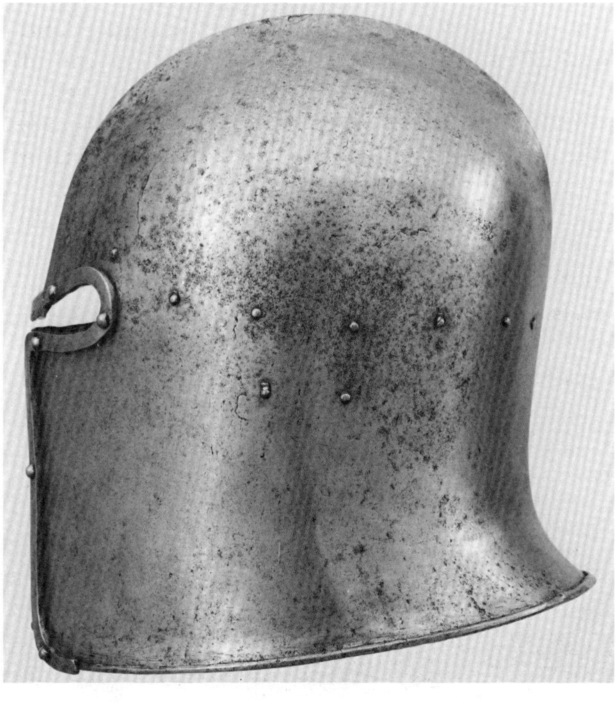

(Fig. no. 61) Missaglia Workshop

BARBUTE

Lent by The Metropolitan Museum of Art, New York.
Gift of Stephen V. Grancsay, New York (Cat. no. 105).

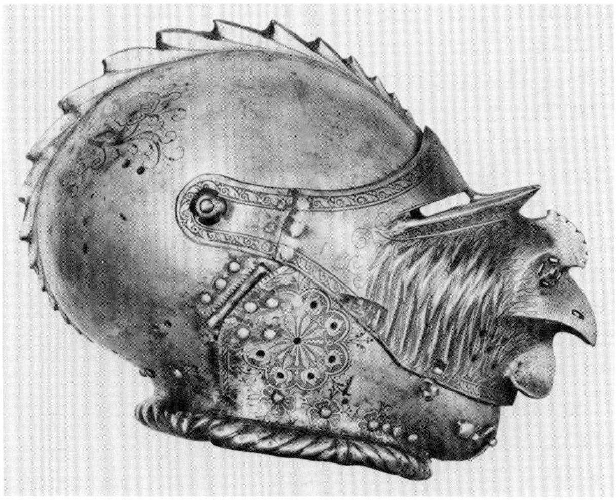

(Fig. no. 62) Hans Seusenhofer

CLOSE HELMET (Cock's Comb)

Lent by The Metropolitan Museum of Art.
Bequest of Bashford Dean, 1928 (Cat. no. 107).

nally belonged to the Saxon Elector Christian I. An Italian sword, dated 1560, was made by Daniele da Serravalle for Philip II of Spain. The entire surface of the blued steel hilt is studded with bossets in relief.

The technique of chiseling motives out of solid iron is represented by a remarkable wrought ceremonial war-hammer (Cat. no. 123). Especially noteworthy are the perforated terminals and elaborate Renaissance sculpturing which decorate the area of the shaft. The members of the royal guard of Charles IX of France (1560-1574) were called the *Gentilshommes au Bec-de-Corbin* from the ornamented war-hammers which they carried. The head of our bec-de-corbin is the most highly decorated example of this arm extant.

Two items of horse equipment, an Italian curb bit (Cat. no. 122) with chiseling of extraordinary quality and a German stirrup (Cat. no. 125) elaborately pierced like a fabric of lace, are token exhibits, since the Renaissance was an epoch when a good part of life was spent on horseback. Another token exhibit is a French powder flask decorated with a central medallion representing Mars. Lack of space has prevented the inclusion of firearms in the exhibition; however, it should be noted that among the Metropolitan Museum's Renaissance firearms is a wheel lock rifle of the mid-sixteenth century which bears the heraldic arms of Philip of Croy (1521-1595). The stock of this remarkable example of decorative art is entirely veneered with carved ivory plaques representing the gods of Olympus and the story of Perseus.

Few today, it is safe to say, know about the wonderful work of the armorer. For one thing, work in steel deteriorates with alarming rapidity unless given technical care. Anyone who has seen only the shockingly bad copies which have been turned out in Venice or Paris may have formed an erroneous idea of the potential beauty of armor, and examining authentic armor of only the most common type is as little inspiring as viewing a badly painted picture. Yet, Renaissance arms and armor are considered to be works of decorative art because they include objects of the most remarkable workmanship ever made in metal. We feel certain that the splendid examples in this exhibition will make more real for the visitor the part arms and armor played in the glamor and magnificence of the Renaissance.

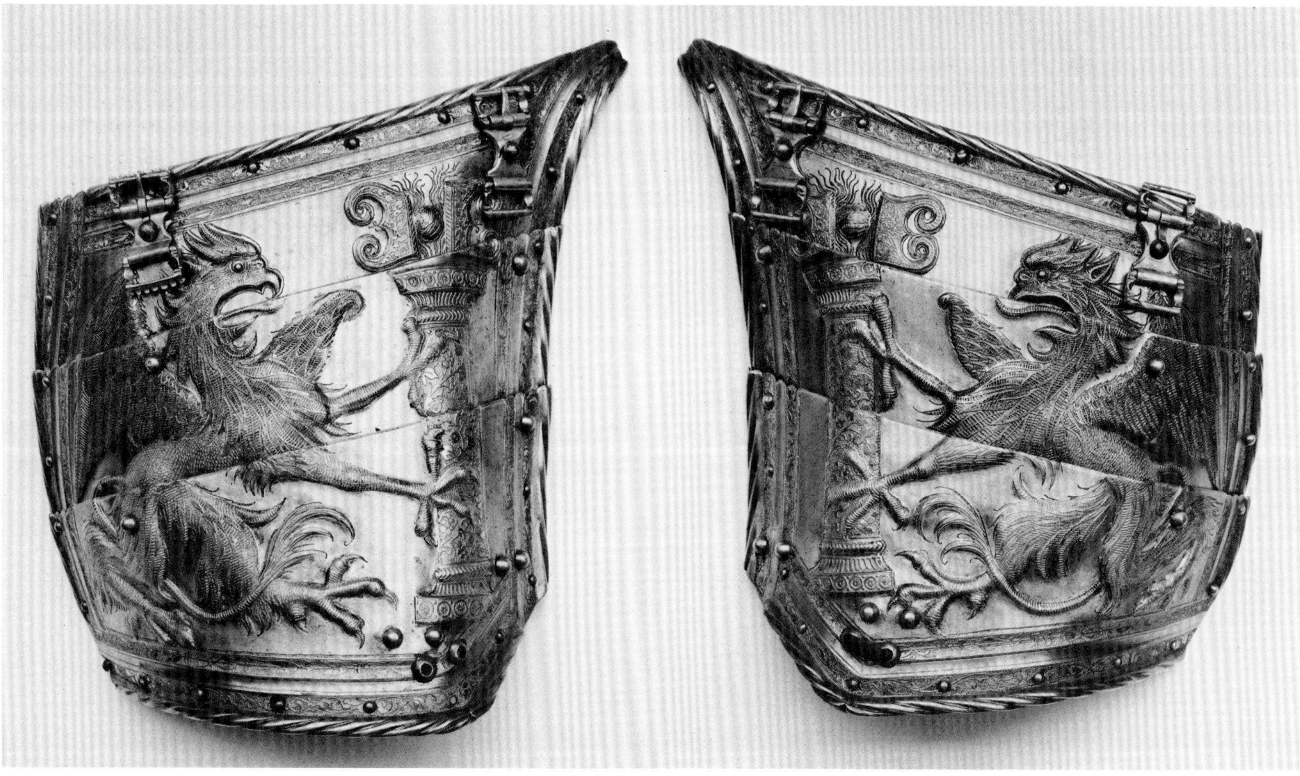

(Fig. no. 63) Matthäus Frauenpreis

PAIR OF TASSETS FROM THE HARNESS OF EMPEROR CHARLES V

Lent by The Metropolitan Museum of Art, New York. Bequest of Bashford Dean, 1928 (Cat. no. 111).

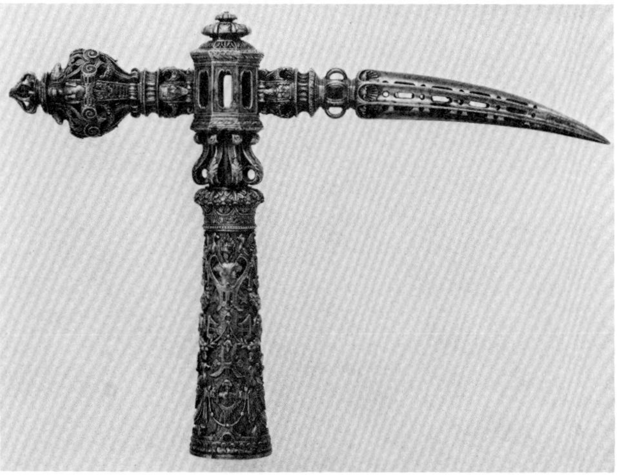

(Fig. no. 64) Italian, 1575

HEAD OF A CEREMONIAL WAR HAMMER

Lent by The Metropolitan Museum of Art, New York.
Rogers Fund, 1904 (Cat. no. 123).

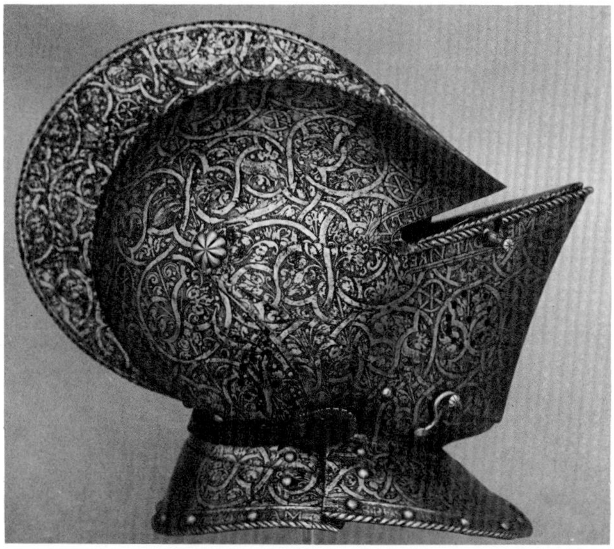

(Fig. no. 65) French, ca. 1550

HELMET OF CLAUDE GOUFFIER, MARQUIS OF BOISY, GRAND EQUERRY OF FRANCE

Lent by The Metropolitan Museum of Art, New York.
Gift of William H. Riggs, 1913 (Cat. no. 108).

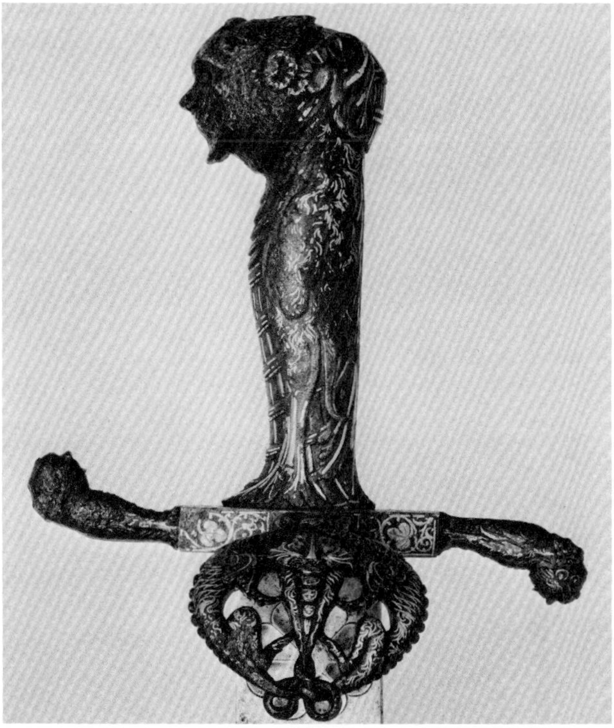

(Fig. no. 66) Italian (Brescia), 1520

FALCHION

Lent by Stephen V. Grancsay, New York (Cat. no. 115).

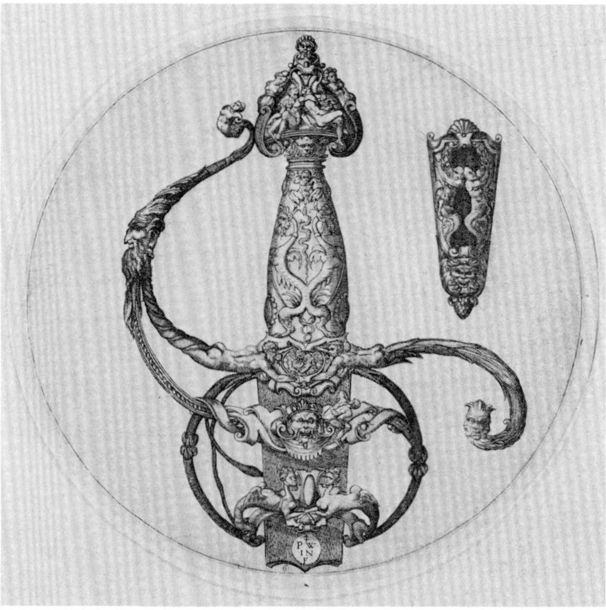

(Fig. no. 67) Pierre Woeiriot (1532-d. after 1596)

DESIGN FOR A SWORD HILT

Courtesy, Museum of Fine Arts, Boston.
Maria Antoinette Evans Fund (Cat. no. 269).

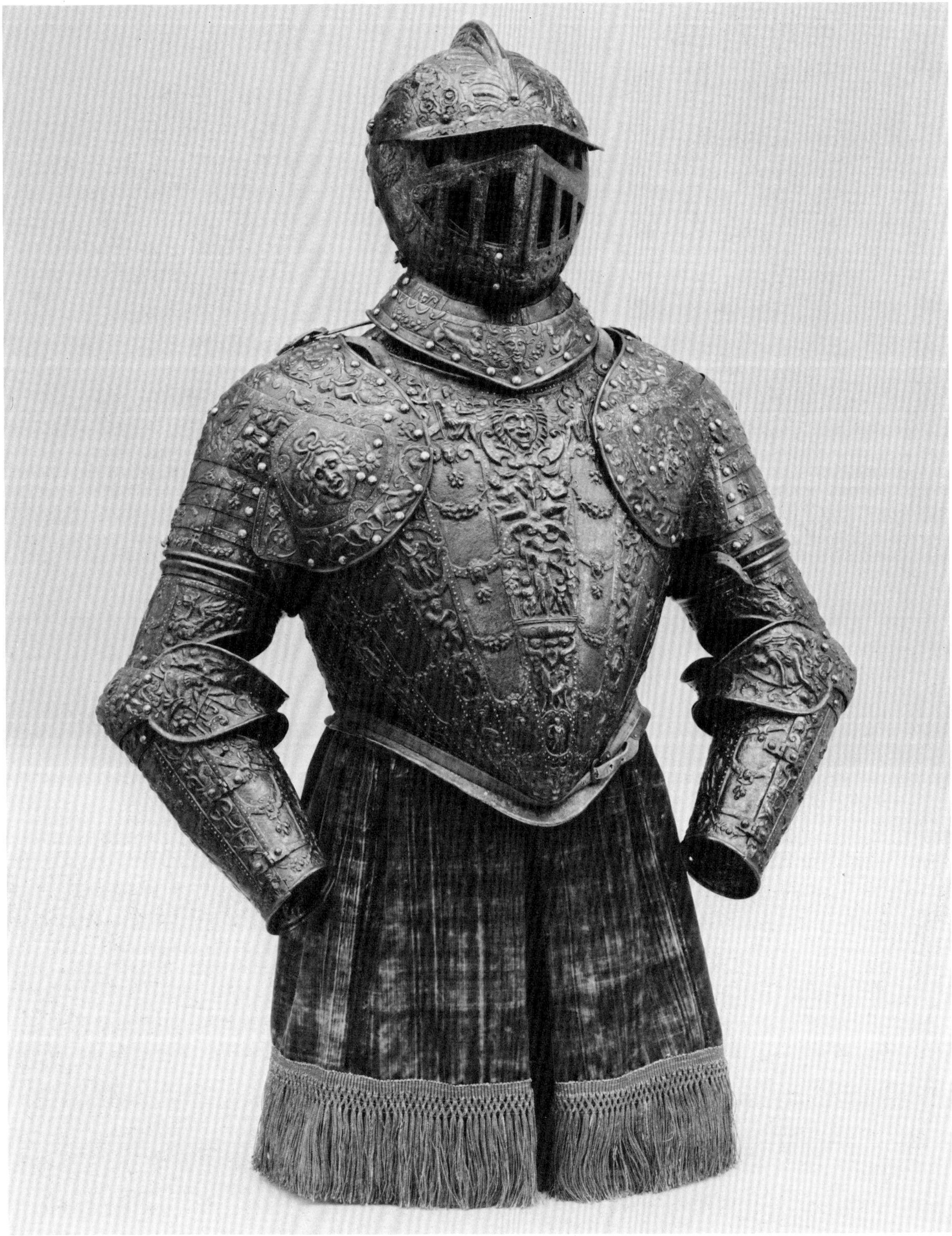

(Fig. no. 68) Lucio Piccinino

HALF-ARMOR OF FERNANDO ALVAREZ OF TOLEDO, DUKE OF ALBA

Lent by The Metropolitan Museum of Art, New York.
Gift of William H. Riggs, 1913 (Cat. no. 114).

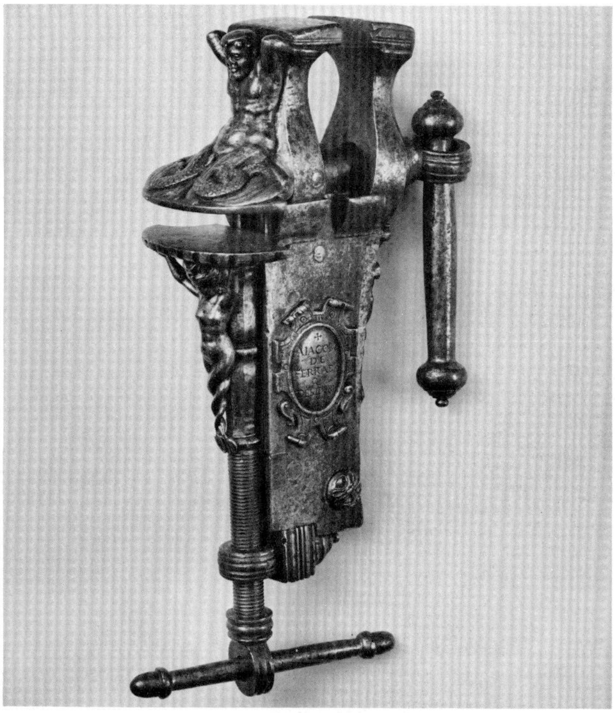

(Fig. no. 69) Jacopo da Ferrara

ARMORER'S VISE

Lent by The Metropolitan Museum of Art, New York.
Harris Brisbane Dick Fund, 1958 (Cat. no. 128).

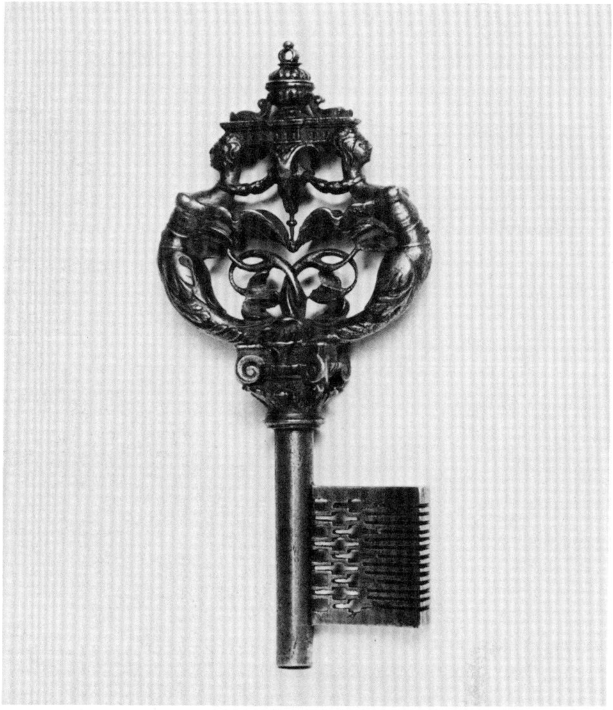

(Fig. no. 70) French, probably 1580-1589

KEY

Lent by The Metropolitan Museum of Art, New York.
Harris Brisbane Dick Fund, 1958 (Cat. no. 129).

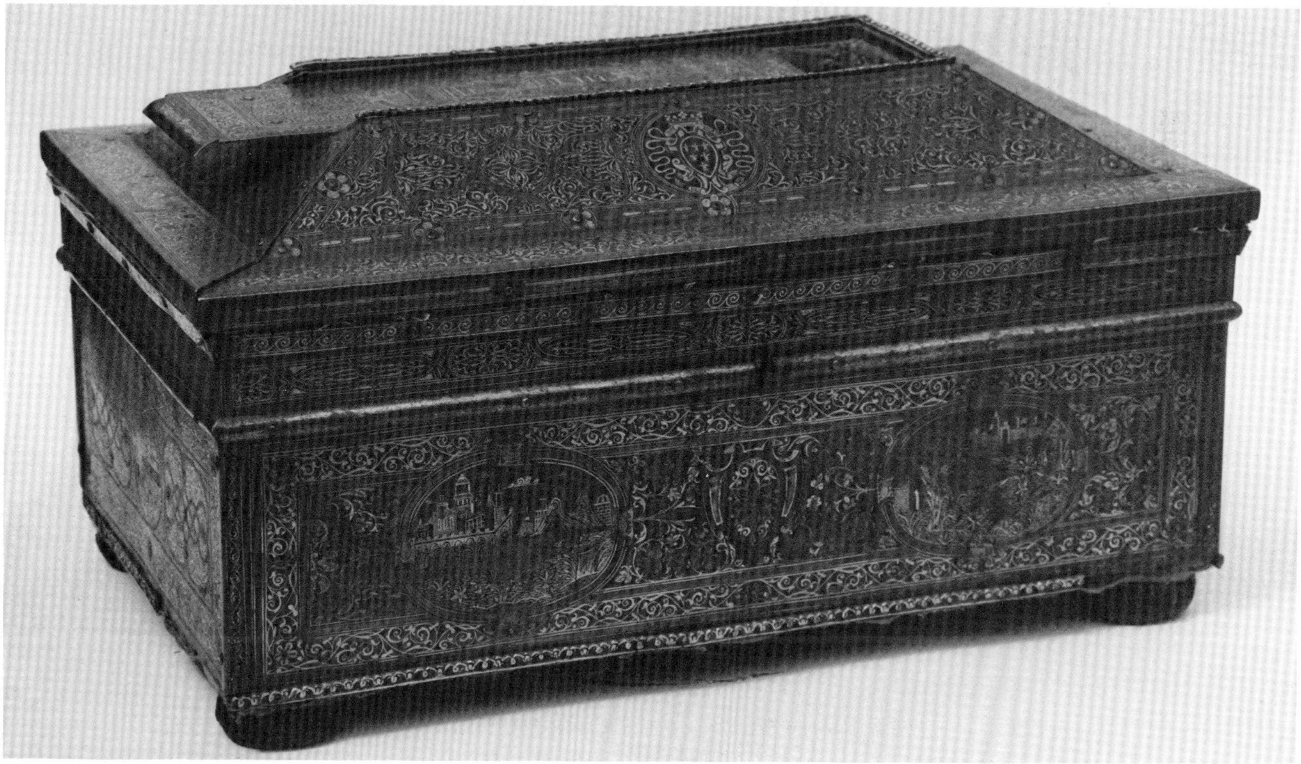

(Fig. no. 71) Italian (probably Milan), 1545-1547

CASKET

Lent by The Metropolitan Museum of Art, New York.
Morris Loeb Gift Fund, 1956 (Cat. no. 130).

Renaissance Timepieces

Clare Vincent

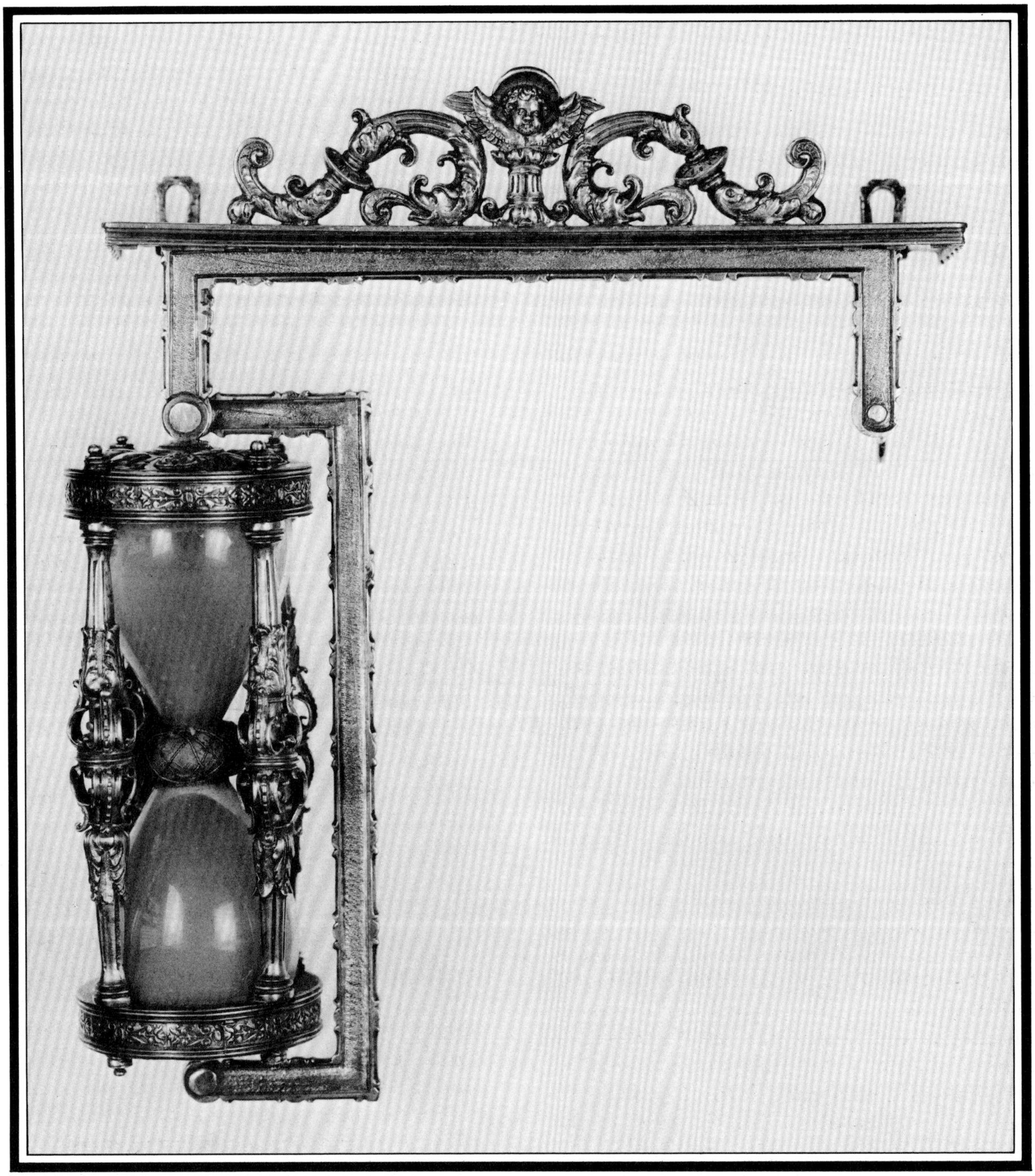

(Fig. no. 72) English, 1525-1530

HOURGLASS

Courtesy, Museum of Fine Arts, Boston.
Theodora Wilbour Fund in memory of
Charlotte Beebe Wilbour (Cat. no. 135).

The Renaissance clock is the product of two parallel, but not necessarily distinct, functions, each based on very much earlier European traditions. The first of these functions is that of the clock as a timekeeper; the second, ultimately of Hellenistic Greek origins, is that of the clock as a machine for demonstrating the motions of the heavenly bodies and, by extension, as a metaphor for the universe. The successful development of both functions depended on the invention in the late thirteenth century of the mechanical escapement, the device which revolutionized timekeeping.

The history of Renaissance clockmaking is one of continual improvement and refinement of the basic medieval invention. Perhaps the earliest and most important development was the substitution of a coiled spring for falling weights as the source of power. The concomitant invention of the cone-shaped device called a fusee was used to even out the force of the spring as it unwound. There is good evidence to show that spring-driven clocks were probably first made during the first half of the fifteenth century in Burgundy. By 1450 at the latest, the spring and fusee device could be found in the movement of a clock that appears in an illuminated French manuscript (Brussels, Bibliothèque royale ms. IV, 111). The miniature illustrates one of the more popular medieval allegories that employed the clock as a metaphor for the correctly ordered Christian life, known in its French translations as the *Horloge de Sapience*. As the miniature clearly indicates, the invention of the spring and fusee permitted the construction of small table clocks which, unlike the weight-driven clock that had to be hung on a wall or otherwise provided with protection for the undisturbed fall of the weights, had the advantage of easy portability. Few examples of the spring-driven clock survive from this period; even less is known of their makers.

From the second quarter of the sixteenth century a small number of surviving examples can be associated with specific clockmakers such as Jacob Zech (fl. 1518-1540) of Prague or Pierre de Fobis (fl. 1506-1515) of Aix and, later, Lyons. With rare exceptions, the cases of these small table clocks were of gilded metal. Some were quite architectural in character, others embellished with engraved and embossed designs that often rival the work of the goldsmiths of the day, and many of the finest northern European examples reflect the newly imported taste for Italian Renaissance ornament.

By the second half of the century, the major and probably the most inventive center of clockmaking was South Germany, where Nuremberg, Augsburg, and, to a lesser extent, Munich were the chief producers of small domestic clocks of various kinds. Often these small clocks were provided with multiple dials for telling the time in the various systems for counting the hours that were prevalent in an age before the now familiar twelve equal hours beginning at midnight and repeated at noon had become the standard for organizing a day according to the clock. Additional dials were also added to indicate the day of the week, the day of the year, and other calendrical information.

Most of these clocks were housed in elaborately decorated, gilded metal cases that displayed a high quality of craftsmanship. Some of the best were ornamented with gilt-bronze reliefs and plaquettes that were fine examples of late German Renaissance bronze casting. Although it is often possible to trace the sources of the designs that they employed, very little is known about sixteenth-century case makers.

Elsewhere in Europe, royal patronage was responsible for the excellent work of such clockmakers as Bartholomew Newsam (fl. 1568-1593) in London and de la Gardes in Blois, while Gerhard Emmoser (fl. 1556-1584) and Jost Bürgi (1552-1632) produced some of their most exquisite clocks for the Holy Roman Emperors in Vienna and Prague.

Miniaturization of the parts of the spring-driven clock permitted the construction of the watch. Watches were once thought to have been an early sixteenth-century invention of Peter Henlein of Nuremberg (about 1479-1542). More recently, discoveries of written allusions to timepieces in Italy made to be worn on the person have made it apparent that the watch is in fact an Italian Renaissance invention. French and German clockmakers rather quickly took up the making of watches, and in the second half of the sixteenth century tambour watches (Cat. no. 149) were characteristic of German products.

The growing production of mechanical clocks during the Renaissance had the effect of stimulating the construction of a number of other varieties of timekeeping instruments. Sundials were used for setting clocks as well as for regulating their still inaccurate and often highly erratic movements. Both the variety and number of sundials proliferated in the Late Renaissance, especially the small, portable ones that could be carried around and used in a number of latitudes. These were commonly made of ivory or gilded brass and ranged from the compact practical folding dials produced in quantity at Nuremberg to such whimsical combinations as the pillar sundial which serves as the handle for a knife with a fork contained inside (Cat. no. 137) and which is undoubtedly the product of the Prague workshop of Erasmus Habermel (fl. 1576-1606), instrument maker to the Holy Roman Emperor, Rudolph II. Sundials of the period were often equipped with calculators that permitted the user to employ them for telling time by moonlight, while still other instruments called "nocturnals" were made to tell time by the nightly movements of certain stars. Sometimes several varieties of sundials were combined with a nocturnal and tables of calendrical and astronomical information in small portable instruments such as the fine compendium (Cat. no. 140) by the Augsburg master, Christopher Schissler the Elder (1530/32-1609).

Unlike the sundial, the sand glass does not predate the mechanical clock, but rather evolved as an instrument that could be substituted for the clock in measuring comparatively short periods of time. It was used when a clock was impractical, as in the case of a ship at sea, or unavailable, as for example for regulating the length of religious devotions, sermons, or university lectures. It was also used for timing the hourly striking of a bell in a community too poor to afford a public clock. The silver-gilt, framed hourglass (Cat. no. 135) is a rare survivor of the Renaissance, as well as a splendid piece of English silver of the Tudor period.

The demands of Renaissance science and navigation were responsible for many advancements in the making of astronomical and timekeeping instruments. The fifteenth-century workshop in Nuremberg that supplied the instruments for the work of the great astronomer Johannes Regiomontanus (1436-1476) set new standards in the search for precision that occupied European instrument makers throughout the Renaissance. With greater precision went a greater attention to the refinement of proportion, as well as a standard of craftsmanship in metal working that made many of these scientific instruments genuine works of art. Among the finest of the sixteenth century are the astrolabes produced by the workshop of the Arsenius family of Louvain (Cat. no. 141).

A few really accurate clocks were made by Jost Bürgi for the astronomical pursuits of the princely court of Landgraf Wilhelm IV of Hesse at Cassel using a new escapement called the cross-beat. Bürgi's invention remained a secret until modern times, however, to all but a small group of clockmakers. The clocks used by the Danish astronomer Tycho Brahe (1546-1601), at the observatory where he made the observations of the motions of the planets laid the groundwork for Kepler's revolutionary work in astronomy are no longer in existence, but they must have attained a fair degree of accuracy. Nevertheless, with few exceptions, true precision clockmaking was unknown until the widespread application of the pendulum to the clock in the second half of the seventeenth century.

The employment of mechanical clockworks to automate the Medieval devices used to illustrate and calculate the motions of heavenly bodies occupied clockmakers throughout the sixteenth century, as it has from the earliest invention of the mechanical escapement. The recent publication of the manuscript describing Richard of Wallingford's astronomical turret clock, begun in 1327 for the Abbey of St. Albans, leaves no doubt that at this early date a clock was being constructed which not only would include a mechanized astrolabe but would also show the positions of the sun, moon, and planets and indicate lunar eclipses. Richard of Wallingford's clock was the first in a long line of complex mechanisms produced in increasing numbers during the course of the next three centuries which illustrated the heavenly movements. These clocks were not primarily scientific in the modern sense; they had at least two more important roles. The first was to demonstrate God's handiwork, and the second was to evoke an aesthetic appreciation of the order of the universe. We find examples of these clocks, though usually not quite so elaborate, being built in church towers and castle walls. The main faces on most were astrolabes which showed the motion of certain stars, as well as the sun and the moon, in the zodiac.

Soon after Richard of Wallingford's clock was finished, a freestanding astronomical clock with separate dials for showing the motion of each of the planets and for a mechanized astrolabe was made by Giovanni de' Dondi of Padua, thus providing a model for a line of such clocks that can be traced throughout the Renaissance. In the middle of the sixteenth century the mathematician Philip Immser, working with the clockmaker Gerhard Emmoser, improved on the de'Dondi model by making the first astronomical clock to show the motions of all the known planets, together with those of the sun and moon, on one concentrically organized dial that gave a visually coherent picture of the universe according to the Ptolemaic system of cosmology then current. Clocks such as this one were rare and costly items, but small table clocks with astrolabe dials were soon being made with some degree of regularity. During the first quarter of the seventeenth century watches began to be made with complicated astronomical dials. After 1617, a French Huguenot emigré from the Auvergne, Antoine Arlaud, specialized in the making of such watches at Geneva.

One of Arlaud's astronomical watches mounted on a caryatid figure of Hercules (Cat. no. 150) survives to show the skill of the watchmaker and to point to the coming use of the Swiss watchmaking industry in Geneva.

Another Renaissance contribution to the tradition of making instruments to demonstrate the order of the universe is the celestial globe with clockworks. In 1570, Christian Heiden of Nuremberg enclosed a clock movement inside the two halves of a sphere that could be made to revolve in a way that is comparable to the daily motions of the stars. In the last quarter of the century a small group of clockmakers, who were either German or working in Germany, produced a series of ingeniously constructed clockwork globes. Small rotating images of the sun and sometimes the moon were added to later instruments, as were perpetual calendars. The globes revolved in simulation of the movements of the stars, while the sun images moved along the path of the ecliptic in accord with the sun's apparent motion through the ecliptic in the course of the year. In addition, small dials were added, and gearing was devised to register mean solar time. For purposes of practicability in clock-making, the fiction of 365 days in a year with each day composed of twenty-four equal hours is the system for counting hours which was widely adopted in Renaissance Europe and which still governs our mode of daily timekeeping.

One of the earliest and most beautiful in the series of celestial globes is made of silver and supported by a silver figure of Peagasus with gilded wings. The instrument is signed by Gerhard Emmoser, who was clockmaker to the Holy Roman Emperor, Rudolph II, in 1579 when the globe was made (Cat. no.144). The goldsmith and the engraver of the stars and constellations on the globe remain anonymous, but clearly the craftsmen of the imperial workshops in Vienna produced a masterpiece of Mannerist goldsmith's work which succeeds very well in evoking an aesthetic appreciation of both the abstract and the concrete model of the heavens as embodied in the globe.

Like the mechanized model of the universe, the mechanized figure, or automaton, has been associated with clocks since classical times. Public clocks during the Renaissance, as during the Middle Ages, were often supplied with robot bell-ringers, crowing cocks, and, indeed, whole parades of figures that performed their appropriate hourly duties. A strain of this tradition strongly pervaded Renaissance domestic clockmaking. In the second half of the sixteenth century small automaton clocks were produced in quantity in South Germany. Embossed and gilded copper lions were made with moving parts to simulate the motions of roaring; ostriches were made to bat their eyes on the hour and roosters to flap their wings and make crowing motions, in emulation of the well-known fourteenth-century automaton that perched atop the astronomical clock completed in 1354 for the Cathedral of Strasbourg. Wooden cases for clocks came into fashion during the seventeenth century. The earliest wooden cases are of ebony veneered on oak or of fruitwood darkened to look like the more precious ebony. Augsburg, Nuremberg, and Munich specialized in such work, often combining wooden bases with gilded bronze or silver automaton figures. The goddess Diana (Cat. no. 147), with her moving eyes and fingers, is accompanied on her ebony chariot by a feeding monkey and a bird with flapping wings. She is typical of these early seventeenth-century automata. Similar clocks continued to be made until the latter half of the seventeenth century when the vastly improved timekeeping properties of the pendulum clock made curiosities not only of these amusing conceits, but also of Renaissance clocks in general.

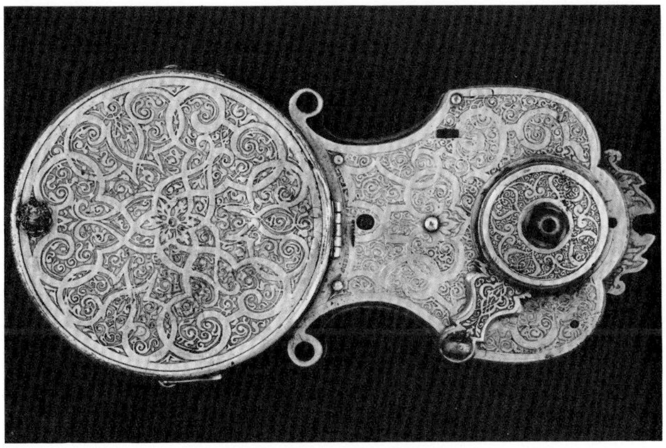

(Fig. no. 73) School of Christoph Schissler

PEDOMETER

Lent by The Adler Planetarium, Chicago (Cat. no. 153).

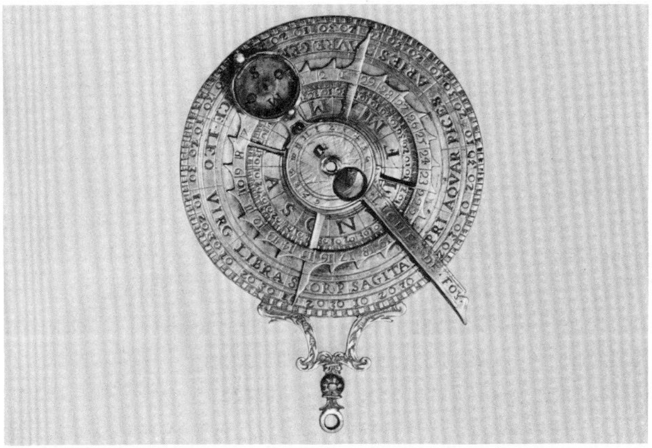

(Fig. no. 74) French, ca. 1550-1582

NOCTURNAL AND SUNDIAL

Lent by The Metropolitan Museum of Art, New York.
Gift of Mrs. Stephen D. Tucker (Cat. no. 138)

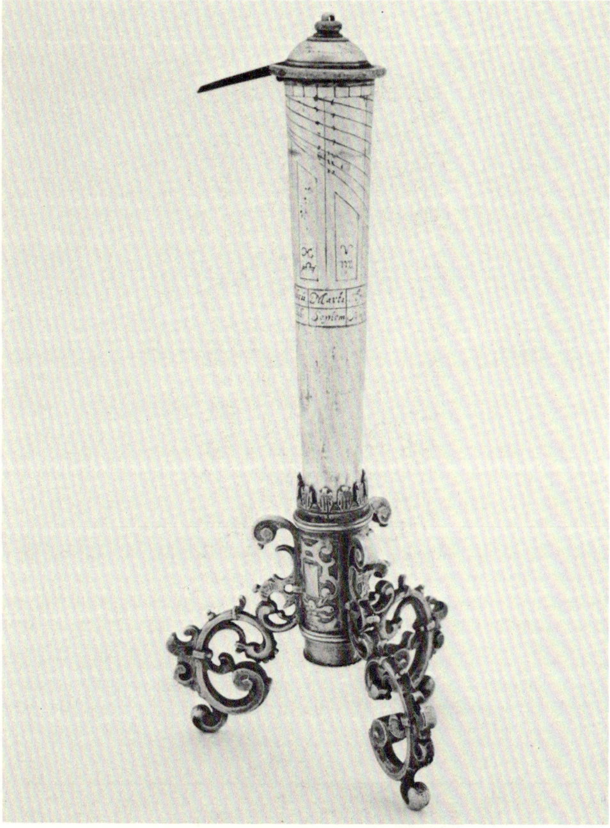

(Fig. no. 75) School of Erasmus Habermel

PILLAR SUNDIAL
(with screw-out knife and fork)

Lent by The Adler Planetarium, Chicago (Cat. no. 137).

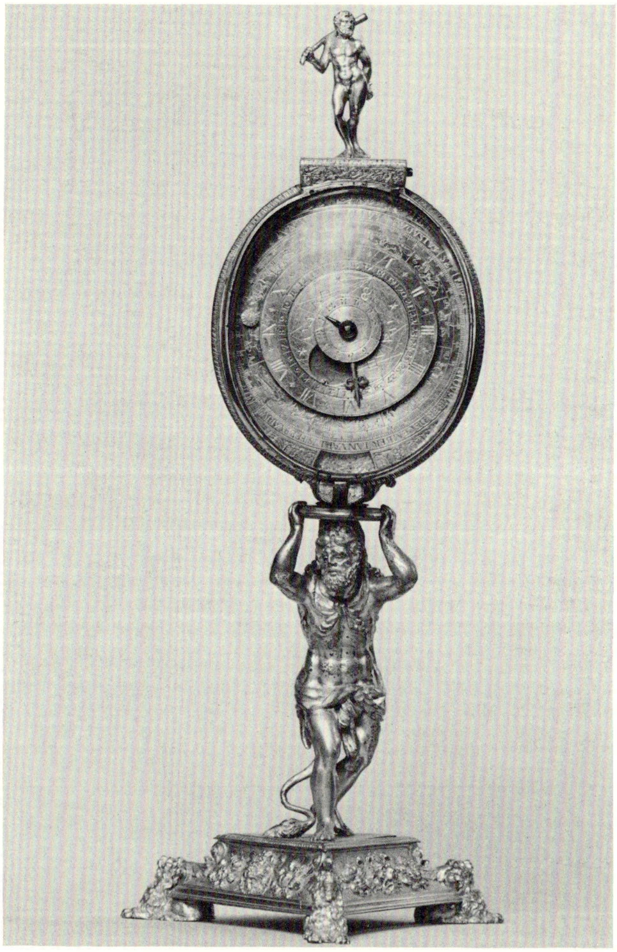

(Fig. no. 76) Antonio Arlaud

OVAL WATCH ON STAND SUPPORTED BY HERCULES

Lent by The Walters Art Gallery, Baltimore (Cat. no. 150).

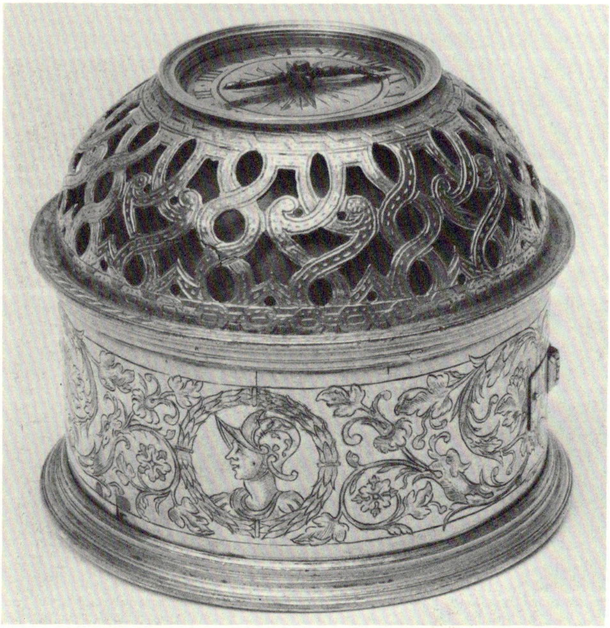

(Fig. no. 77) Bartholomew Newsam

TABLE CLOCK

Lent by The Metropolitan Museum of Art, New York.
Gift of J. Pierpont Morgan, 1917 (Cat. no. 146).

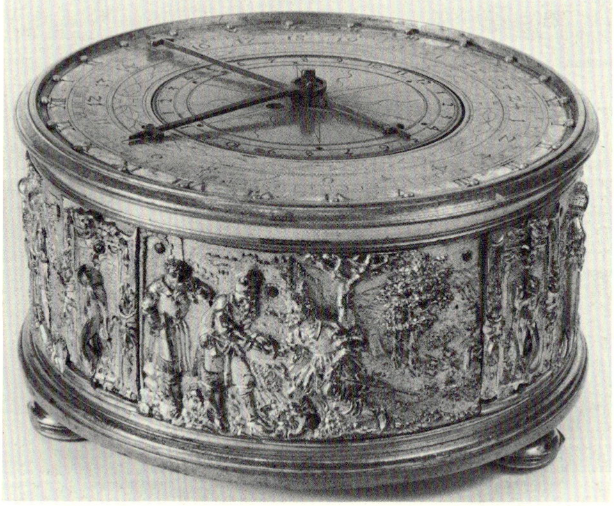

(Fig. no. 78) Hans Gruber

TABLE CLOCK

Lent by Ruth Blumka, New York (Cat. no. 142).

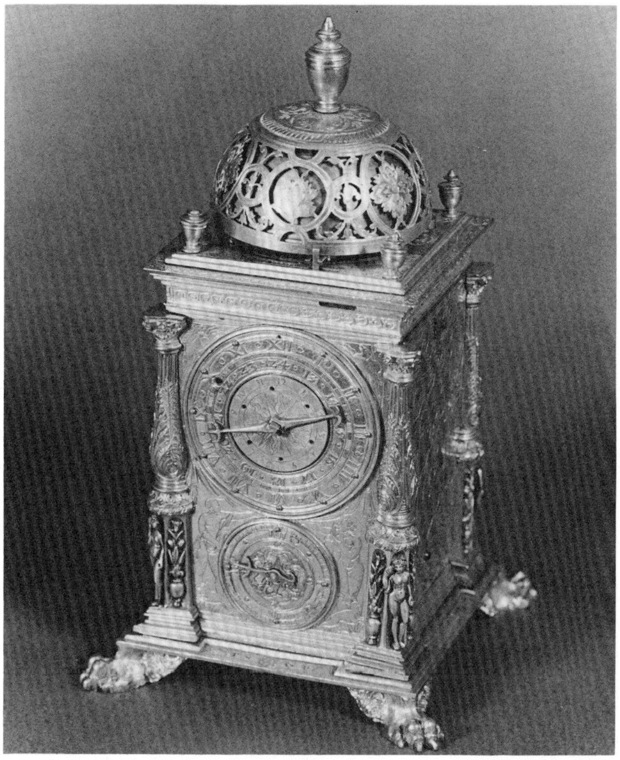

(Fig. no. 79) German (Augsburg), dated 1568

TABLE CLOCK

Lent by The Time Museum, Rockford, Illinois (Cat. no. 143).

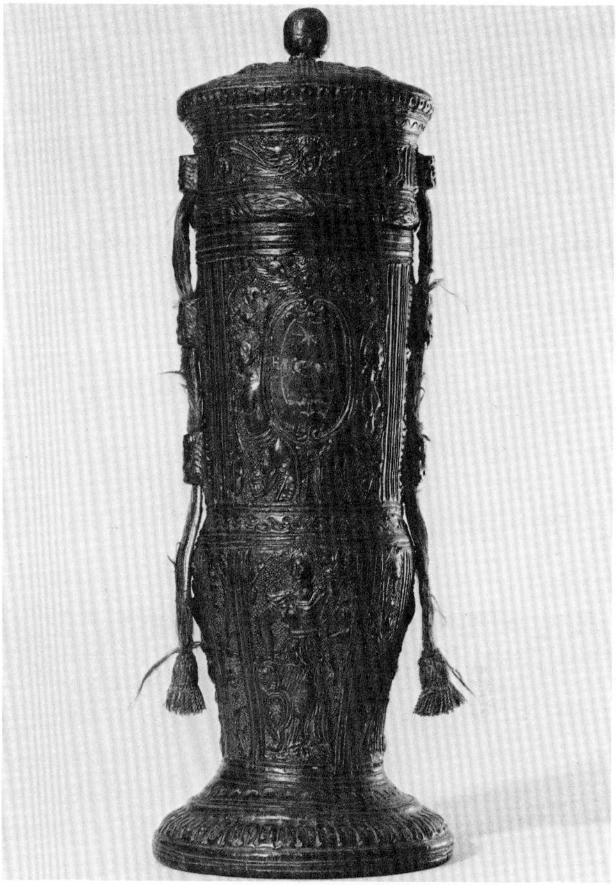

(Fig. no. 80) Italian, mid-16th century

INSTRUMENT CASE

Courtesy, Museum of Fine Arts, Boston.
Hezekiah E. Bolles Fund (Cat. no. 159).

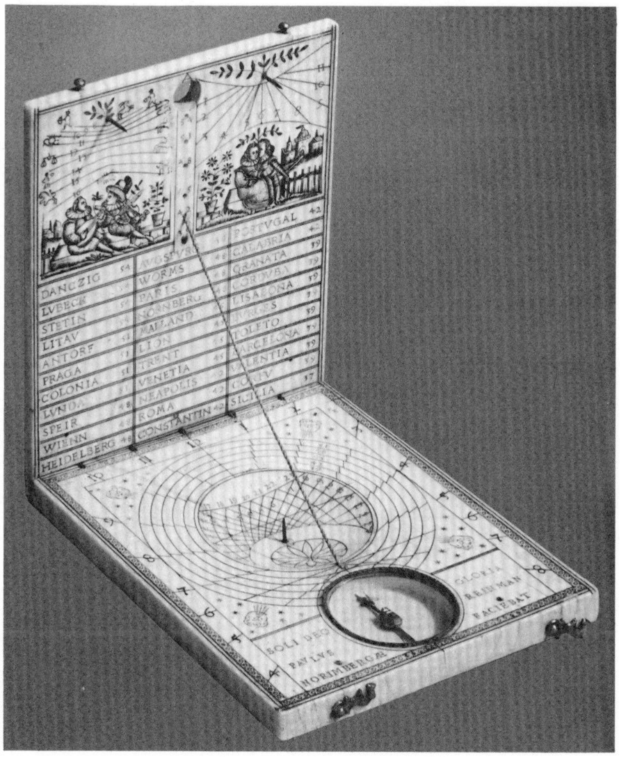

(Fig. no. 81) Paul Reinmann

PORTABLE DIPTYCH SUNDIAL

Lent by The Metropolitan Museum of Art, New York.
Gift of Mrs. Stephen D. Tucker, 1903 (Cat. no. 136).

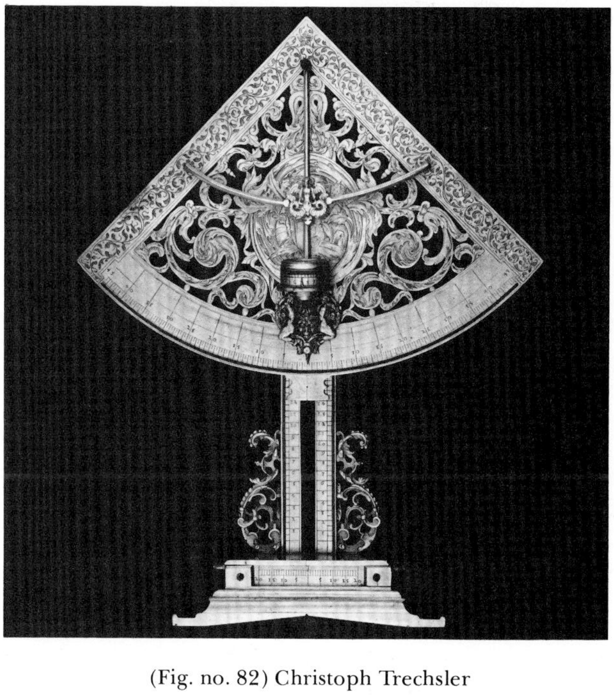

(Fig. no. 82) Christoph Trechsler

ARTILLERY LEVEL

Lent by The Adler Planetarium, Chicago (Cat. no. 156).

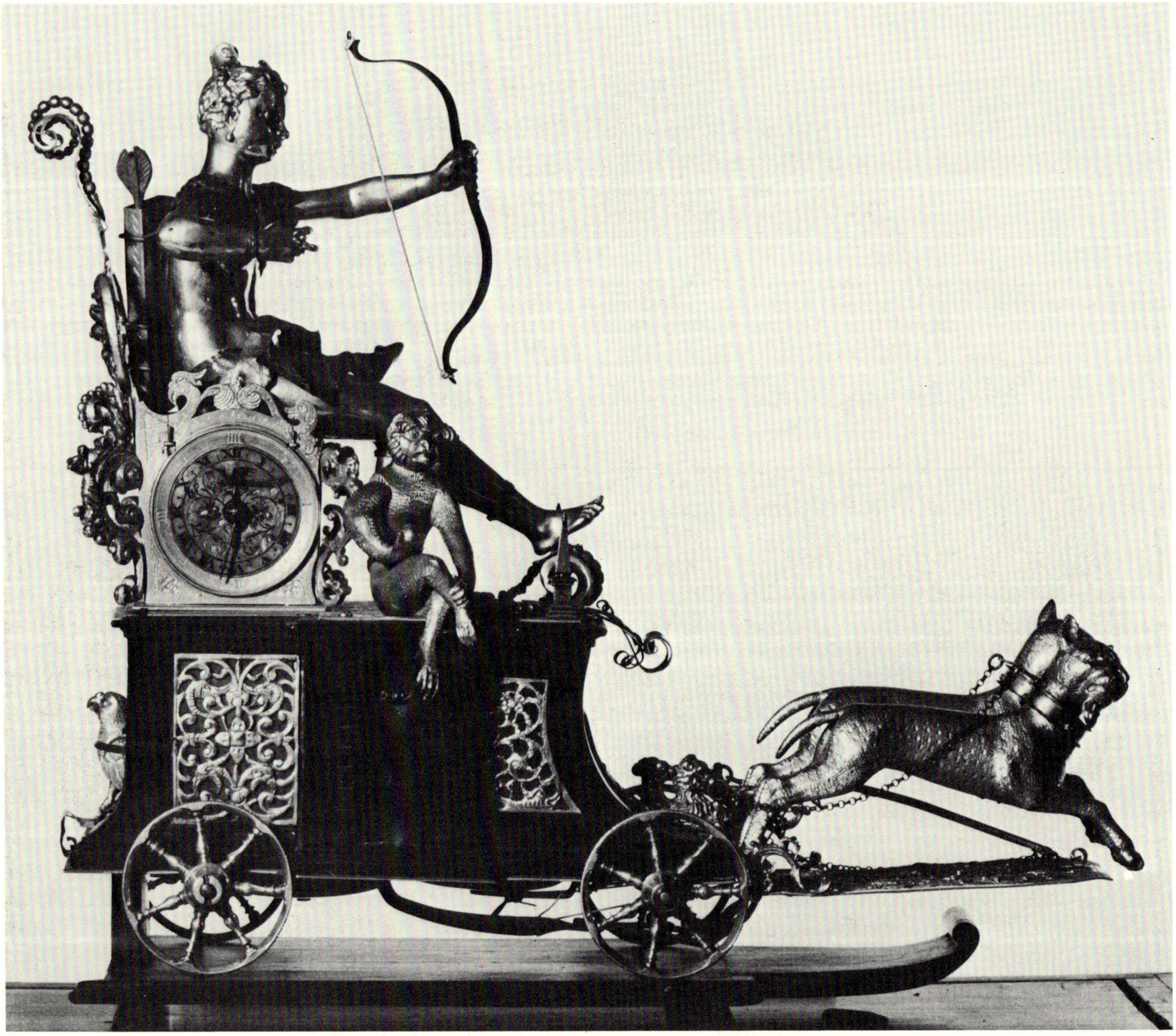

(Fig. no. 83) German, ca. 1600

AUTOMATE CLOCK IN THE FORM OF
DIANA ON HER CHARIOT

Lent by Yale University Art Gallery, New Haven, Connecticut.
Gift of Mrs. Laird S. Goldsborough (Cat. no. 147).

Ceramics and Glass

Jessie McNab Dennis

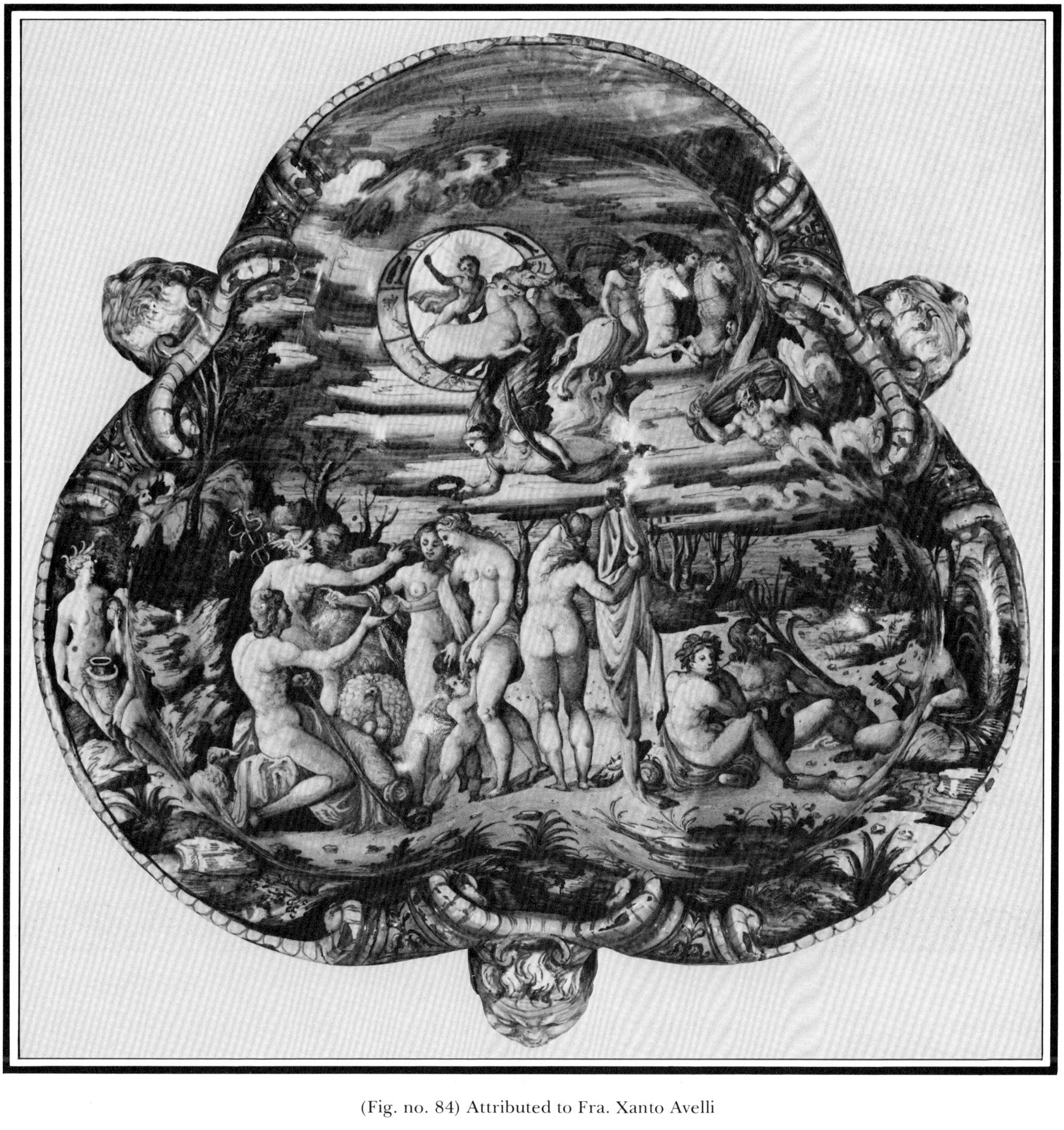

(Fig. no. 84) Attributed to Fra. Xanto Avelli

MAJOLICA WINE CISTERN

Lent by Los Angeles County Museum of Art.
Gift of Stanley Mortimer (Cat. no. 180).

Majolica

During the fifteenth and sixteenth centuries, the normally utilitarian activity of pottery manufacture was raised in a handful of places in North and Central Italy to the level of a minor art. This development became possible through the combination of advances in technology and the adoption of entirely new forms of decoration derived from contemporary fine art.

The movement appears to have had its beginnings in Tuscany. Pottery glazed with a white tin enamel had been made for over a century in this district, as well as in other parts of northern Italy. The enamel was made by oxidizing together lead and tin and adding the resulting ash to the materials for the European potter's traditional clear glaze. The secret may have been learned from Spain, or it may have remained a secret and the opacifying tin oxide have been obtained at first through trade. In Spain the white enamel was decorated with painting in lustre colors and blue (Cat. no. 167), techniques which certainly remained secret until well into the fifteenth century. In Italy only the colors long known for decorating ordinary lead-glazed pottery were used on the white wares — green from copper and purple from manganese — and the "bianco" (white enamel) itself was meager in quality and used only sparingly.

Between about 1430 and 1460, in potteries serving the discriminating market in Florence, a totally new kind of white-surfaced pottery was made. Shapes derived from Spanish examples and included the cylindrical "albarello" for dry drugs. Decoration was in the deep, blackish blue derived from cobalt, then a new and difficult material to use, though long known and its control understood in the East. Bold motifs such as birds, beasts, and fish taken from Islamic and heraldic sources, as well as human figures and portrait busts in profile inspired by contemporary fashions in Italian art, were the main decoration. These were surrounded by large leaf-like motifs which give their name to the whole class of "oak leaf" jars (Cat. no. 160). There is little doubt that imported lustred Hispano-Moresque ware was the source of this background design, though it was much distorted due to the difficulty in handling the cobalt, which appears to have been applied as a smalt. This would explain a peculiarity in the early use of cobalt — its standing up in relief from the surface of the ware which made the rendering of fine detail impossible.

The period 1450 to 1500 was one of intense evolution artistically and technically, an evolution that was pressed forward not only in Tuscany but also in Faenza, on the other side of the Appenines, and in Siena and Deruta by masters from Faenza. The "bianco" was improved in whiteness and density by an increase of tin-oxide, that of Faenza being whitest of all. The use of cobalt was refined and several shades of blue became available. Yellow, orange, black, and several new shades of green were also developed. At the very end of the period, lustre colors, through what instrumentality is uncertain, became known at Deruta, and red came into use at Siena and Faenza. The privileged small factory established in 1506 by artisans from Montelupo in the Medici Villa at Caffaggiolo used all the colors generally available, as well as the lustres and reds which at the time were probably limited to a small number of technicians.

In the sixteenth century a few additional refinements to the range of possible color effects were made. A very white tin enamel was fabricated for painting abstract designs on a less white "bianco." Alternatively, the "bianco" was stained a light blue with cobalt to serve as a ground for painting in colors. Both innovations were introduced at Faenza. At Urbino, later in the century, particularly painterly effects were gained by washes of one color over another. At Gubbio, in a workshop owned by the Master Giorgio Andreoli and continued by his son, red and yellow lustres were added to polychrome decoration giving a dazzling effect. At this workshop also, wares made and decorated elsewhere were brought to be over-lustred, a practice that was possible because the lustre pigments were added in a separate firing. Toward the end of the century, possibly due to economic causes as much as to a change in taste, a preference for less heavily decorated wares asserted itself. Colored decoration had, for most of the century, completely covered the white ground on a very large percentage of pieces. Now, however, in the final phase of the vital period of "majolica," as this ware is now generically called, isolated polychrome compositions or motifs were set against wide expanses of undecorated "bianco."

The range of decoration in the period 1450-1600 was substantial. In the larger centers, for instance Faenza where in its heyday over thirty individual workshops were active, a number of flourishing businesses competed in a sellers' market for an interested and active clientele. The patterns chosen in the earlier period show a full and confident use of Hispano-Moresque and late Gothic decorative motifs, such as scrolling leaves, and more abstract designs with heraldic figures and Christian symbols. There was also a gradual and increasing use of pagan motifs and compositions catering to the interests of the intellectually-active elite that could be found in every city; they passionately admired the classical world and were familiar with its history and myths. In the sixteenth century pictorial compositions illustrating scenes from mythology (Cat. no. 172) and Roman history predominated, although biblical subjects were also illustrated, as well as more exotic decoration derived from blue and white porcelain and abstract Arabic design.

Except for a very small number of names, all this work is anonymous; even the names of the proprietors of the workshops are largely unknown. In the fifteenth century certainly, possibly starting with the first "oak leaf" jars, some specialization must have taken place. Majolica decoration essentially involves staining the unfired tin-glaze with various metal oxides. In its unfired state this surface is friable and absorbent, and it requires a very steady and practised touch in applying the coloring agents. In Florence and elsewhere there would be no difficulty in either recruiting artisans for this work or employing men who had previous experience in fresco or painting on gesso for furniture and panel paintings — both methods involving an absorbent ground for the paint. In the later fifteenth and early sixteenth centuries the decoration, whether pictorial or purely ornamental, is so well measured and firmly delineated as to suggest that an artist was the designer if not the painter. As the sixteenth century progressed, engravings were used sometimes very literally as a guide for pictorial decoration. A few names of painters are recorded and have been linked with actual pieces, such as Nicola Pellipario of Castel Durante, Xanto of Urbino, and Maestro Lodovico and Domenico, both of Venice.

Emigrant Italian potters took the practice of majolica-making to Lyons early in the sixteenth century. In the second half of the century workshops were also flourishing in Nimes and Nevers. At Rouen, however, a Frenchman, Matthéot Abaquesne, was the owner-master who worked for the court circle, producing mainly tiles and tile pictures as well as drug jars.

Majolica in the Italian manner was also produced at other isolated places in Europe, notably in Antwerp, Brixen in the Tyrol, and Talavera (Cat. no. 168).

Medici Porcelain

After ten years of experiment, a truly white ceramic hybrid decorated in light blue under a clear lead glaze was manufactured in Florence in a small factory in the Boboli gardens (Cat. no. 179). A versatile artist, Bernardo Buentalenti, rather than a working potter, was both director and designer. This intimate involvement of an artist with the productions of a factory, in this case documented in contemporary records, was an Italian innovation of surpassing significance for European decorative arts. The Florentine ware — an effort to imitate Chinese porcelain — was only possible through the enthusiasm and material support of its patron, Francesco Maria de' Medici, grand duke of Tuscany. Its period of production (1575-1587) did not survive his lifetime, nor did the endeavor become a commercial feasibility. Similar experiments were made at Padua and elsewhere, and a few white glass dishes from Venice (Cat. no. 192) show that the imitation of porcelain was a general aspiration of the period. These efforts at best could only imitate the appearance of porcelain. The source of its resonance, translucency, and rock-like hardness remained a mystery.

Scraffiato Ware

In Bologna, in precisely the same period that majolica was coming to the fore artistically elsewhere, the ancient "scraffiato" technique was revived for imposing chargers, probably all deriving from one workshop with ties to the leading Bentivoglio family (Cat. no. 183). A slip of white pipe clay mixed with water was applied over the body of dishes and objects formed from a red-brown clay. Elaborate pictorial compositions drawn with a very sure touch were incised into this friable white clay surface, showing the darker clay beneath. The glaze was usually a warm yellow or honey color, sometimes diversified with areas of green, purple, or blue. Three-dimensional objects decorated in this manner were also produced at Bologna (Cat. no. 177). Similar wares were produced in other cities of northern Italy; but none reached the level of achievement of those of Bologna, and the technique ultimately declined to a rather pedestrian level in both design and workmanship.

France

Apart from the majolica of Italian type made at Lyons, Nevers, Rouen, and Nimes, two unique and isolated efforts were made to raise ceramics to an artistic level. At St. Porchaire a white pottery was made over a span of years from about 1526-1566. The white clay of Poitou was employed and the lead glaze was remarkably clear. The ware has almost no resonance or hardness and for this reason can hardly have been intended for use. It was moreover very elaborately decorated in a technique of tortuous refinement. While still soft the finished clay object was impressed with fine metal stamps of a type similar to those used for decorating leather book bindings as a preparation for gold inlay. The shaped depressions were then brought level again with the surface of the wares by being filled with brown, orange, or black burning clays (Cat. no. 189). Only then was it fired and glazed. The effect was delicate, dark-on-white decoration analogous to the contemporary niello inlay on silver. In the last twenty years or so of the period of production, selective use was made of pale blue and green tinted glazes and motifs of reptiles and animals realistically modeled but so fine in scale as to suggest that they may have been borrowed from goldsmiths' work. These later features indicate an awareness of the work of Palissy, possibly through the linking effect of Anne de Montmorency, constable of France and Palissy's first patron, who owned a number of examples of St. Porchaire ware. Bernard Palissy conducted his preliminary experiments and executed his early commissions in Saintes, later moving to Paris (1566). He had devised a method of obtaining colored lead glazes through the use of various metal oxides, although he had originally set out to discover the secret of white tin glaze of the Italian type. These glazes were advantageously used, mingled, to imitate jasper and to color realistically animal and vegetable forms in clay. His best documented works were his grottoes (none of which survive) employing these "rustiques figulines," but tradition has also linked him with large dishes, frequently with the mingled jasper glaze on the reverse, on which shells, crayfish, worms, snakes, leaves, ferns, and other riverside fauna and flora cast from living models were arranged and appropriately colored with the tinted glazes. Also often attributed to Palissy (who died in 1590), but more probably made at Avon near Fontainebleau by the successors to his inventions, are the boat-shaped vessels modeled with a variety of figures on the interior and the sloping-sided dishes molded with masks and foliage.

Germany

In Austria and the cities of southern Germany where the most ambitious work in pottery was created by the builders and decorators of tile stoves, the white tin enamel did not displace lead glaze for fashionable wares as it had in Italy. Instead, as Renaissance themes tended to take the place of Gothic themes in the tile panels which formed the outer decorative cladding of the stoves (in important rooms, these assumed the status of a major, almost architectural, installation and were conspicuously

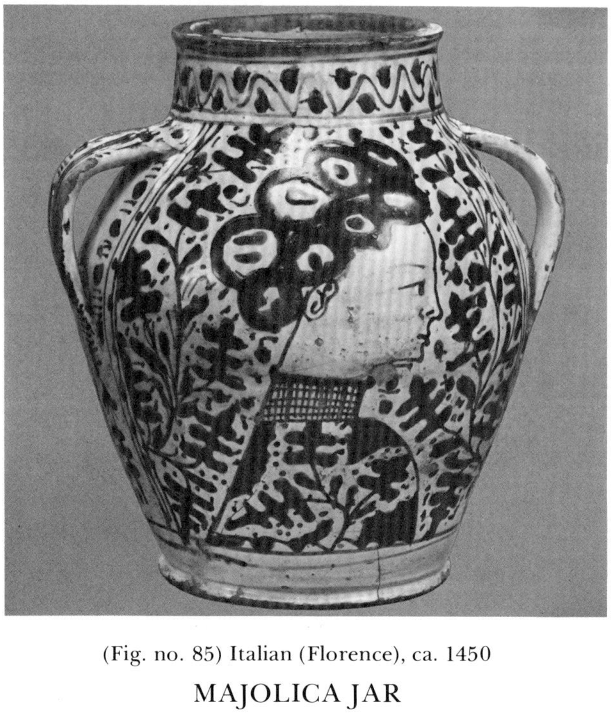

(Fig. no. 85) Italian (Florence), ca. 1450

MAJOLICA JAR

Lent by Wadsworth Atheneum, Hartford, Connecticut.
Gift of J. P. Morgan (Cat. no. 160).

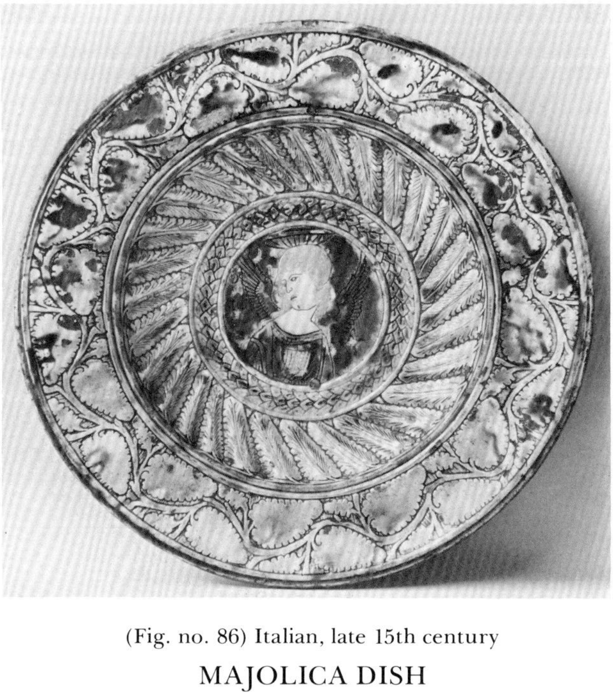

(Fig. no. 86) Italian, late 15th century

MAJOLICA DISH

Lent by The Metropolitan Museum of Art, New York.
Gift of R. Thornton Wilson in memory of
Florence Ellsworth Wilson (Cat. no. 183)

ornate), tin enamel was used in areas where white as a color was required by the composition, the deeply colored yellow, blue, green and purple lead glazes continuing in use.

In northern Germany, an interesting departure was made in artistic pottery using the pale clays of the Rhineland. Centers were in Cologne, Raeren, Siegburg and Westerwald. The local clay could be fired to a high temperature and assumed a vitrified state. Although the resulting stoneware needed no glaze to render it impermeable, a salt glaze was usually employed. At Siegburg a type of tall, tapering, near-white jug (Cat. no. 191) was produced, often decorated with crisp armorial or figure motifs formed in wooden molds and applied to the surface before firing. Fine detail was possible because of the fine-grained nature of the ware. At Cologne, which had long been a potting center, the grayer clay was given a wash of a ferruginous clay on its surface before firing and salt-glazing which gave it a pleasing orange-peel surface of a brownish to light orange hue (Cat. no. 64) Cologne wares are marked by massive, simple shapes, and the most common form of decoration is the molded bearded man's face under the spout, although applied relief decoration was also sometimes used.

Glass

The activity of glassmaking in the Venetian Republic was, according to documentary sources, considerable throughout the late Medieval and early Renaissance periods. Colored and gold glass was made for beads and mosiacs, and many glass houses made blown vessels. These must have so shared the character of the Syrian glass wares of the period as to be indistinguishable from them. However, the same stirring of artistic interest that was manifested in ceramics in the second half of the fifteenth century appears to have been felt in Venice. The first sign of this was the manufacture of stately goblets in jewel deep blue, green, and turquoise glass, enameled and gilt with pictorial scenes drawn from popularized themes of humanist literature, such as the Triumph of Love. In this fifty years too, many new methods for decorating glass were invented, and new formulas for the metal itself (glass) were perfected. The most conspicuously successful of these and the one that has endured to the present day was the "cristallo," so called from its resemblance to the only clear substance then known, rock crystal. This was used for princely objects of great luxury, often mounted in gold. The earliest objects in "cristallo" were rather heavy looking gob-

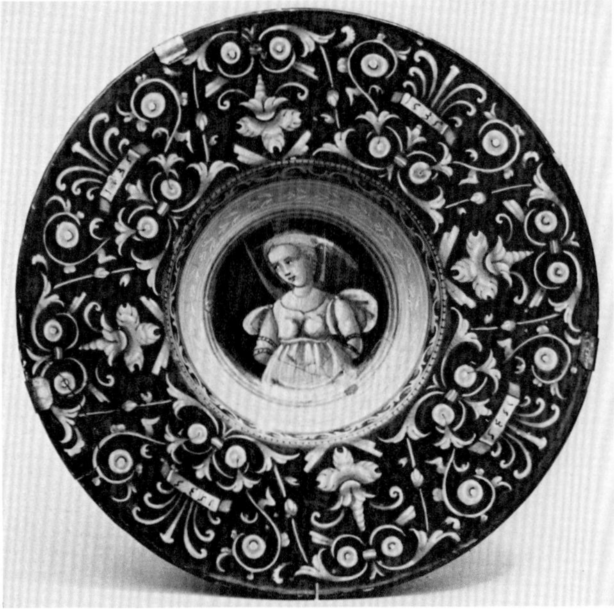

(Fig. no. 87) Italian, 1535

MAJOLICA DISH

Lent by The Metropolitan Museum of Art, New York. Gift of Julia A. Berwind, 1953 (Cat. no. 173).

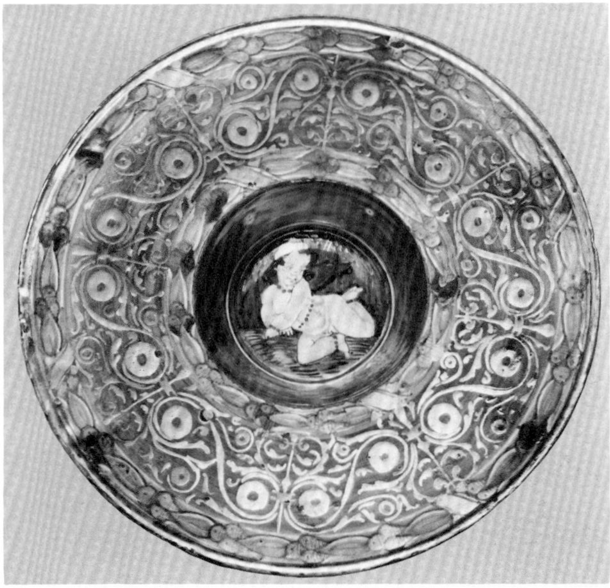

(Fig. no. 88) Italian, 1526

MAJOLICA DISH

Lent by The Metropolitan Museum of Art, New York. Gift of V. Everit Macy, in memory of his wife, Edith Carpenter Macy, 1927 (Cat. no. 171).

lets and bowls of imposing size that relied on the formal shapes that were natural to rock crystal. These were dictated by the intractable nature of the mineral, which had to be cut and polished on the lapidary's wheel and was brittle and difficult to work. The period of dependence on rock crystal models was short-lived, and the qualities inherent in "cristallo" were exploited instead. It was very light and ductile and could be manipulated while in a semi-molten state into any number of fantastic shapes; it could also be cut, pincered, elongated, and twisted.

Evidence recently brought to light shows that at the end of the sixteenth century artists were commissioned to design all kinds of glass vessels in a contemporary idiom. There is no reason to believe that artists were not also active much earlier in designing both the shapes and the decoration of Renaissance glass. This is the only possible explanation for the aesthetic harmony of glass with the major arts which is seen in the late fifteenth and throughout the sixteenth century.

The export of glass was for long an important item in the economy of Venice. The impetus given by the new developments raised exports to their highest volume and also made it economically inviting — in spite of dire threatened consequences — for Venetian glassmakers to emigrate to great mercantile cities such as Antwerp and London and there make glass in the Ventian manner.

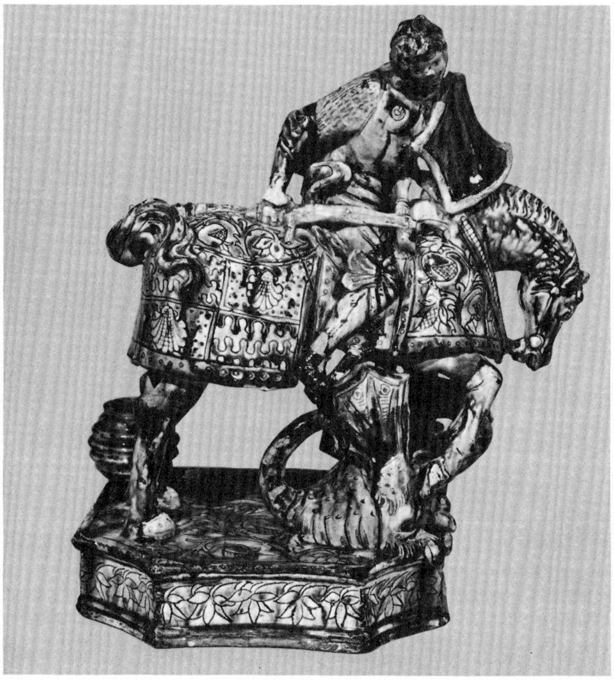

(Fig. no. 89) Italian (Ferrara), ca. 1500

INKSTAND WITH ST. GEORGE AND THE DRAGON

Lent by The Detroit Institute of Arts.
Founders Society Purchase. Elliott T. Slocum Fund.
(Cat. no. 177).

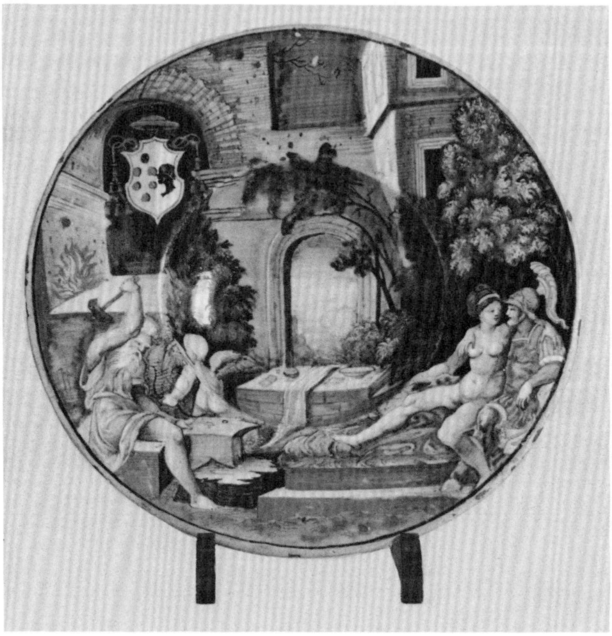

(Fig. no. 90) Italian (Pesaro), 1540-1544

MAJOLICA PLATE (Vulcan, Venus, and Mars)

Lent by The Cleveland Museum of Art.
John L. Severance Collection (Cat. no. 174).

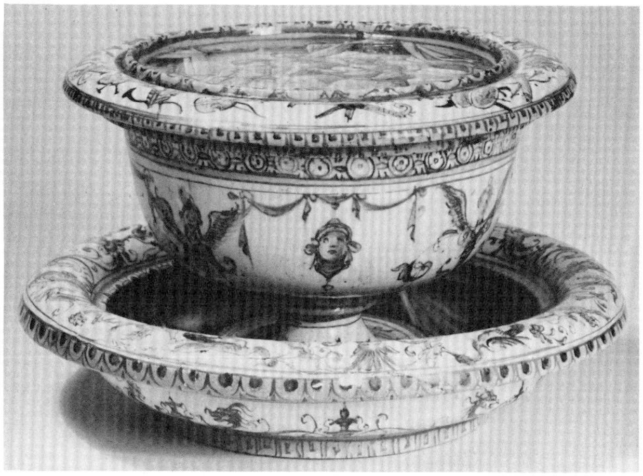

(Fig. no. 91) Italian (Urbino), 1500-1550

MAJOLICA CHRISTENING SET

Lent by The Detroit Institute of Arts.
Gift of Mr. and Mrs. Henry Ford II (Cat. no. 165).

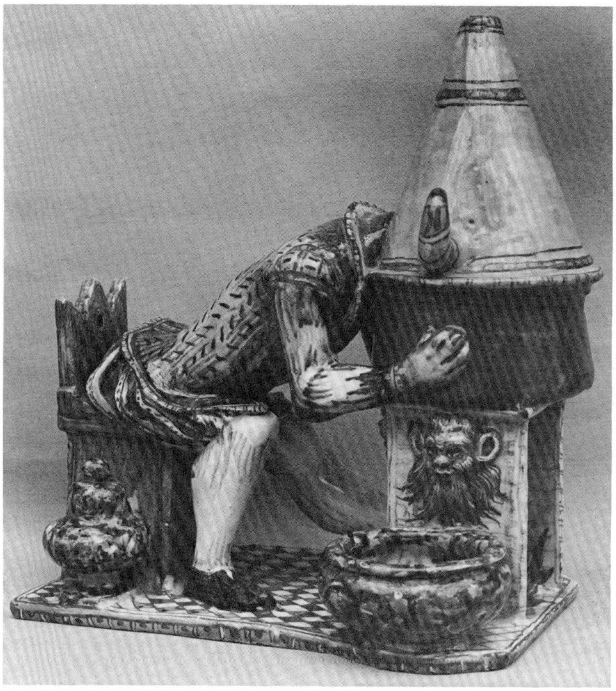

(Fig. no. 92) Italian, 16th century

MAJOLICA SALT CELLAR

Lent by The Metropolitan Museum of Art, New York.
Rogers Fund, 1904 (Cat. no. 175).

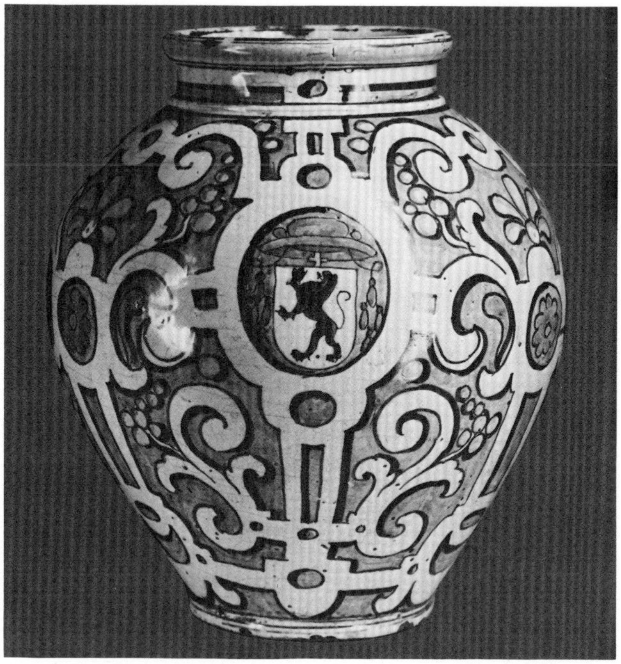

(Fig. no. 93) Spanish (Talavera), ca. 1565

MAJOLICA DRUG JAR

Lent by John Philip Kassebaum, Wichita, Kansas
(Cat. no. 168).

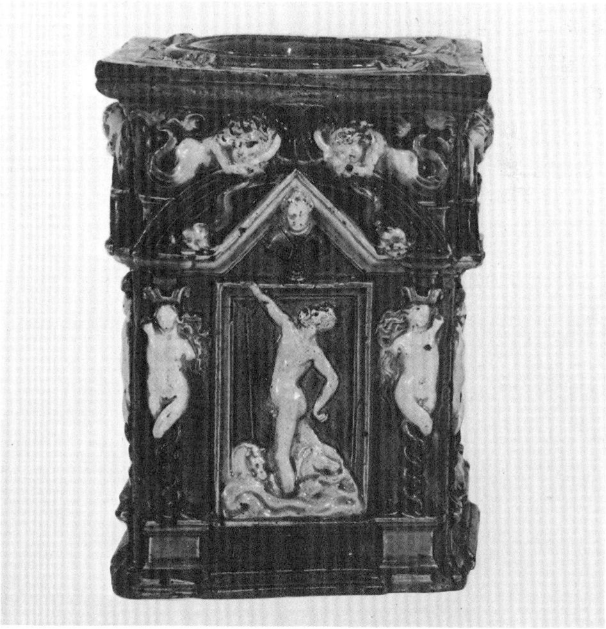

(Fig. no. 94) Manner of Bernard Palissy

SALT CELLAR

Lent by Cyril Humphris, London (Cat. no. 190).

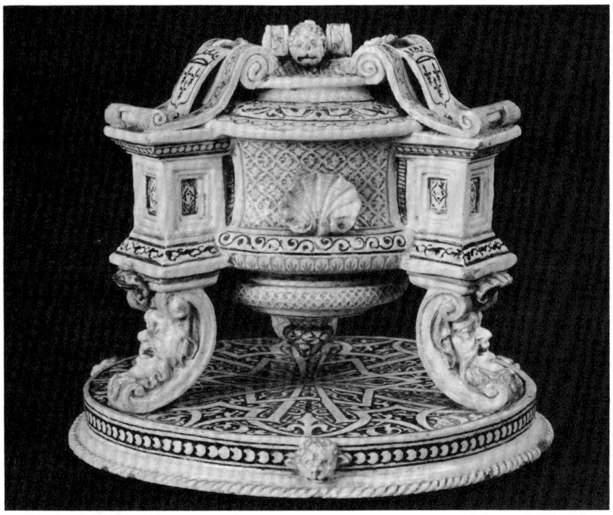

(Fig. no. 95) French (Saint-Porchaire), 16th century

SALT CELLAR

Lent by The Cleveland Museum of Art.
Purchase from the J. H. Wade Fund (Cat. no. 189).

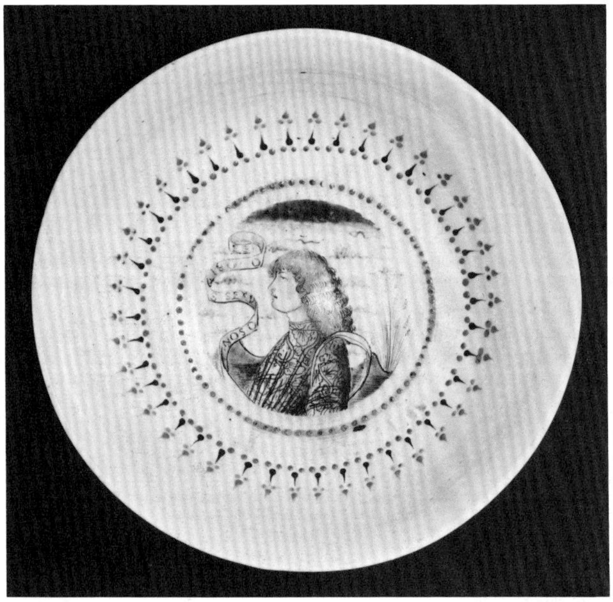

(Fig. no. 96) Italian (Venice), 1500-1510

BOWL

Lent by The Corning Museum of Glass, Corning, New York (Cat. no. 192).

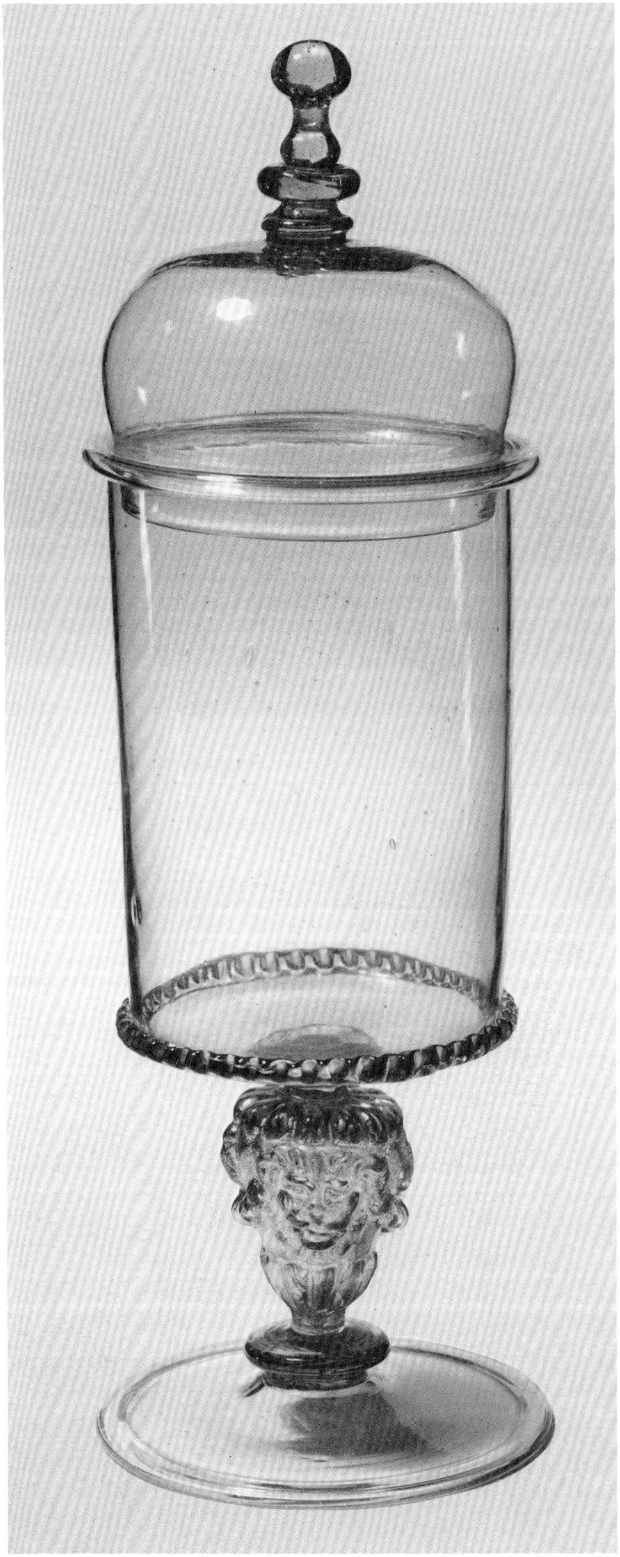

(Fig. no. 97) Italian (Venice), 16th century

COVERED GOBLET

Lent by The Wine Museum of San Francisco
Franz W. Sichel Collection (Cat. no. 197).

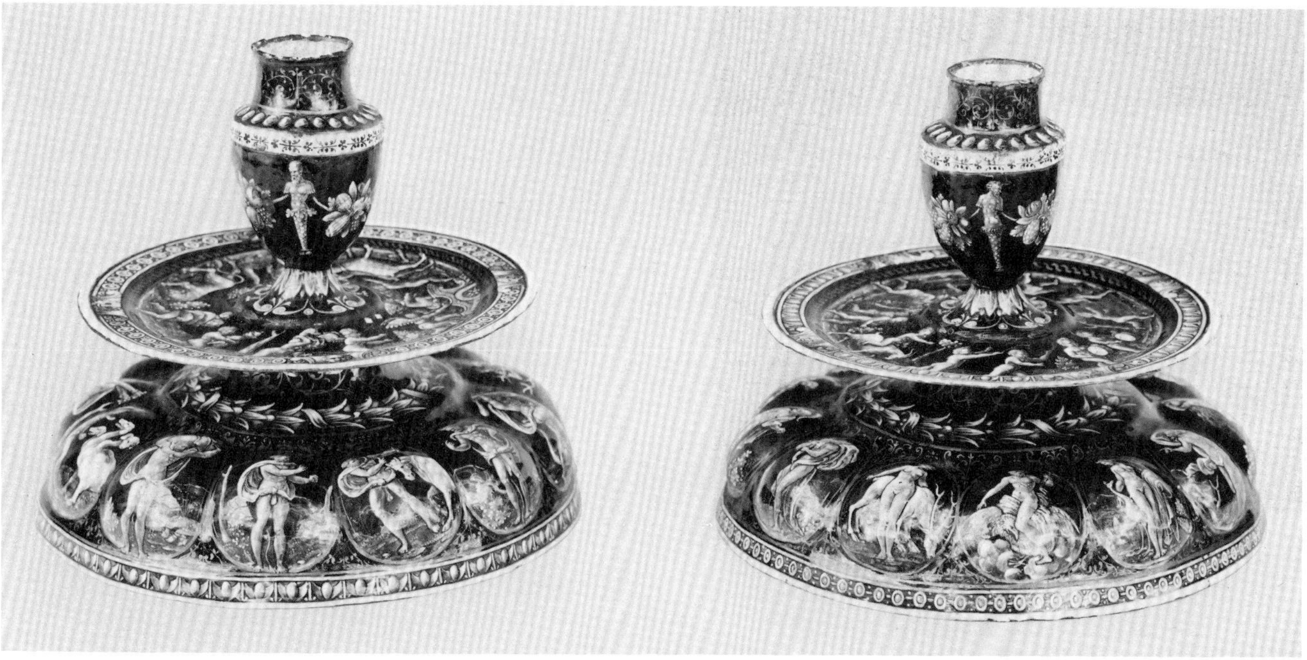

(Fig. no. 98) Possibly by Jean de Court

PAIR OF CANDLESTICKS

Lent by The Metropolitan Museum of Art, New York.
Gift of Ann Payne Blumenthal. (Cat. no. 202).

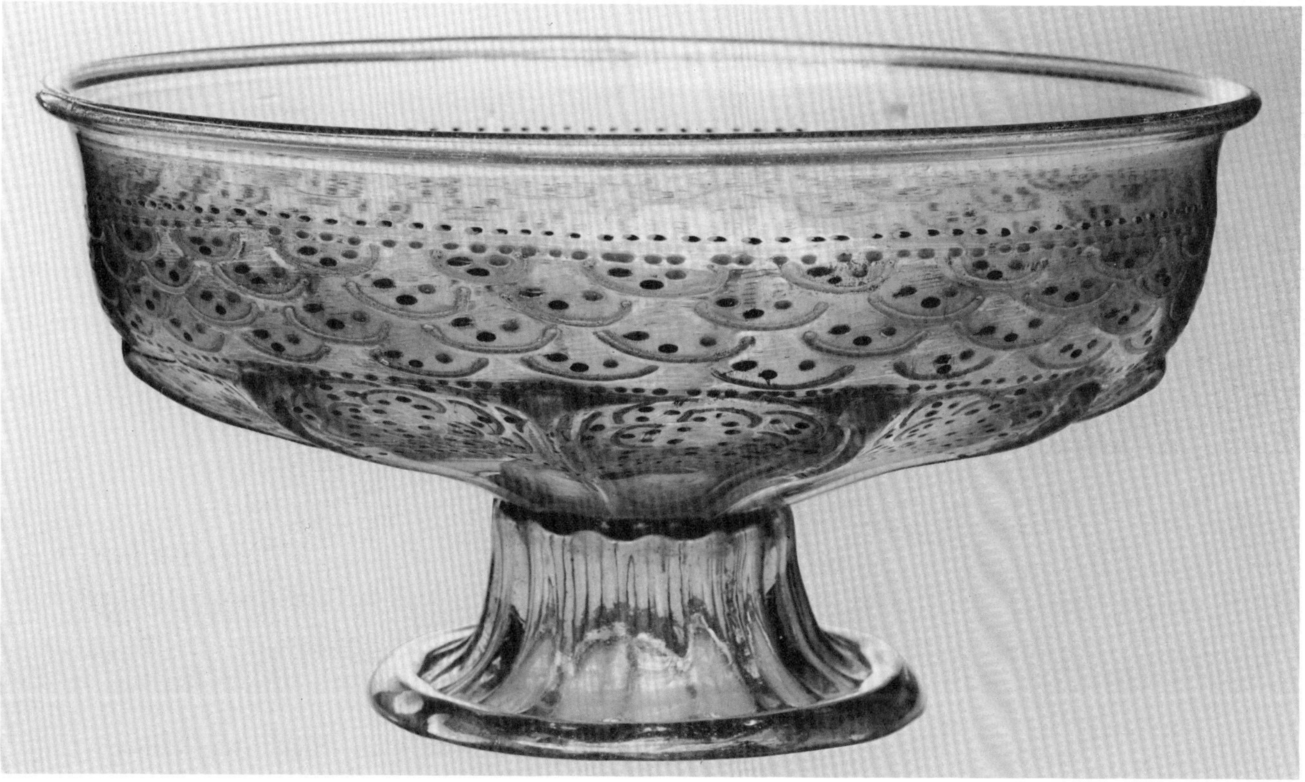

(Fig. no. 99) Italian (Venice), first half of 16th century

TAZZA

Lent by The Metropolitan Museum of Art, New York.
Gift of J. Pierpont Morgan, 1919 (Cat. no. 196).

Furniture and Woodcarving

David DuBon

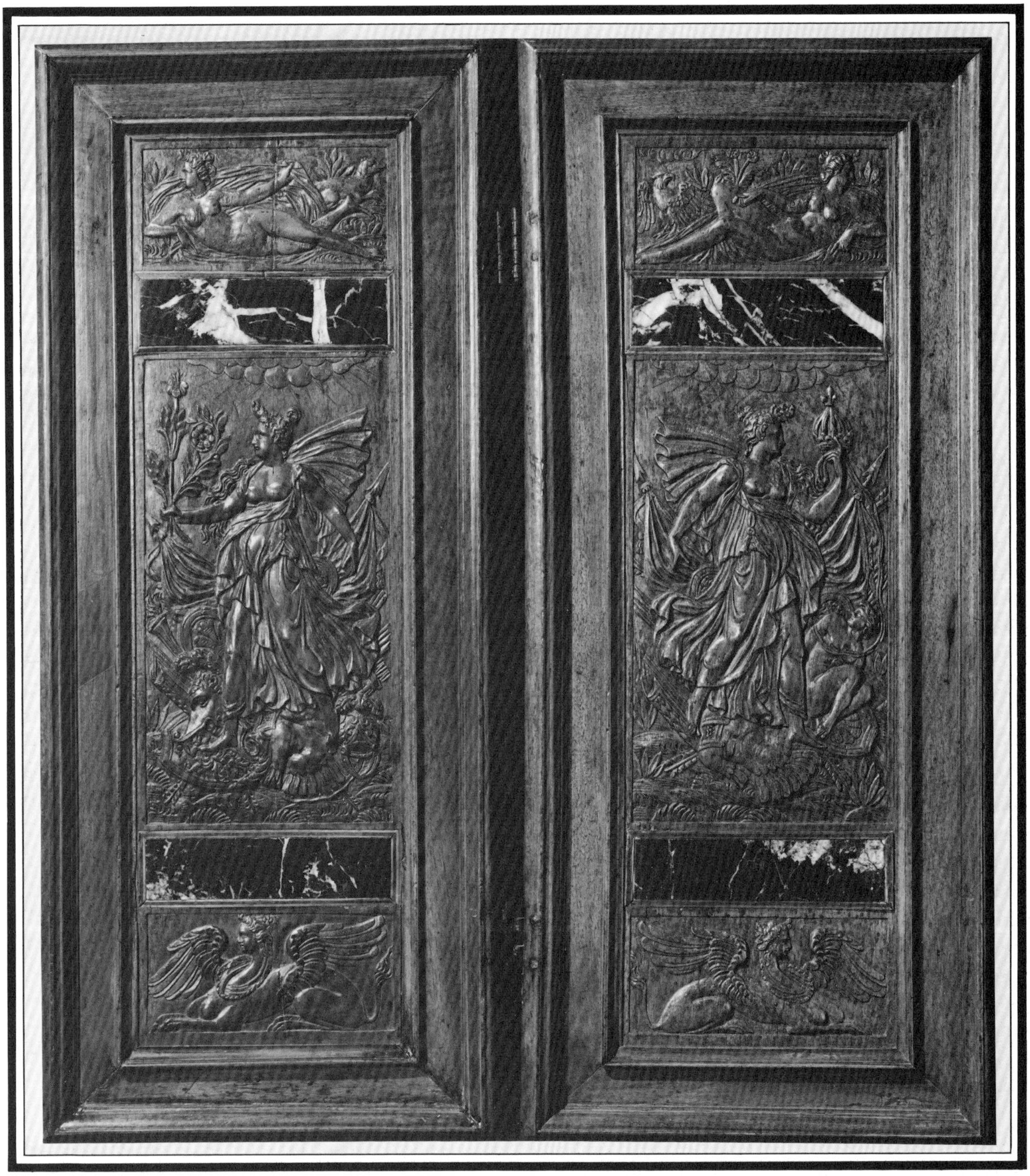

(Fig. no. 100) French (School of Fontainebleau), ca. 1550

TWO PANELS (Allegory of Peace and War)

Lent by Philadelphia Museum of Art.
Purchased: John T. Morris Fund (Cat. no. 222).

For secular furniture, the Renaissance was not, for the most part, the period of continual change and great achievements that it was for painting, sculpture, and architecture. It was rather a time of transition from the Medieval period, and not until the second half of the sixteenth century were the necessary elements — construction techniques, forms and surface ornament, and a more stable social pattern — sufficiently developed for the general production of pieces which were completely integrated in all aspects. Renaissance furniture, like that of all periods, was conditioned by its function — that is, a seating piece must be made, whether in the ancient world, the Renaissance, or today, to conform to the human body. There were national or regional differences which occurred for a variety of reasons, but the needs of a piece of furniture were essentially the same in each locale, although the form and surface manipulation might vary.

The essential characteristics of Medieval society that affected furniture-making continued into the early Renaissance — houses had few rooms; furnishings were sparse and required to be highly mobile. However, the changes which did occur and which dictated new design and surface ornament for furniture were the greater number and specialized use of rooms in a dwelling and the rise of a middle class with the needs and means for greater quantities and more varieties of furniture. With these new demands, new construction techniques were necessarily evolved or resurrected (they had not disappeared during the Middle Ages but had been utilized primarily by the Church).

The influence of the antique in this area was felt less in the forms than in the surface treatment, presumably because of lack of technique. For instance, the standard Greek and Roman chair, the *klismos* depicted on unending extant reliefs, was probably not produced because the construction techniques of the antique chair were too sophisticated. Yet at the same time the form of the solid-end marble table was quickly taken up and adapted in Italy and France; and of course, in Italy the *cassone,* a low chest with hinged top, imitated the antique sarcophagus. There is little consistent pattern to the way antique models were adapted from country to country. The Italians and the French were the only people to adapt the form of the antique solid-end table. The French also utilized the columnar form as a supporting member, and for their cabinets the Italians adapted Renaissance façades which depended on antique sources.

The heritage of the Middle Ages is apparent in many aspects. The extensive use of fabrics was retained during the Renaissance. Contemporary paintings and miniatures indicate that this very adaptable device had many uses: as wall decoration, as a covering for boards supported by trestles for the display of precious objects on several levels, and on beds which were composed completely of fabric covering a frame. In household inventories in the Middle Ages and during the Early Renaissance, fabrics were held in such high esteem that they were itemized with other important household items such as jewels and valuable small objects. It is not until the later fifteenth century that furniture is described to the same extent as fabrics. Another aspect of the Medieval heritage was the dependence on forms which were easily moved. The portable trestle and plank combination was used throughout western Europe as were other inherited forms, for example the three-legged stool and simple plank-constructed furniture such as benches and cupboards. In addition to plank and trestle devices, the folding chair and stool and wood tables with solid ends (Cat. no. 204) which could easily be dismounted were a necessity even for the rich. Not until the social pattern depended less on mobility could stable furnishings become possible.

Construction and form are dependent on each other, but in these cases whether forms followed available techniques or the techniques were developed to meet the needs of the form is uncertain. Renaissance Italy certainly had broad technological ability in many areas but used only a very elementary plank and nail construction on many pieces of furniture, while northern countries in the fifteenth century used interlocking dovetails at the corners of plank-constructed furniture and had already perfected the fairly sophisticated frame and panel construction with a rigid corner formed by a mortise and tenon joint. In this technique, the tenon, which is tapered at the end, is inserted at a right angle into another section with a cavity of the same dimensions; when a panel is enclosed, its edges are inserted into channels incised in the inside edges of the framing sections, producing a lighter, stronger structure with options for a greater variety of shapes.

Italy continued to use primitive forms of construction on many pieces throughout the sixteenth century. When new techniques became available, they were frequently used not for creating new structures but in modifying and elaborating older forms. For example, though it had no function, frame and panel construction was imitated on cabinets by the addition of flat sections and molding to a plank structure, creating the appearance of a technique of construction that was not actually used until the very late sixteenth century. Another example of this is the *cassone* with a curved front and top used by young ladies entering convents during the fifteenth century. It is a derivation of the low chest made from a hollowed-out tree trunk, known by documents to have been used centuries earlier, with iron bindings which functioned both as hinges and hasps for locking. The form persisted in the fifteenth century with nailed plank construction, the iron bindings no longer functional. The same structure was retained later in the century in *cassoni* without the bindings and with late-fifteenth-century ornament consisting of a painted or polychromed gesso surface. In the following century, the curved front was incorporated into the bench form *(cassapanca)* which still functioned as a *cassone,* but with a hinged seat. In the same manner, the typical chair form, the *sgabello* with back, was derived from a stool composed of a plank seat and similar front and back supports (Cat. no. 207).

The first evidences of the new taste were in the surface, the structures themselves retaining earlier styles. From the very little we know of Medieval furniture, it appears that surface ornament, and sometimes the forms themselves, had been for the most part architectural. This tradition was continued in the early Renaissance, but gradually new surface treatments evolved which were particularly related to the structures until, in the later sixteenth century, the ornamental designs depended less on the architectural vocabulary. One reason for the dependence on architecture for the articulation of surfaces in the Early Renaissance was the lack of any variety of readily transportable sources for surface ornament; the only models were those close at hand. Earlier, fabrics seem to have inspired the allover small patterns of low-relief gesso ornament on some *cassoni,* but the importation of objects from the East seems to have had only a limited influence on furniture. Not until the late fifteenth century and early in the sixteenth did easily accessible sources become available in the form of ornamental engravings — prints produced solely for the use by craftsmen in all materials. The widely collected medals representing famous people were one of the most influential ornamental forms. Although first produced in Italy, they were not used for ornamental design in that country; they were, however, broadly used in France and to a lesser extent in England. From the same source, roundel engravings of profile heads surrounded by ornament were produced and used extensively by woodworkers. Prints of antique sculpture and architecture were utilized, particularly in countries that had few examples of antique art, in addition to those of contemporary interpretations of classical subjects. In France, for instance, craftsmen used both prints produced in their own country and those from Flanders as well. At the same time, numerous books on architecture in the new taste were being produced from which woodworkers could extract bits and pieces — consoles, pediments, columns, cornices, etc. — to incorporate into furniture. Not only did they use books produced specifically for the craftsman, but they also borrowed from allegorical illustrations or ornamented title pages — any printed material which was in the new style. Only in the sixteenth century when new ornamental forms were developed (particularly the strap or scrollwork from the north, and Flemish and German forms) was a more extensive and varied range of designs made available.

There were national differences both in form and surface ornament. Native to Italy was the *sgabello,* with or without a back; furniture with columnar supports was particular to France and was used sparingly in England, while the latter developed the court cupboard (Cat. no. 228) — a display piece of several stages to show precious objects, a heritage of the earlier plank and trestle structures. The French fulfilled this need for display with the *dressoir,* an adaptation of a Gothic cabinet. The tall wardrobe was not taken up in most countries, although it was known during the earlier period. Germany and Flanders were the only two areas where it seems to have been produced extensively in the Renaissance. There were also national and regional variations in surface treatments not necessarily related to or paralleling the other visual arts. At times new ornamental forms were invented, such as strap or scrollwork at Fontainebleau (flat, leather-like intertwining strips) which had no precedent and was favored in the northern countries. Italy was the only country to rely on gesso, a pliable material of varying compositions applied to flat sections to form surface relief. The elements were made from molds and could be repeated on one piece, such as the early fifteenth-century low-relief patterns derived from textiles and also used with paint and gesso narrative panels enclosed by gesso architectural elements (Cat. no. 208). This unique process was developed to the extent that late in the century narrative figural reliefs could be produced in very deep, almost three-dimensional form, many modeled after sarcophagus reliefs; this was the first step in the development of the sixteenth century's elaborately carved and gilded walnut *cassoni.* Most of the northern countries employed carving. In England a peculiarly individual incised pattern developed, perhaps as an inheritance from the Gothic period, although inlaid woods were used extensively in Germany and to a lesser extent in other areas.

The sixteenth century, then, was in all countries a period in which the achievements of advanced construction techniques, surface treatment, and furniture of one use were realized with forms and surfaces beginning to be more closely related to each other and to the structural material, relying less on unrelated forms. In Italy, the heritage of the earlier period — use of fabrics, primitive plank construction, the easily disassembled pieces such as the trestle and solid-end table and the folding chair — was carried well into the sixteenth century, gradually replacing newer forms. Rigid frame construction was perfected, enabling greater variety of forms. Tables were produced in many shapes and sizes; those of the earlier part of the century, round, octagonal (Cat no. 209), and rectangular, were supported by baluster and volute forms, and for the first time drawers were incorporated in many pieces. In the north, which had a tradition of cabinetwork, the knowledge of construction allowed the craftsman more options in adapting the new style with a transition from earlier forms; at first he applied surface ornament in the new style to Gothic pieces, gradually creating fully conceived furniture with all of the elements related.

The second half of the sixteenth century in these countries saw the full realization of all the construction techniques, forms, and surface treatments which were to comprise the basis — in many instances unchanging — for all furniture for more than two centuries. The requirements for multiple use and mobility were, in all but a few instances, abandoned with the coming of a more stable living pattern. Furniture could be fabricated for a single use; pieces formerly only functional, such as seat furniture, were now highly designed; and everywhere additional pieces were made for very specific uses. The cabinet became the most important case piece, its fabrication in great variety in all countries made possible by the new techniques. These pieces were a further development of the concept of show or luxury pieces (evolving from the small, richly decorated Medieval boxes) in which the most important element was that of displaying one's ability to afford such richly surfaced pieces, a concept first evident in the elaborate *cassoni* made at the turn of the century. They probably also served the secondary purpose of a repository for collections of precious objects, which were becoming ever more important. Appearing for the first time around the middle of the century were small moveable cabinets containing many drawers and compartments, their surfaces decorated with applied materials, and large cabinets whose surfaces were richly ornamented with carving, parcel-gilding, polychrome, metal, and veneers and inlays of rare woods, ivory, and semiprecious stones. The technique of frame construction allowed seating furniture to change radically during this period, except in Italy where plank construction was not totally abandoned until the following century. New, light forms were now possible, and also for the first time turned sections and upholstery instead of loose cushions were used on backs and seats. Pieces seating more than one person, the Medieval bench or multi-purpose bench-chest having been abandoned in most countries except England in favor of individual seating pieces, were produced extensively in Italy in the form of the *cassapanca* — the *cassone* form with arms and back added. Wood tables were elaborated upon and became relatively stable objects during this time, although the highly useful moveable trestle and plank structures were still produced. The earlier solid-end constructed pieces were still fabricated, but with the advent of the ability to produce frame structure they were gradually replaced by the lighter pieces, like seating pieces, with turned sections.

Thus the Renaissance saw the evolution of domestic furniture from simply constructed objects, which grew out of the needs of the restricted Medieval life-style, to varied structures that changed and multiplied as a more sedentary life-style gradually emerged. In the last years of the sixteenth century, all of the forms, construction techniques, and surface decorations that were necessary and possible for secular furniture were developed — only refinements were needed for the achievements of the next several hundred years.

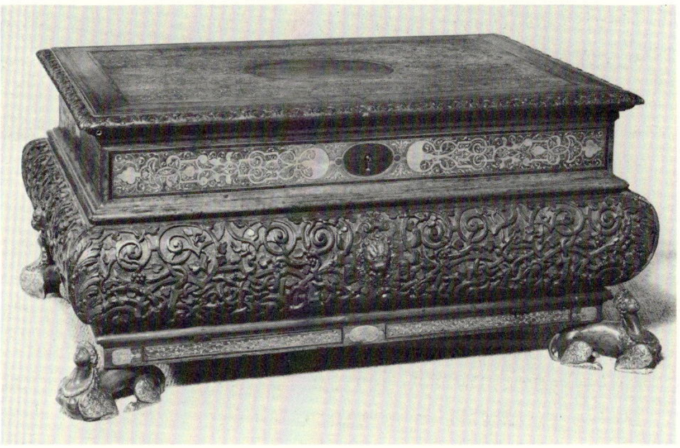

(Fig. no. 101) French (Burgundy), ca. 1550

COFFER

Lent by Philadelphia Museum of Art.
Purchased for the McIlhenny Collection (Cat. no. 226).

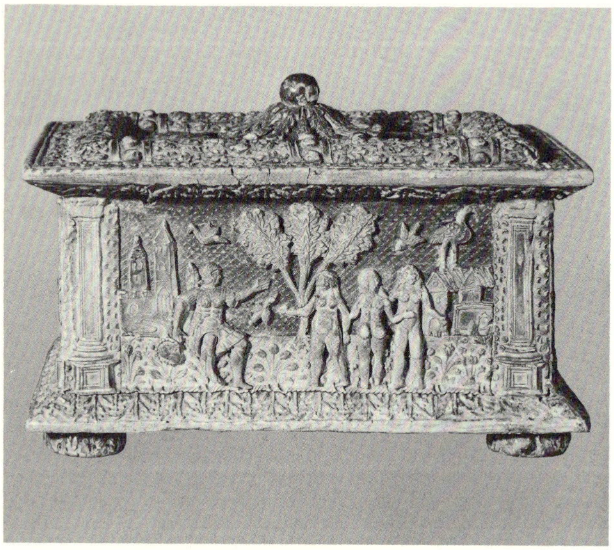

(Fig. no. 102) North Italian, ca. 1500

CASKET

Lent by Cooper-Hewitt Museum,
The Smithsonian Institution's National Museum of Design,
New York (Cat. no. 208).

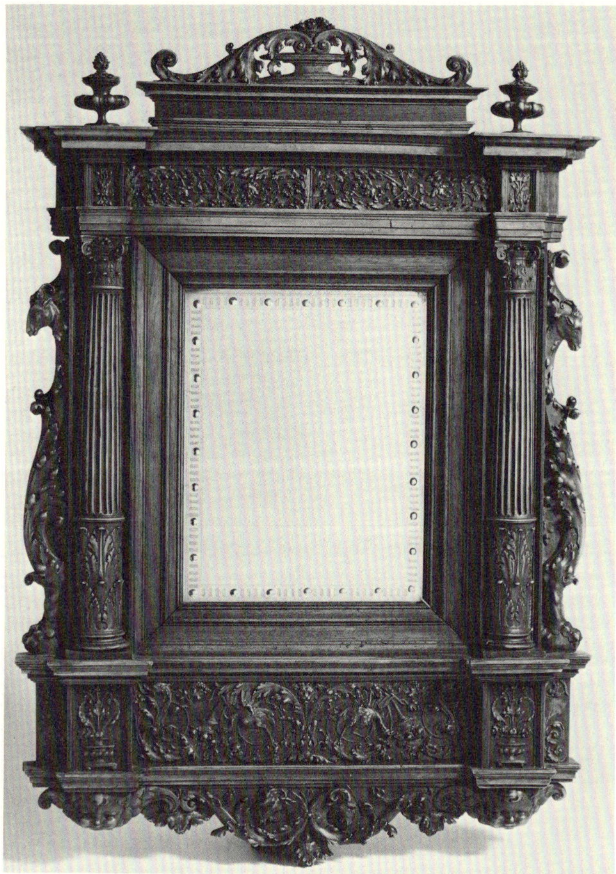

(Fig. no. 103) French, ca. 1550

MIRROR FRAME

The Fine Arts Museums of San Francisco.
Gift of Mr. and Mrs. George Wagner (Cat. no. 218).

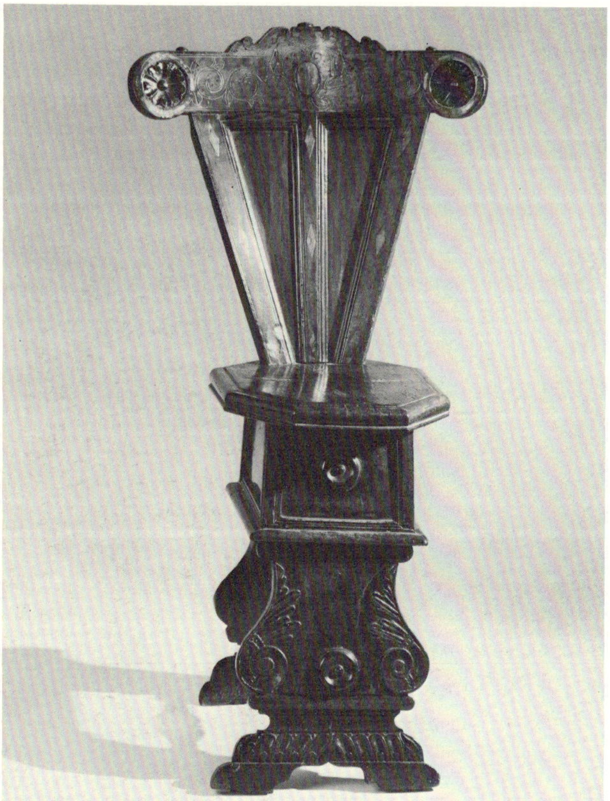

(Fig. no. 104) Italian (Tuscany), ca. 1500

SGABELLO

Lent by Philadelphia Museum of Art (Cat. no. 207).

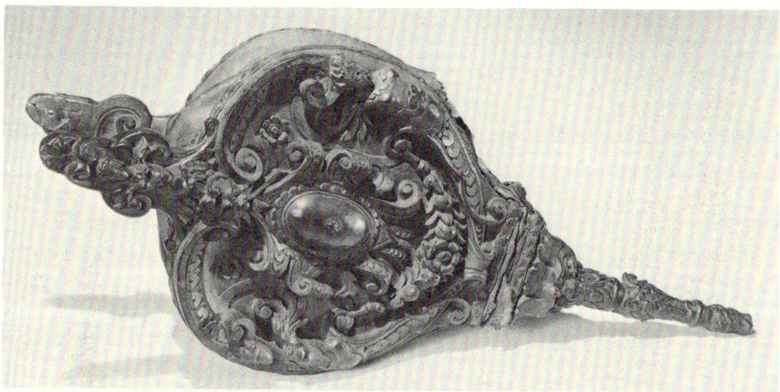

(Fig. no. 105) Italian, 16th century

BELLOWS

Lent by Philadelphia Museum of Art (Cat. no. 213).

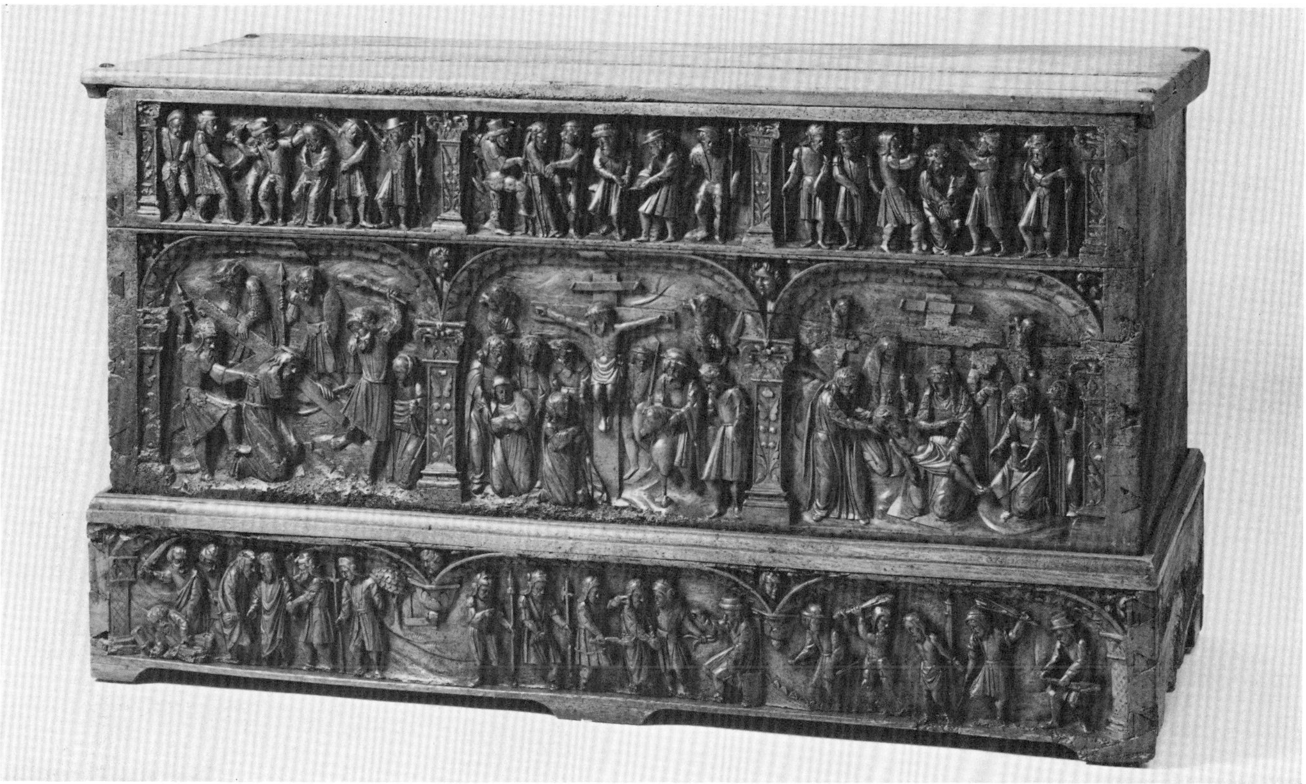

(Fig. no. 106) Probably French, 16th century

CHEST WITH BASE

The Fine Arts Museums of San Francisco.
Hélène Irwin Fagan Collection (Cat. no. 223).

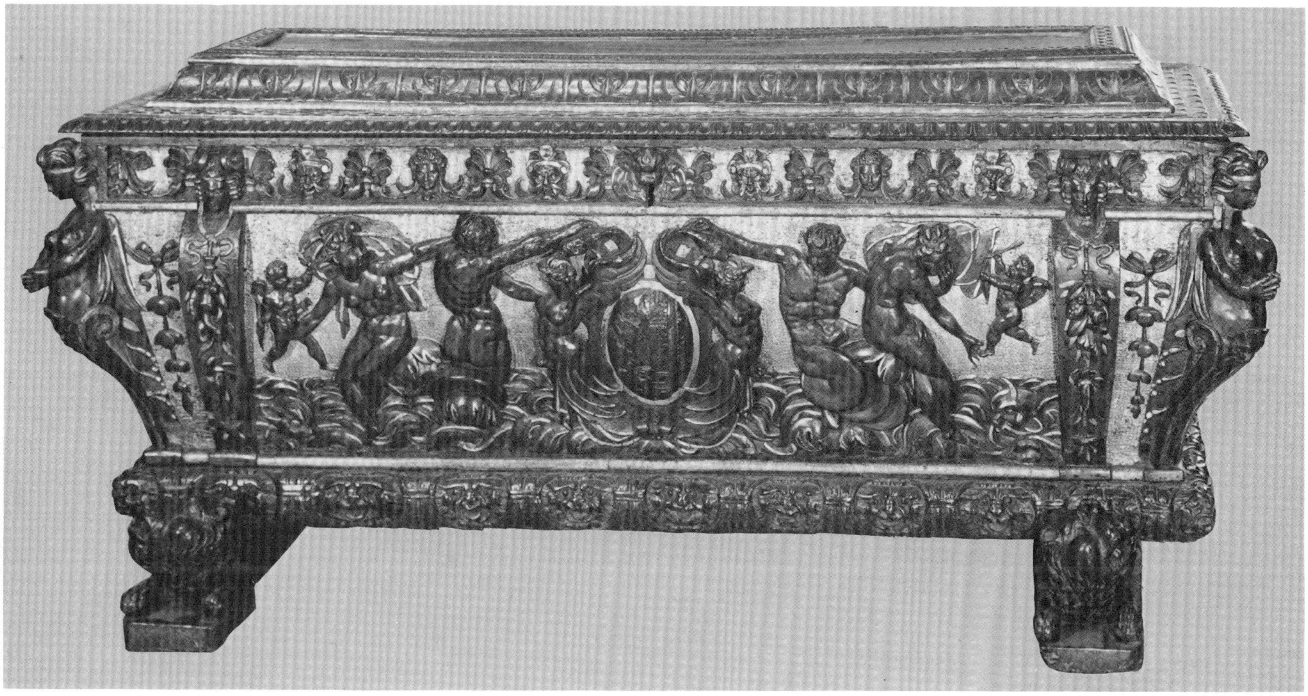

(Fig. no. 107) Italian, 16th century

CASSONE

Lent by The J. Paul Getty Museum, Malibu, California
(Cat. no. 205).

Gold-tooled Bookbindings of the Renaissance

Paul Needham

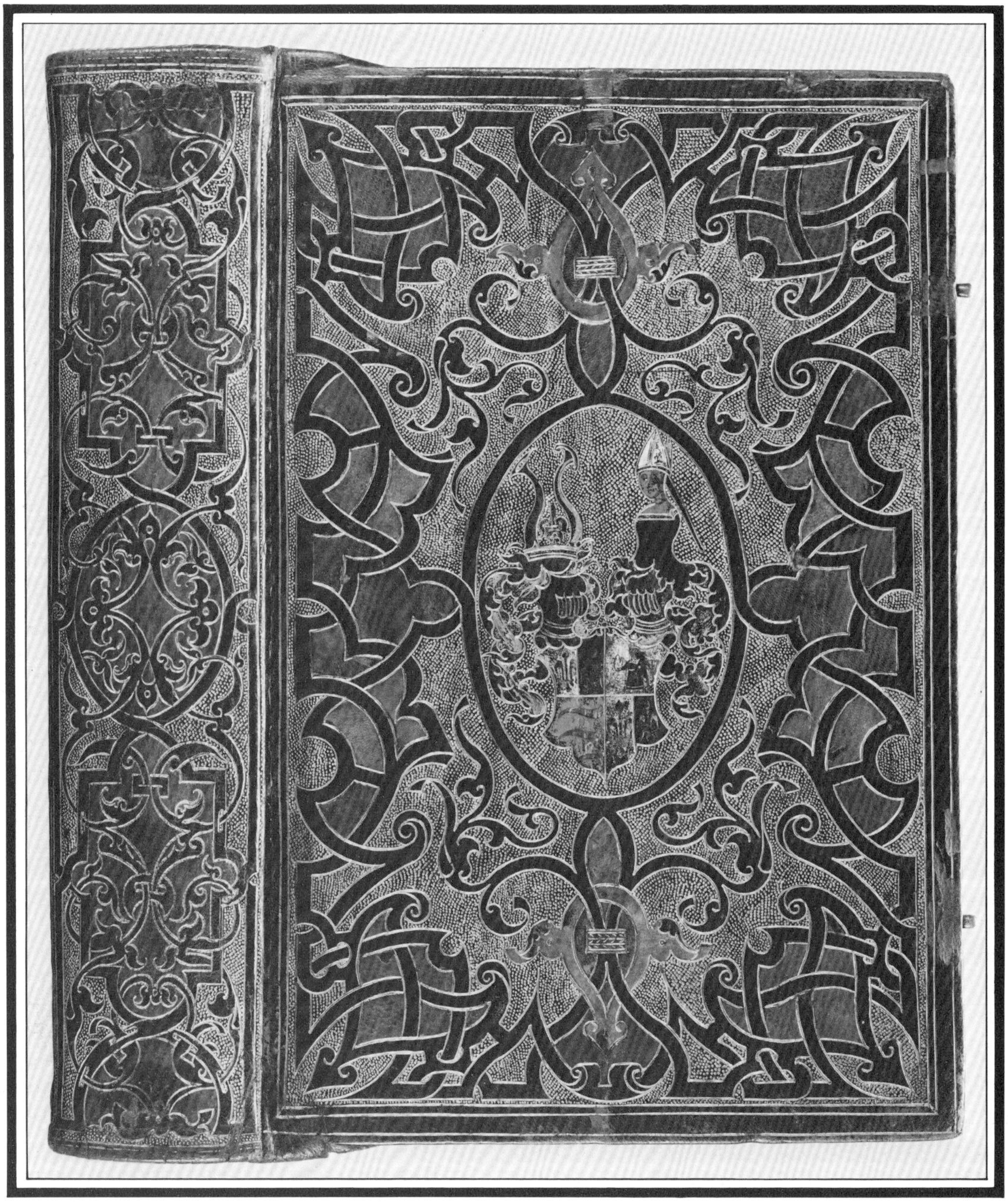

(Fig. no. 108) Attributed to Claude de Picques

BINDING FOR MARCUS FUGGER

Lent by The Pierpont Morgan Library, New York
(Cat. no. 237).

Ex oriente lux: A new era in the history of European bookbinding began in the second half of the fifteenth century with the introduction into Europe from Islamic lands of the art of gold tooling on leather. The consequences of this new technique were not immediately felt, but their effect in the long run was to establish gold-tooled leather as the standard, though not invariable, medium for sumptuous bookbinding. Leather had already been long-established in Europe as a binding material and had been decorated in a variety of ways: stamping with engraved metal tools (blind tooling), cutting in elaborate patterns *(cuir ciselé),* painting, and the addition of ornamental metal clasps, center- and cornerpieces, and bosses. In the fifteenth century these decorative systems were practised most characteristically and with greatest sophistication in Germany, where the chief customers were monastic and other religious foundations rather than private owners. When secular bibliophiles of this age had special bindings put on their fine manuscripts (and it was not a matter of course that they would), their tastes ran generally to lighter, more delicate materials, such as silk and velvet, often decorated with attached metal ornaments or with needlework. These are fragile substances, and almost all the volumes bearing them underwent rebinding in leather in later generations. Only a handful of fifteenth-century textile bindings have survived in fresh enough condition to show just how attractive this style could be.

Gold tooling enables a much more durable material, leather, to be decorated with something of the brightness and richness of textile. The same engraved tools and stamps can be used as for blind tooling. The surface of the leather is painted with glair (egg white) upon which, after it has dried, gold leaf is laid. The tool is heated and applied firmly to the leather; the heat cooks and sets the glair, bonding the gold leaf to the leather in the pattern engraved on the tool. The excess leaf not stamped as part of the pattern is rubbed off. Though gold tooling may be made on any leather, its early employment in Europe correlates with the increasing use there of beautiful dyed goatskins imported from Moslem lands and generically known as "morocco," whatever their specific origin.

Gold tooling was widely practiced in the Islamic world for at least two centuries before reaching Europe. The earliest surviving example is found on a multi-volumed Koran written in Marrakesh in 1256. Indeed, the marriage of gold and leather by other techniques goes back centuries before this. A Coptic bookcover of the seventh or eighth century, preserved at The Pierpont Morgan Library, is decorated with cut leather tracery stitched over a background of gilt vellum. The art of bookbinding underwent remarkable developments in the Moslem world of the fourteenth and fifteenth centuries, particularly in Egypt and Persia. The finest Moslem examples from this period have never been surpassed in beauty.

Concerning the path or paths whereby gold tooling migrated to Christian Europe there has been considerable controversy. One obvious channel was that of Spain, where the two cultures overlapped and merged as nowhere else in Europe. Spanish royal inventories of 1410 and 1458 do describe bindings which may conceivably have been gold-tooled. However, no surviving Spanish bindings with such tooling can be attested before the end of the fifteenth century, by which time the technique was well known elsewhere in Europe. In Italy we are on firmer ground, for there quite a few actual examples of early gold tooling are known. The honor of primacy in gold tooling was long contested between Naples, at that time in the hands of Aragonese rulers, and Venice, gateway to the eastern Mediterranean. Recently the scales of evidence have moved in favor of Venice, which is associated with two gold-tooled bindings dating earlier than anything known from Naples: one probably from about 1459, the other about 1465. Both show a very close acquaintance with Islamic, and more particularly Persian, models. After 1475 some very elegant gold-tooled bindings were made for Petrus Ugelheimer, a wealthy merchant resident in Venice where he was the financial patron of Nicolaus Jenson's press. From this point on, an uninterrupted series of gold-tooled bindings can be traced in Venice to the end of the fifteenth century and beyond.

In Naples, the chief patron of gold-tooled bindings was the king, Ferrante, who followed the bibliophilic example set by his father Alfonso the Magnificent. From documentary evidence we know that the first Neapolitan binder in this technique was Baldassare Scariglia, who held a post in the royal library; his earliest gold-tooled work was probably done around 1480. The Neapolitan tradition of deluxe binding, splendid while it lasted, was short-lived, dying out in the early sixteenth century. In the meantime, the new binding fashion spread to other cities in Italy and beyond: Rome, Florence, Bologna, and Urbino (where a beautiful group of bindings was made for Duke Guidobaldo di Montefeltro). One remarkable series was the product of a workshop in Buda, bindery to the great royal bibliophile Mathias Corvinus, king of Hungary.

Neapolitan influence was certainly at work here: Mathias was connected with the Aragonese court through his marriage to the daughter of the king of Naples.

In style as well as technique, almost all European gold-tooled bindings of the century from roughly 1460 to 1560 betray a heavy debt to the Islamic world. Four major design elements from the Islamic tradition can be isolated as strong influences on binding styles of the European Renaissance. Two of these elements, the center- and cornerpiece style and the strapwork or interlace style, are structural; they determined the overall patterns of the covers. The other two elements, cablework (and more elaborate knotwork) and arabesque, are more purely decorative; they were usually made with small tools which could be accommodated to a variety of patterns.

The center- and cornerpiece style is familiar as the most common pattern of Persian carpets. As found on bindings, the pattern is precisely similar: a central, symmetrical compartment, often oval in shape, with four cornerpieces closely related to the centerpiece in their decoration (Cat. no. 243). Frequently they are simply quarter-segments of the centerpiece. The interlace style — which was unknown in Persia during its great period of bookbinding — used tooled bands, rectilinear or curved, to divide the covers into symmetrical compartments often filled with smaller tooling (Cat. no. 236). Cablework, a rather monotonous interlinking of small conventionalized C-shaped rope tools, was routine on early Spanish bindings through Moslem influence. It was also common on early Neapolitan bindings (Cat. no. 229), probably via the Spanish connection; but in the sixteenth century it would have looked very archaic to the sophisticated patron of fine bindings. Not so with arabesques, abstract flower and leaf forms on long, gracefully-curving stems. Arabesque ornament (Cat. no. 242) rapidly became part of the permanent repertory of European decorative motifs; some of its earliest appearances in Europe were found on the first Venetian bindings in the Persian style. These four elements did not exhaust the decorative resources available to European binders. Less abstract flower tooling, classical ornament, gilt lettering of titles, mottoes and monograms, impressed medallion portraits and scenes, as well as heraldry were employed; but it is uncommon to find a deluxe binding of the Renaissance entirely free of direct or mediated Islamic influence.

Curiously, the full flowering of gold-tooled binding as a Renaissance minor art took place in France, where the technique made rather a delayed and retarded appearance. No fifteenth-century gold tooling is known from France — the one example frequently cited is probably of Italian workmanship. A group of gold-tooled bindings from the first two decades of the sixteenth-century is known — from a shop that has plausibly been identified with that of Simon Vostre, the famous Parisian publisher of books of hours. Individual tools from this bindery were copied from Venetian or Milanese models, but their method of employ was thoroughly old-fashioned and "gothic": most commonly, the entire cover was filled with tooling in vertical bands, alternately gilt and blind.

In the 1520s at least one Paris bindery executed some bindings of cleaner appearance in the Italian style, consisting of a simple central motif within a rectangular border of arabesque tooling. But it was not until the mid-1530s that a distinctively French style of gold-tooled binding developed, a style independent for the most part of Italian models, but one which itself, in succeeding decades, exerted a strong influence on Italian fine binding. Much research remains to be done on Parisian binding in these decades, but a complicated chain of evidence connects many of these early "new style" bindings with Etienne Roffet, a bookseller and publisher who is known to have bound for the royal library.

Patronage has always figured large in the history of deluxe bookbinding, for only a steady stream of commissions could encourage and support this superfluous luxury trade. The dominant patron of fine binding who emerged at this time in France was Jean Grolier, a wealthy treasury official of Lyonnese origin. In the second decade of the sixteenth century, Grolier was resident in Milan while the duchy was under French domination, and he commissioned there a unified group of interesting bindings (Cat. no. 230). These were decorated with painted central relief stamps of mythological scenes, produced by stamping with dies designed for making metal plaquettes. After this Milanese group there is a gap of some twenty years before we can recognize bindings, this time French, commissioned by Grolier. It has been suggested that between about 1515 and 1535, most of Grolier's book acquisitions were bound in textiles and that he subsequently had almost all of these rebound in leather. Grolier patronized a number of Parisian binders to greater or lesser extent. From the late 1530s to late 1540s his chief binder was Claude de Picques, who produced much work of exceptional quality.

Grolier was the most influential bibliophile of the High Renaissance and perhaps, with his *et amicorum* ownership motto, the most attractive; but even his bindings were overshadowed by the great series executed by Claude de Picques for Henry II (Cat. no. 235) following his accession in 1547. After this year the pressures of royal patronage seem to have kept de Picques too busy to create more than occasional bindings for Grolier (Cat. no. 236), who took his custom elsewhere. During Henri's reign virtually all the very finest French bindings were made for the royal library at Fontainebleau; their preservation almost intact at the Bibliothèque Nationale has prevented a more widespread appreciation of their splendor.

The best Parisian binders of the 1540s and 1550s used familiar decorative elements, notably arabesque tools and interlaces, but with a freedom of design far removed from conventional Islamic patterns. It has been suggested that many of the Parisian arabesque tools were taken from embroidery pattern books, particularly that of Francesco Pellegrino (Paris, 1530), rather than directly from Islamic models. About 1550, another fashion developed of adding outlines and scrolled endings to the interlaces to give them a three-dimensional appearance (Cat. no.234). These are related to the cartouche-style woodcut borders found especially in Lyonnese illustrated books of the 1540s and 1550s.

The twenty years from about 1540 to 1560 saw the high-water mark of Renaissance gold-tooled bookbinding. The evolution of styles in this period was rapid and inventive, and Parisian work set the dominant fashion for all of Europe. Bindings in the French style were made, with varying degrees of success, in England, Italy, Spain, the Netherlands, Switzerland and Germany, and as far afield as Sweden. The extent of imitation makes it impossible on purely stylistic grounds to assign many bindings to a particular country, let alone a city or a workshop. The noticeable decline in the production of absolutely first-rate bindings in the 1560s and beyond can in large measure be attributed to the deaths of the art's two greatest patrons, Henry II (1559) and Jean Grolier (1565). High-quality work continued to be done in Paris (and to be copied elsewhere), but even the best bindings tended to fit into a few routine patterns: the semé, with one or several small tools evenly disposed over the covers; or the "fanfare," developed from earlier interlace patterns and occasionally splendid, but more often thoroughly standardized. Nevertheless, it was in the High Renaissance that Paris earned its reputation as the leader in fashionable, deluxe bookbinding; this is a reputation it has never since relinquished.

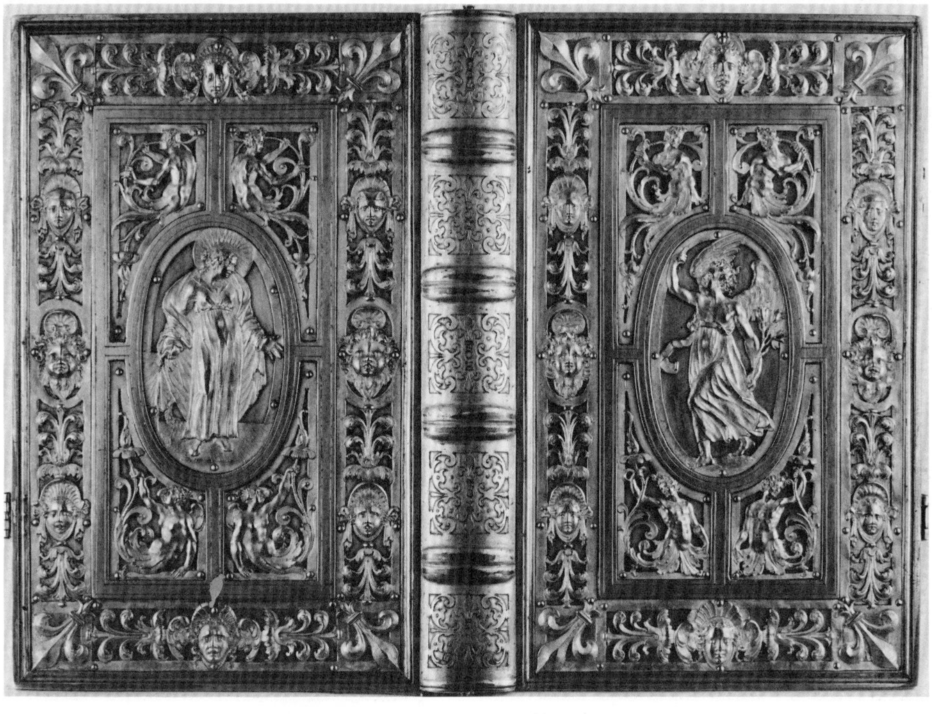

(Fig. no. 109) Antonio Gentili

BINDING FOR CARDINAL ODOARDO FARNESE

Lent by The Pierpont Morgan Library, New York (Cat. no. 244).

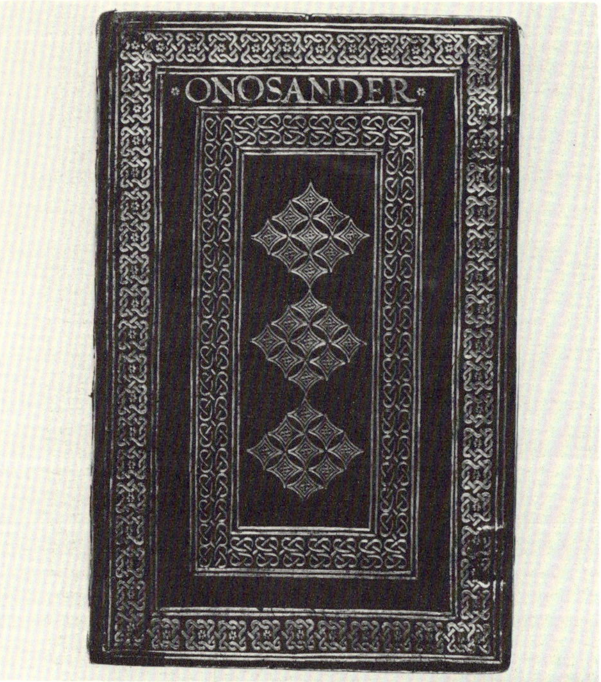

(Fig. no. 110) Probably by Baldassare Scariglio

EARLY EUROPEAN BINDING

Lent by The Pierpont Morgan Library, New York
(Cat. no. 229).

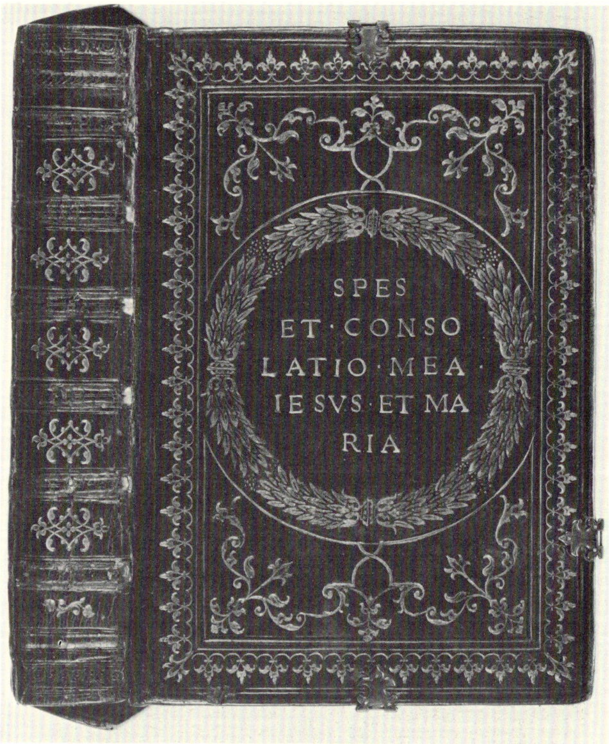

(Fig. no. 111) Attributed to Etienne Roffet
or the "Fontainebleau" binder

BINDING FOR PEREGRINUS PECCATOR

Lent by The Pierpont Morgan Library, New York

(Cat. no. 231).

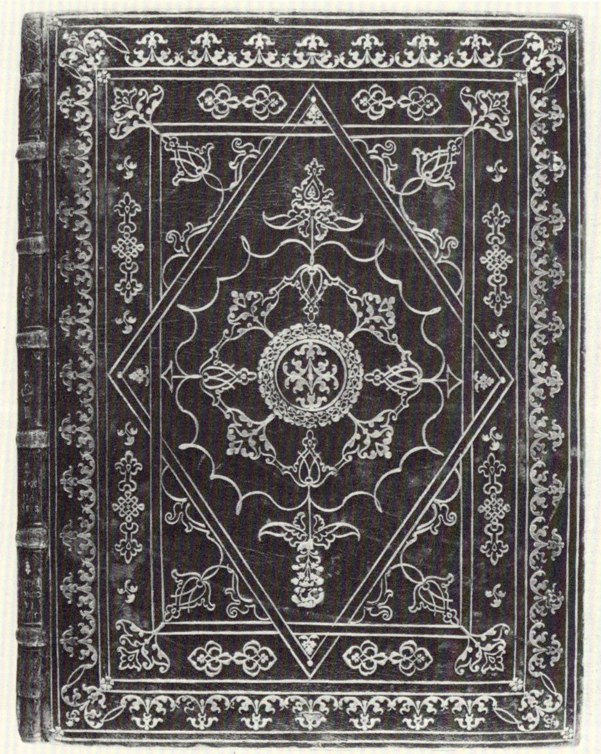

(Fig. no. 112) French (Paris), ca. 1548

BINDING FOR PRESENTATION TO HENRY II

Lent by The Pierpont Morgan Library, New York
(Cat. no. 233).

(Fig. no. 113) Grolier Cuspinianus Binder

BINDING FOR THOMAS MAHIEU

Lent by The Pierpont Morgan Library (Cat. no. 234).

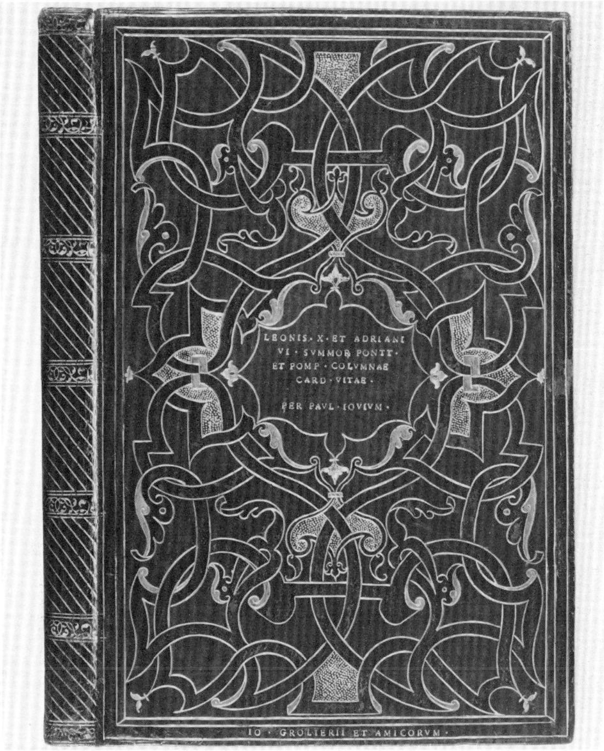

(Fig. no. 114) Claude de Picques

BINDING FOR JEAN GROLIER

Lent by The Pierpont Morgan Library, New York (Cat. no. 236).

(Fig. no. 115) French (Paris or Lyons), ca. 1554

ARCHITECTURAL BINDING

Lent by The Pierpont Morgan Library, New York (Cat. no. 238).

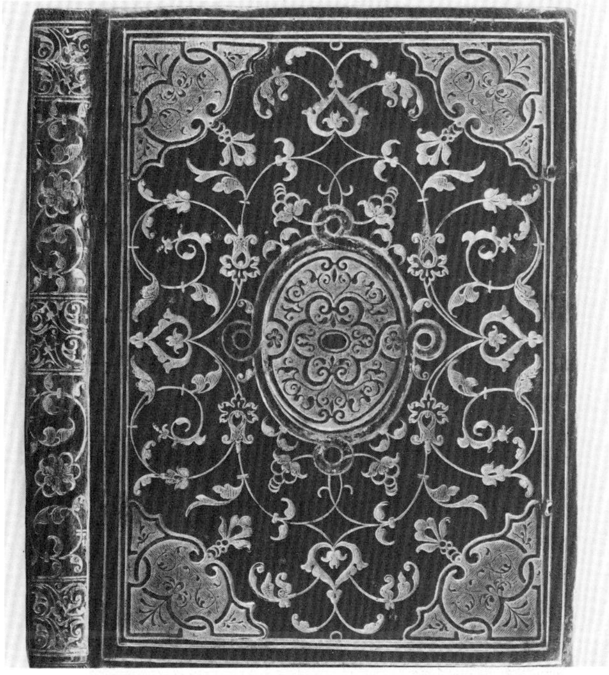

(Fig. no. 116) Dudley-Morocco binder

BINDING FOR ARCHBISHOP PARKER

Lent by The Pierpont Morgan Library (Cat. no. 242).

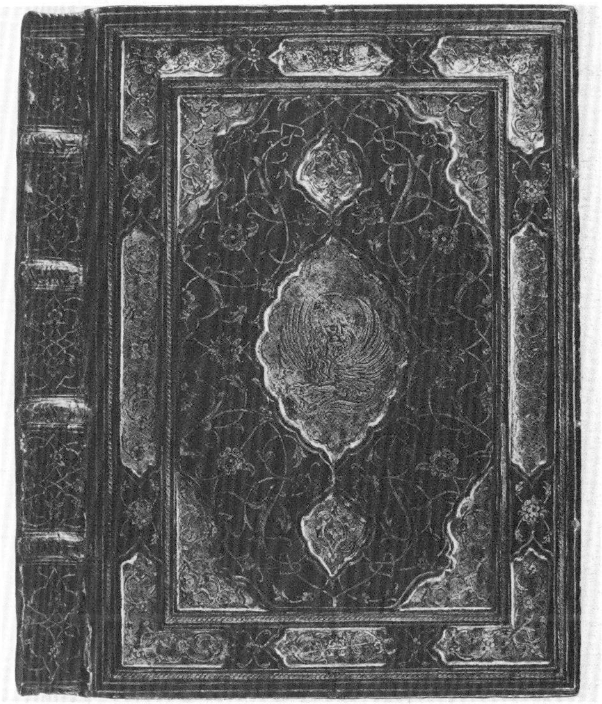

(Fig. no. 117) Italian (Venice), 1574

BINDING IN THE PERSIAN STYLE

Lent by The Pierpont Morgan Library, New York (Cat. no. 243).

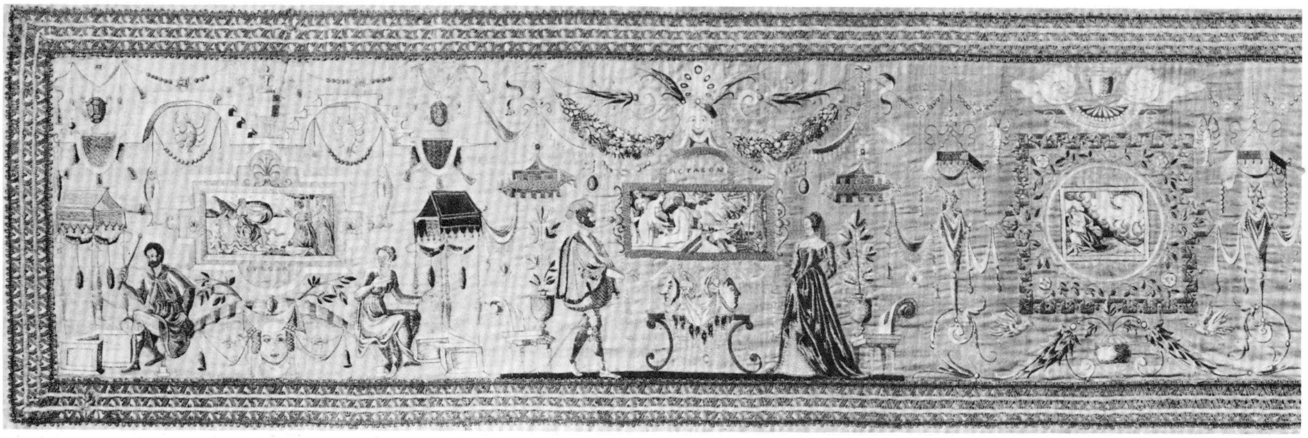

(Fig. no. 118) French, ca. 1550

EMBROIDERED PANEL (detail)

Lent by the Metropolitan Museum of Art, New York.
Rogers Fund. (Cat. no. 286).

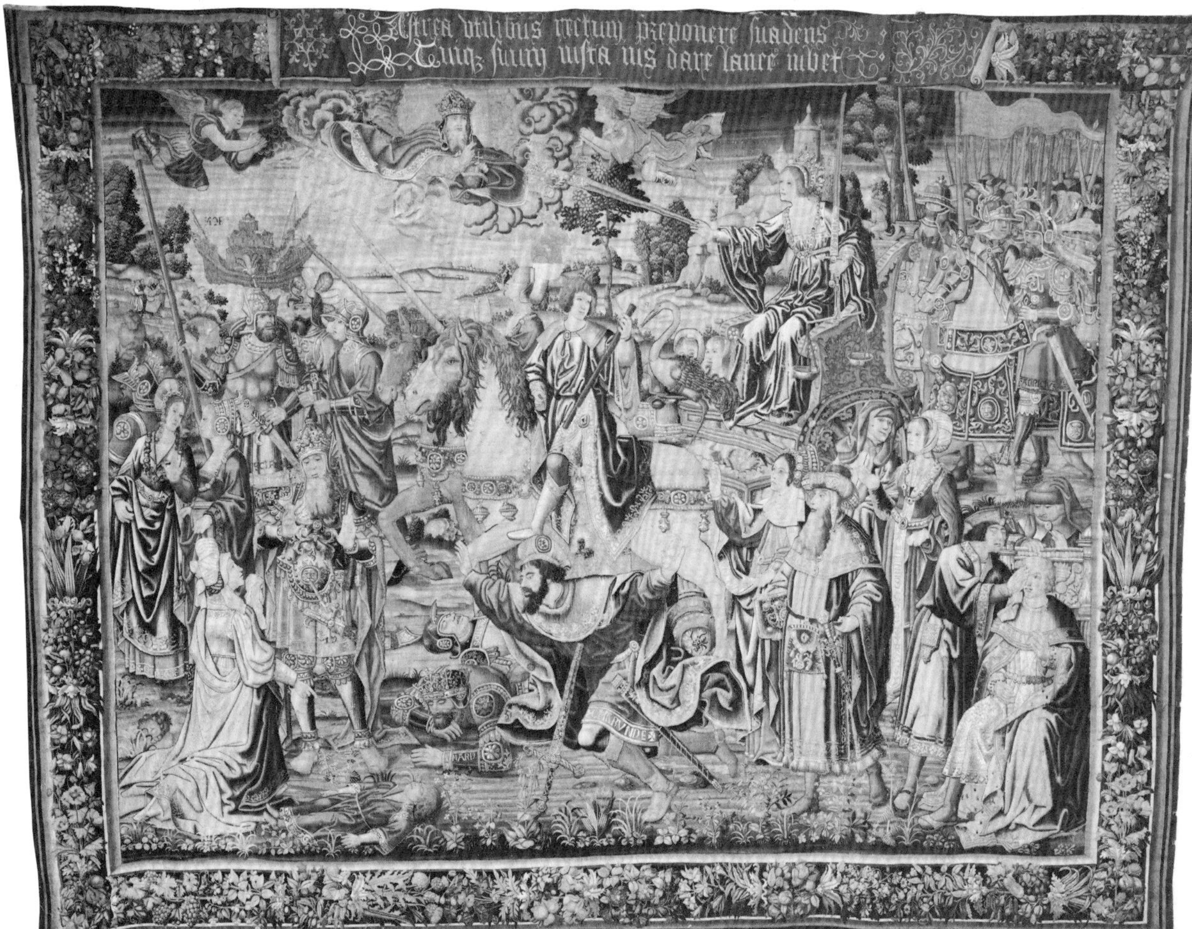

(Fig. no. 119) Flemish (Brussels), ca. 1550

TRIUMPH OF JUSTICE

The Fine Arts Museums of San Francisco.
Gift of the Hearst Foundation (Cat. no. 273).

Catalogue of the Exhibition

Measurements are given in inches with centimeter equivalents given in parenthesis. Height precedes width and depth. A single dimension indicates height, unless designated by a d. for diameter.

1 Attributed to Benvenuto Cellini (1500-1571)
COSIMO I DE' MEDICI (Fig. no. 10)
Italian (Florence), ca. 1550
Pentelic marble; 30 (76.2) (without later base)
The Fine Arts Museums of San Francisco. Gift of the Roscoe and Margaret Oakes Foundation 75.2.16

SMALL SCULPTURES IN BRONZE

2 Bertoldo di Giovanni (ca. 1420-1491)
JASON RESTING AFTER SLAYING THE DRAGON
Italian (Florence), 1460-1480
Bronze; 8¾ (22.2)
Lent by The Detroit Institute of Arts. Gift of the Founders Society, General Membership Fund 56.33

3 North Italian, ca. 1500
DANCING BOY (Fig. no. 29)
Bronze; 4 1/16 (10.3)
Lent by The Cleveland Museum of Art. The Severance and Greta Millikin Purchase Fund 75.29

4 Italian (Padua), ca. 1510
WARRIOR ON HORSEBACK (Fig. no. 30)
Bronze; 8½ x 9 9/16 x 3 15/16 (21.6 x 23.6 x 10)
Lent by Heinz Schneider, Cleveland, Ohio

5 Attributed to Camelio (Vettor di Antonio Gambello) (ca. 1455-1537)
HERCULES AND THE NEMEAN LION (Fig. no. 22)
Italian (Venice), ca. 1520
Bronze; 4 (10.1)
Lent by The Cleveland Museum of Art. Gift of Dr. and Mrs. Sherman Lee in Memory of Paul Mallon 75.111

6 Italian (Florence), 16th century
GANYMEDE (after Benvenuto Cellini) (Fig. no. 25)
Bronze; 13½ (34.3)
The Fine Arts Museums of San Francisco. Gift of E. John and Rose Magnin 75.18.13

7 Italian (Florence), 1550-1575
EVENING AND DAWN (after Michelangelo, 1475-1564) (Figs. no. 15a, 15b)
Bronze; Evening: 9¼ x 11¾ x 4¼ (23.5 x 29.8 x 10.8)
Dawn: 8¾ x 11 x 4⅞ (22.2 x 28 x 12.3)
Provenance: Frank Gair Macomber
Lent from a private collection

8 Italian (Florence), second half of 16th century
FLORA FARNESE (after a Roman marble) (Fig. no. 24)
Bronze; 14¼ x 6 (36.2 x 15.2)
Provenance: Volpi, Rome; Lord Cavendish Bentinck
Lent from a private collection

PLAQUETTES

9 North Italian, 1450-1500
SACRIFICE OF APHRODITE (?)
Bronze; d. 5 (12.7)
Provenance: Fitzhenry Collection; Oppenheimer Collection
Lent by University Art Galleries, University of California, Santa Barbara. The Morgenroth Collection M-262

10 Italian (Florence), 15th century
TAZZA FARNESE (Fig. no. 20)
Bronze; d. 6⅝ (16.9)
Provenance: Fitzhenry Collection; Oppenheimer Collection
Lent by University Art Galleries, University of California, Santa Barbara. The Morgenroth Collection M-291

11 Italian (Florence or Mantua), ca. 1500
ALLEGORY OF THE POWERS OF NATURE
Bronze; d. 7⅛ (18.1)
Provenance: Oppenheimer Collection
Lent by University Art Galleries, University of California, Santa Barbara. The Morgenroth Collection M-292

12 Pier Jacopo Alari Bonacolsi, called L'Antico (ca. 1460-1528)
HERCULES RESTING AFTER SLAYING THE NEMEAN LION (Fig. no. 2)
Italian (Mantua), ca. 1500
Bronze; 10 x 5¾ (25.4 x 14.6)
Provenance: Dr. A. von Frey, Vienna; Edith A. and Percy S. Straus, New York
Lent by The Museum of Fine Arts, Houston. Edith A. and Percy S. Straus Collection 44.582

13 Italian (Venice), ca. 1500
THE TRIUMPH OF NEPTUNE (Fig. no. 28)
Bronze; d. 8½ (21.6)
Lent by National Gallery of Art, Washington, D.C. Samuel H. Kress Collection, 1957 A583.305B

14 Italian (Padua), early 16th century
COMBAT OF TRITONS (after Andrea Mantegna's engraving, "Combat of the Sea-Centaurs") (Fig. no. 23)
Bronze; d. 7 (18)
Provenance: Figdor Collection, Vienna
Lent by University Art Galleries, University of California, Santa Barbara. The Morgenroth Collection M-214

15 Italian (Padua), early 16th century
MUSIC (?)
Bronze; 4½ x 2¾ (11.5 x 7.1)
Provenance: Pini Collection
Lent by University Art Galleries, University of California, Santa Barbara. The Morgenroth Collection M-215

MEDALS

16 Antonio Pisano, called Pisanello (1395-1455)
NICCOLO PICCININO
Italian, ca. 1441
Bronze; d. 3½ (8.9)
Lent by University Art Galleries, University of California, Santa Barbara. The Morgenroth Collection M-4

17 Antonio Pisano, called Pisanello
LIONELLO D'ESTE
Italian, 1441-1444
Bronze; d. 2⅝ (6.8)
Lent by University Art Galleries, University of California, Santa Barbara. The Morgenroth Collection M-6

18 Matteo de'Pasti (act. 1441-d. 1467/8)
DOUBLE-FACED MEDAL OF SIGISMONDO PANDOLFO MALATESTA, LORD OF RIMINI AND FANO (1417-1468) (Fig. no. 34)
Italian (Rimini?), 1446
Bronze; d. 3⅜ (8.6)
Lent by William Rockhill Nelson Gallery of Art and Atkins Museum of Fine Arts, Kansas City.
Nelson Fund 69.9

19 Italian (Florence), ca. 1465-1469
COSIMO DE' MEDICI
Bronze; d. 2⅞ (7.2)
Lent by University Art Galleries, University of California, Santa Barbara. The Morgenroth Collection M-93

20 Bertoldo di Giovanni (ca. 1420-1491)
MOHAMMAD II
Italian (Florence), 1480-1490
Bronze; d. 2½ (9.4)
The Fine Arts Museums of San Francisco.
Gift of Julius Landauer 76.18.1

21 N. di Forzore Spinelli, called Niccolo Fiorentino (1430-1514)
LORENZO IL MAGNIFICO
Italian (Florence), ca. 1490
Bronze; d. 3¼ (8.3)
Provenance: Whitcombe Greene Collection
Lent by University Art Galleries, University of California, Santa Barbara. The Morgenroth Collection M-97

22 Italian (Rome), 1513
GIULIANO II DE' MEDICI
Bronze; d. 1 3/16 (3.4)
Provenance: Oppenheimer Collection
Lent by University Art Galleries, University of California, Santa Barbara. The Morgenroth Collection M-90

23 Valentin Maler (ca. 1540-1603)
WENZEL JAMNITZER (1508-1585; cast on the occasion of his 75th birthday)
German (Nuremberg), 1582
Lead; 1¾ x 1¼ (4.3 x 3.3)
Lent by Edward Gans, Berkeley, California

UTILITARIAN BRONZES
Writing Boxes and Inkwells

24 Attributed to Severo da Ravenna (act. ca. 1500)
WRITING CASKET (Fig. no. 32)
Italian (Padua), ca. 1500
Bronze; 5½ x 8⅜ x 6⅜ (14 x 21.3 x 16)
Lent by The Cleveland Museum of Art.
Purchase from the J. H. Wade Fund 41.63

25 Italian (Padua), ca. 1500
WRITING CASKET
Bronze; 3½ x 9⅝ x 5⅝ (8.9 x 24.4 x 14.3)
Lent by Heinz Schneider, Cleveland, Ohio

26 North Italian, ca. 1500
INKWELL WITH HERCULES SLAYING THE NEMEAN LION
Gilt-bronze; 7½ x 7¾ (19 x 19.7)
Provenance: Simon Miller, Paris; Edith A. and Percy S. Straus, New York
Lent by The Museum of Fine Arts, Houston. Edith A. and Percy S. Straus Collection 44.591

27 Italian (School of Ravenna), ca. 1500
INKWELL
Bronze; 4 (10.2)
Lent by The Metropolitan Museum of Art, New York.
Gift of Ogden Mills, 1925 25.142.7

28 Italian (Padua), 16th century
INKWELL WITH GROTESQUE HEAD
Bronze; 3½ (9)
Lent anonymously.

29 Italian (Padua), ca. 1500
BOX IN THE FORM OF A CRAB
Bronze; 6⅞ (17.5)
Provenance: Dreyfus Collection
Lent by National Gallery of Art, Washington, D.C.
Samuel H. Kress Collection, 1957 A239.80C

30 Italian (Padua), 1500-1550
INKSTAND IN THE FORM OF A MONSTER
Bronze; 5⅛ (13)
Provenance: Foulc Collection
Lent by Philadelphia Museum of Art.
Purchased: Temple Fund 30.1.33

31 Italian (Venice), 1500-1550
INKSTAND IN FORM OF TRITON RIDING A DOLPHIN
Bronze; 6 11/16 (17)
Provenance: Foulc Collection
Lent by Philadelphia Museum of Art. Purchased for the McIlhenny Collection 30.1.26

32 South Italian, ca. 1570
INKSTAND (Arms of Organtino Scarola, Bishop of San Marco from 1568-1572) (Fig. no. 33)
Bronze; 9 x 11½ (22.9 x 29.2)
Lent by Victoria and Albert Museum, London M57-1952

Candlesticks and Lamps

33 Italian (Venice), ca. 1500
CANDLESTICK
Bronze; 6¼ x 5½ (16 x 14)
Lent by Victoria and Albert Museum, London M688-1910

34 Attributed to Andrea Briosco, called Riccio (ca. 1470-1532)
OIL LAMP IN THE FORM OF A SPHINX (Fig. no. 36)
Italian (Padua), early 16th century
Bronze; 4 15/16 x 5½ (12.5 x 14)
Provenance: Fernand Adda Collection
Lent by Cyril Humphris, London

35 Italian (Venice), mid-16th century
TWO ALTAR CANDLESTICKS (with arms of the Garzoni family)
Bronze; 22⅞ (57)
Provenance: Dreyfus Collection
Lent by National Gallery of Art, Washington, D.C.
Samuel H. Kress Collection, 1957 A223.64C; 65C

Incense Burners

36 Probably by Desiderio da Firenze (act. 1532-1545)
INCENSE BURNER
Italian (Padua), 16th century
Bronze; 14¾ (37.5)
Lent by The Metropolitan Museum of Art, New York.
Gift of George Blumenthal, 1941 41.100.78

37 French (probably Fontainebleau), ca. 1550
PAIR OF MONUMENTAL INCENSE BURNERS
Bronze; 20 (50.8)
Provenance: C. von Weinberg, Walfried
Lent by The Toledo Museum of Art.
Gift of Florence Scott Libbey 53.93A, B

38 Workshop of Peter Vischer the Younger (1487-1528)
INCENSE BURNER
German (Nuremberg), early 16th century
Bronze; 7⅛ x 6⅝ (18.1 x 16.9)
Lent by Heinz Schneider, Cleveland, Ohio

Doorknockers

39 Andrea Briosco, called Riccio
DOORKNOCKER (Fig. no. 26)
Italian (Padua), early 16th century
Bronze; 13 x 4 x 6 9/16 (33 x 10.4 x 16.7)
Lent by The Cleveland Museum of Art.
Gift of Mr. and Mrs. Severance A. Millikin 75.58

40 Italian (Venice), mid-16th century
DOORKNOCKER (Fig. no. 27)
Bronze; 10 x 7¾ (25.4 x 19.7)
Provenance: Robert Meyer, Vienna
Lent by The Cleveland Museum of Art.
Purchase from the J. H. Wade Fund 72.1

41 Italian (Venice), late 16th century
DOORKNOCKER (Fig. no. 31)
Bronze; 10½ (26.7)
The Fine Arts Museums of San Francisco.
Gift of Mr. Castillan, Paris 1925.30

Mortars

42 Italian (Fabriano), dated 1465
MORTAR (Fig. no. 35)
Bronze; 4 x 5 (10.2 x 12.7)
Provenance: Gibson Carmichael Collection
Lent by Victoria and Albert Museum,
London M684-1910

43 Workshop of Giuliano di Mariotti de' Navi
(act. first half of 16th century)
MORTAR
Italian (Florence), dated 1515
Bronze; 4 3/16 x 6 (10.6 x 15.2)
Provenance: Gibson Carmichael Collection
Lent by Victoria and Albert Museum,
London M685-1910

Miscellaneous

44 Attributed to Lautizio da Perugia (d. 1527)
PRESENTATION MODEL FOR THE SEAL OF CARDINAL GIULIO DE' MEDICI (1478-1534), later Pope Clement VII (1523-1534) (Fig. no. 18)
Italian (Rome), ca. 1513
Bronze; 4⅝ x 3 (11.8 x 7.5)
Provenance: Wyndham Francis Cook;
Humphrey W. Cook
Lent by Heinz Schneider, Cleveland, Ohio

45 Pier Jacopo Alari Bonacolsi, called l'Antico
BASE
Italian (Mantua), early 16th century
Bronze and copper, silvered and gilded; 5¾ x 5⅛ (14.6 x 13.1)
Lent anonymously.

46 North Italian, early 16th century
SWORD POMMEL
Bronze; 3½ x 3 5/16 (8.9 x 8.6)
Lent by Victoria and Albert Museum,
London M699-1912

47 Italian (Venice or Brescia), early 16th century
HAND BELL
Bronze; 4 5/16 x 3¾ (11.6 x 9.5)
Lent by Victoria and Albert Museum,
London M28-1923

48 Italian (Rome), mid-16th century
JUBILEE HAMMER (arms of Marcellus II, as cardinal) (Fig. no. 37)
Bronze; 6½ (16.5)
Lent anonymously.

49 Italian (Florence), 1560-1570
WALL FOUNTAIN: NEPTUNE (Fig. no. 38)
Bronze; 17⅛ x 12½ x 3¼ (43.5 x 31.7 x 8.25)
Lent by The Toledo Museum of Art.
Gift of Edward Drummond Libbey 52.13

GOLDSMITHS' WORK
Objects for Ecclesiastical Use

50 North Italian, 1475-1500
CHALICE
Silver-gilt with enamel; 8⅜ x d. 5⅝ (21.5 x d. 14.4)
Lent by The Walters Art Gallery, Baltimore 44.225

51 Italian (Florence), 1523-1534
PROCESSIONAL AND RELIQUARY CROSS
Silver and silver-gilt with champlevé enamel;
13 x 7⅞ (32.5 x 18.2) (Corpus is later addition)
Inscribed: "CL VII" with coat-of-arms and "CLEMENTIS VII MVNVS" (for Giulio de' Medici, Pope 1523-1534)
Lent by The Walters Art Gallery, Baltimore 57.1925

52 Spanish, ca. 1540
CHALICE (Fig. no. 44)
Silver, parcel-gilt; 8½ x 6 7/16 (21.56 x 16.4)
Lent by Victoria and Albert Museum,
London M206-1956

53 Flemish (Mons?), 1540-1560
MONSTRANCE
Silver, parcel-gilt and glass; 20 (50.8)
Lent by Philadelphia Museum of Art.
Purchased: Bloomfield Moore Fund 65.113.1

54 English (London), 1571
COMMUNION CUP
Silver; 6½ x d. at lip 3 5/16 (16.5 x x d. at lip 8.4)
Maker's mark: TF (in monogram)
Lent by the Francis E. Fowler, Jr. Foundation Museum,
Beverly Hills, California L260

55 Spanish (Toledo), ca. 1550
PLAQUE
Silver; d. 3½ (8.82)
Lent by Victoria and Albert Museum,
London M350-1880

Drinking Vessels

56 Italian, 16th century
ONYX CUP
Onyx mounted in gold and enamel;
4¼ x 4⅛ (10.8 x 10.5)
Lent by The Walters Art Gallery, Baltimore 57.1005

57 German (Nuremberg), ca. 1530
DRINKING VESSEL
Stoneware (Kreussen) mounted in silver-gilt;
4⅞ (12.38)
Courtesy, Museum of Fine Arts, Boston.
Otis Norcross Fund 55.472

58 German (Nuremberg), mid-16th century
FOOTED CUP (Fig. no. 45)
Silver-gilt; 3⅜ (8.4)
Provenance: W. R. Valentiner, 1957
Lent anonymously.

59 Jörg Ruel (d. 1625)
DRINKING CUP
German (Nuremberg), ca. 1598
Silver and agate; 8½ (21.95)
Provenance: Rothschild Family of Vienna and Frankfurt
Lent by The Minneapolis Institute of Arts.
The Lillian Z. Turnblad Fund 53.5

60 German, 1550-1575
WELCOME CUP FROM A SHOEMAKERS' GUILD
Leather mounted in silver; 5⅛ x 2¾ (13 x 7)
Lent by the Francis E. Fowler, Jr. Foundation Museum, Beverly Hills, California

61 German (Regensburg), ca. 1563
TANKARD (Fixier-Krug; arms of von Thurn and Taxis, inscribed 1563)
Silver-gilt; 4½ (11.4)
Lent by The Metropolitan Museum of Art, New York. Bequest of Emma A. Sheafer, 1974. The Lesley and Emma Sheafer Collection 1974.356.762

62 German (Bamberg), ca. 1600
COCONUT TANKARD
Marks: WE conjoined
Carved coconut mounted in silver-gilt; 6¾ (17.2)
Provenance: Leopold von Rothschild
Lent by The Metropolitan Museum of Art, New York. Bequest of Emma A. Sheafer, 1974. The Lesley and Emma Sheafer Collection 1974.356.764

63 English, ca. 1580
FLAGON
Colored marble, silver-gilt mounts; 9⅝ x 4⅝ (24.4 x 11.75)
Provenance: Torkington, Great Stukeley Hall, Huntingdon; A Gentleman's Sale, Christie's, 1907; Lord Swaythling until 1924
Courtesy, Museum of Fine Arts, Boston. Theodora Wilbour Fund No. 2, in memory of Charlotte Beebe Wilbour 49.476

64 English (London), 1589
"TIGERWARE" JUG
Saltglazed stoneware mounted in silver-gilt; 9⅛ (23.2)
The Fine Arts Museums of San Francisco. Gift of The Roscoe and Margaret Oakes Foundation 69.20

65 German (Augsburg), ca. 1600
WAGER CUP (Fig. no. 39)
Silver-gilt; 8 x 4 (20.3 x 10.2)
Marks: IH in oval reserve; pine cone
Provenance: Gutman Collection, Berlin
Lent by The Metropolitan Museum of Art, New York. Gift of J. Pierpont Morgan, 1917 17.190.579

66 German (Augsburg), ca. 1600
TANKARD
Silver-gilt; 6⅜ x 4⅜ (15.5 x 10.7)
Lent by Victoria and Albert Museum, London 552-1874

67 English (Metalwork), ca. 1550
CHINESE PORCELAIN JUG
Hard-paste porcelain mounted in silver; 7⅝ (19.37)
Jug bears Chia Ching seal on base. Metalwork maker's mark: a wallet hook palewise on a cross bendwise.
Courtesy, Museum of Fine Arts, Boston. Theodora Wilbour Fund, in memory of Charlotte Beebe Wilbour 57.530

68 M. Urbiola
POISON CUP (Fig. no. 46)
Spanish, ca. 1610
Marks: M/Vrbiola and head
Silver-gilt, circassian nut and enamel, 8 x 7⅝ (20.3 x 19.4)
Lent by The Art Institute of Chicago. Gift of Mrs. Chauncey McCormick 62.96

Tazzas

69 Attributed to Hans Jamnitzer (1538-1603)
EMBOSSED PLAQUE FROM A TAZZA (after Titian from an engraving by Cornelius Cort) (Fig. no. 47)
German (Nuremberg), ca. 1570
Silver; d. 7 9/16 (19.2)
Lent by Victoria and Albert Museum, London M138-1913

70 Italo-German, ca. 1575
TAZZA (Fig. no. 41)
Silver-gilt; 15½ x d. 15 (39.37 x d. 38.1)
Provenance: Cardinal Ippolito Aldobrandini (whose arms it bears), later elected Pope Clement VIII; Prince Doria Giovanni Battista Pamphili (recorded in his inventory of 1710); Charles Scarisbrick, Scarisbrick Hall, Lancashire; Christie's, London; Frederic Spitzer, Paris.
Lent by The Minneapolis Institute of Arts. The James Ford Bell Family Foundation Fund, the M. R. Schweitzer Fund, and the Christina N. and Swan J. Turnblad Memorial Fund 75.54

Originally one of a set of twelve tazzas. In the course of time the Emperor figures, bowls, and bases have been switched, as they are easily separable. The Minneapolis example has the original bowl and foot, but the figure of Augustus rather than that of Caligula, which it originally possessed.

71 Probably French, ca. 1600
TAZZA
Silver, parcel-gilt; 6½ x d. 6⅝ (15.5 x 16.8)
The Fine Arts Museums of San Francisco. Catherine D. Wentworth Collection 1960.12

Basins and Dishes

72 Spanish, ca. 1500-1550
BASIN
Silver; 8¾ (22.3)
Lent by The Metropolitan Museum of Art, New York. Rogers Fund, 1908 08.102.3

73 Portuguese, ca. 1540
DISH WITH LABORS OF HERCULES
Silver, parcel-gilt; d. 12½ (31.7)
Maker's mark: CB
Lent by Victoria and Albert Museum, London M216-1956

74 Flemish (Antwerp), 1582-1583
STANDING DISH
Silver, parcel-gilt; 5⅝ x 6⅞ (14.3 x 17.5)
Lent by Victoria and Albert Museum, London M37-1960

75 English (London), 1599
ROSEWATER DISH (Fig. no. 48)
Silver-gilt and enamel; d. 19⅜ (49.2)
Provenance: Lord Delamere
Courtesy, Museum of Fine Arts, Boston. Gift of Richard C. Paine 46.845

Salts

76 English (London), 1542
HENRY VIII SALT (arms of Gray of Newcastle-on-Tyne) (Fig. no. 43)
Silver-gilt; 9¾ x 4½ (25 x 11.5)
Maker's mark: a sceptre
Lent by The Worshipful Company of Goldsmiths, Goldsmiths' Hall, London

77 English (London), 1577-1578
PEDESTAL SALT WITH COVER (Fig. no. 40)
Silver-gilt with crystal; 7¼ (18.4)
Maker's mark: bird in a shaped shield
Courtesy, Musem of Fine Arts, Boston. Theodora Wilbour Fund No. 2, in memory of Charlotte Beebe Wilbour 51.16.18

78 English (Exeter), 1582
EXETER SALT, by C. (?) Eston
Silver-gilt; 8⅝ x 3½ (21.9 x 8.89)
Provenance: Lord Swaythling, London; E. Brummer, New York
Lent by The Minneapolis Institute of Arts. The James S. Bell Memorial Fund 49.7

79 German (Ulm), late 16th century
SALT CELLAR
Silver-gilt; 1⅛ x 4½ (2.8 x 11.5)
Lent by Victoria and Albert Museum, London 1259-1885

80 The Netherlands, ca. 1610
SALT
Silver-gilt; 4 1/16 x 8⅜ x 8⅜ (10.3 x 21.3 x 21.3)
Provenance: Mrs. Margaret Oppenheim
Lent by The Art Institute of Chicago. Gift of Mrs. Stanley Keith 44.781

Eating Utensils

81 English (London), ca. 1490
"BALL KNOB" SPOON
Silver, sterling standard; 6 (15)
Lent by Jerry Durham, San Francisco

82 Flemish (Tournai), dated 1562
COMBINED FOLDING SPOON WITH FORK AND TOOTHPICK (Fig. no. 42)
Silver, parcel-gilt; 6 15/16 x 1 15/16 (17.6 x 4.8)
Lent by Victoria and Albert Museum, London M564-1910

83 English, ca. 1570
ELIZABETHAN SPOON
Brass; 6 (15)
Lent by Jerry Durham, San Francisco

84 German or Flemish, ca. 1600
KNIFE AND FORK
Silver and steel; 9 (22.9)
Provenance: George Grey Bernard collection
Lent by Philadelphia Museum of Art. 45.25.255a,b

Miscellaneous Objects

85 German (Augsburg), 1550-1600
CASE FOR A WAX PORTRAIT
Copper-gilt; d. 6 11/16 (17)
Provenance: Foulc Collection
Lent by Philadelphia Museum of Art 30.1.59

86 Boas Ulrich (1550-1624)
CASKET
German (Augsburg), ca. 1580
Silver and silver-gilt on ebony; 5⅞ x 4⅞ x 6¼ (14.9 x 12.4 x 15.9)
Lent by Wadsworth Atheneum, Hartford, Connecticut. J. J. Goodwin Fund 1957.18

87 French, late 16th century
CASKET WITH COMBINATION LOCK
Wood, gilt bronze and velvet; 4½ x 6⅞ x 4¾ (11.5 x 17.5 x 12)
Provenance: Baron Jerome Pichon, Paris
Lent by The Walters Art Gallery, Baltimore 53.40

88 German, dated 1537
MARKSMANSHIP MEDAL
Silver; 5 (12.7)
Provenance: Prince Ratibor, Castle Grafneck, Austria
Courtesy, Museum of Fine Arts, Boston. Frederick Brown Fund 48.1247

89 Wenzel Jamnitzer (1508-1585)
MIRROR FRAME (Fig. no. 52)
German (Nuremberg), ca. 1568
Silver-gilt; 11⅝ x 9⅛ (29.5 x 23.2)
Marks: N and W over lion
Lent by The Metropolitan Museum of Art, New York. Gift of J. Pierpont Morgan, 1917 17.190.620

90 Spanish, 16th century
LECTERN (arms of the Duke of Alba) (Fig. no. 53)
Parcel-gilt silver; 6¼ x 12 (16 x 30.6)
Provenance: Frederic Spitzer, Paris; Seligmann & Co.
Lent by The Walters Art Gallery, Baltimore 57.680

91 French, 1550-1575
FRAME FOR A PURSE
Gilt bronze; 4 15/16 x 5 11/16 (12.5 x 14)
Provenance: Foulc Collection
Lent by Philadelphia Museum of Art 30.1.39

Jewelry

92 Italian, early 16th century
RING WITH A PORTRAIT OF SAVONAROLA (Fig. no. 55)
Gold and chalcedony; d. 1¼ (3.2)
Lent by Mr. and Mrs. James W. Alsdorf, Chicago

93 Sardinian, 1550-1575
BADGE
Silver, parcel-gilt; 3 13/16 x 4 5/16 (9.6 x 10.9)
Lent by Victoria and Albert Museum, London M375-1924

94 Italian, ca. 1575
LION PENDANT POMANDER
Gold, diamonds and rubies; 2⅜ (6)
Provenance: Braganza, Portugal
Lent anonymously

95 North Italian, second half of the 16th century
PENDANT OF "THE JUDGMENT OF PARIS" (Fig. no. 5)
Gold, enamel, quartz, rubies, diamonds and pearls; 3½ (8.9)
Provenance: Count Michelozzi Giacomini, Florence; Prof. Luigi Grassi, Florence; Mrs. Henry Walters; Melvin Gutman
Lent by Mr. and Mrs. James W. Alsdorf, Chicago

96 Manner of Alessandro Masnago (act. second half of 16th century)
PENDANT OF ORPHEUS AND THE ANIMALS (Fig. no. 57)
Italian (Milan), second half of the 16th century
Gold, enamel and agate; 4⅝ (11.8)
Provenance: F. Mannheimer, Amsterdam; Melvin Gutman
Lent by Mr. and Mrs. James W. Alsdorf, Chicago

97 German, 16th century
PENDANT (Diana in an architectural setting)
Gold, enamel and pearls; 2⅝ x 2 1/16 (6.6 x 5)
Lent by The Walters Art Gallery, Baltimore 44.442

98 Italian, 16th century
CAMEO
Mounted in enamelled gold; 3¼ x 1½ (8.25 x 3.8)
Lent by Victoria and Albert Museum,
London 493-1897

99 French, ca. 1550
A BADGE OF PRUDENCE (Fig. no. 6)
Gold, enamel and a diamond; 2½ (6.4)
Lent anonymously

100 French?, late 16th century
CAMEO PENDANT OF JUNO AND MINERVA
(Fig. no. 56)
Gold, enamel and carnelian; 2½ (6.4)
Provenance: Henry Symonds; Melvin Gutman
Lent by Mr. and Mrs. James W. Alsdorf, Chicago

101 Spanish, 16th century
PENDANT
Gold, enamel and jewels; 3 3/16 (8.1)
Lent by The Walters Art Gallery, Baltimore 44.482

102 Spanish, ca. 1560
EAGLE PENDANT
Baroque pearl mounted in enamelled gold;
4 5/16 x 3¾ (10.9 x 9.5)
Lent by Victoria and Albert Museum,
London M243-1975

103 Spanish, late 16th century
PENDANT (man riding a dolphin)
Gold, enamel, emerald and pearl; 4 x 2½ (10.2 x 6.35)
Provenance: Baron Alfred C. de Rothschild, London(?);
A. Seligmann, Paris
Lent by The Walters Art Gallery, Baltimore 44.443

104 Spanish, late 16th century
NEF PENDANT (Fig. no. 58)
Gold, enamel, pearl, rubies, crystal; 4⅜ x 3¾ (11.1 x 9.5)
Provenance: Fritz von Gans, Frankfurt-am-Main
Lent by The Metropolitan Museum of Art, New York.
Gift of The Michael Friedsam Collection,
1931 32.100.312

ARMS & ARMOR

105 Missaglia Workshop (act. 15th century)
BARBUTE (Fig. no. 61)
Italian (Milan), ca. 1470
Steel; 12⅛ x 8⅛ (30.7 x 20.6)
Lent by The Metropolitan Museum of Art, New York.
Gift of Stephen V. Grancsay, New York 42.50.14

106 Koloman Helmschmied (1476-1532)
TRIPLE CRESTED BURGONET OF THE STATE
GUARD OF THE EMPEROR CHARLES V
German (Augsburg), ca. 1530
Steel; 11½ x 8¼ (28.7 x 21)
Provenance: Graf Gablentz-Thuerheim,
Schloss Kefermarkt, Upper Austria
Lent by Stephen V. Grancsay, New York L56.61.1

107 Hans Seusenhofer (1470-1555)
CLOSE HELMET (cock's comb) (Fig. no. 62)
Austrian (Innsbruck), 1525-1530
Steel; 10 3/16 x 9 (25.9 x 22.8)
Lent by The Metropolitan Museum of Art, New York.
Bequest of Bashford Dean, 1928 29.150.3A

108 French, ca. 1550
HELMET OF CLAUDE GOUFFIER, MARQUIS OF
BOISY, GRAND EQUERRY OF FRANCE (Fig. no. 65)
Steel and leather; 15¾ x 8¼ (40 x 20.9)
Lent by The Metropolitan Museum of Art, New York.
Gift of William H. Riggs, 1913 14.25.596

109 Bartolomeo Campi (d. 1596/97)
RIGHT PAULDRON FROM THE ARMOR OF
GUIDOBALDO II, DUKE OF URBINO
Italian, 1545
Steel, silver and gold; 8¼ x 8¼ (20.9 x 20.9)
Lent by The Metropolitan Museum of Art, New York.
Gift of William H. Riggs, 1913 14.25.714i

110 Italian (Milan), ca. 1500
BREASTPLATE
Etched steel; 14¾ x 13 5/16 (37.5 x 32.8)
Lent by The Metropolitan Museum of Art, New York.
Bequest of Bashford Dean, 1928 29.150.78

111 Matthäus Frauenpreis (act. ca. 1529-d. 1549)
PAIR OF TASSETS FROM THE HARNESS OF
EMPEROR CHARLES V (Fig. no. 63)
German (Augsburg), ca. 1545
Steel, embossed, etched and gilded; 8¾ x 9⅜
(22.2 x 23.7)
Lent by The Metropolitan Museum of Art, New York.
Bequest of Bashford Dean, 1928 29.150.1D, E

112 Italian (Milan), 1555
PARADE SHIELD (design after a drawing by Martin van
Heemskerck, dated 1554, in the British Museum)
Steel, gold and silver; d. 23 (58.4)
Lent by The Metropolitan Museum of Art, New York.
Gift of Stephen V. Grancsay, 1942 42.50.5

113 French, ca. 1555
PARADE SHIELD OF HENRY II OF FRANCE
(Fig. no. 59)
Steel; 25 x 18 (63.5 x 45.7)
Lent by The Metropolitan Museum of Art, New York.
Harris Brisbane Dick Fund, 1934 34.85

114 Lucio Piccinino (act. ca. 1550-ca. 1590)
HALF-ARMOR OF FERNANDO ALVAREZ OF
TOLEDO, DUKE OF ALBA (Fig. no. 68)
Italian (Milan), ca. 1570
Steel, silver and gold
Lent by The Metropolitan Museum of Art, New York.
Gift of William H. Riggs, 1913 14.25.714

115 Italian (Brescia), 1520
FALCHION (believed to have belonged to Francis I
of France) (Fig. no. 66)
Steel, iron damascened with gold; 30¼ (76.7)
Provenance: Count Valencis de Don Juan,
former Curator of the Royal Armory, Madrid
Lent by Stephen V. Grancsay, New York L56.61.7

116 North Italian, 1525
"FISH-TAIL" DAGGER
Steel and gilded bronze; 15 x 5½ (38.1 x 13.9)
Lent by The Metropolitan Museum of Art, New York.
Rogers Fund, 1904 04.3.143

117 North Italian, 1525-1550
CINQUEDEA
Steel, ivory, gold and brass; 23 3/16 (58.9)
Lent by The Metropolitan Museum of Art, New York.
Gift of Jean Jacques Reubell, 1926, in memory of his
mother Julia C. Coster, and his wife, Adeline E. Post,
both of New York City 26.145.56

118 Daniele da Serravalle
RAPIER MADE FOR PHILIP II OF SPAIN
Italian (Milan), dated 1560
Steel, iron and gold; 34½ x 1 13/16 (87.6 x 4.7)
Lent by The Metropolitan Museum of Art, New York.
Bequest of Col. Wycliffe P. Draper, 1973 1973.27.2

119 Swiss, dated 1567
DAGGER WITH SHEATH (Fig. no. 60)
Steel and gilt-bronze; 17½ x 3⅛ (44.4 x 7.9)
Lent by The Metropolitan Museum of Art, New York.
Gift of Jean Jacques Reubell, 1926, in memory of his mother, Julia C. Coster, and his wife, Adeline E. Post, both of New York City 26.145.47A-D

120 German (Saxony), ca. 1580
SWEPT-HILTED RAPIER AND DAGGER
Juan Martinez of Toledo (blades)
Steel, gold, wood, leather and velvet;
Rapier: 43¼ (109); Dagger: 16 (41.6)
Lent by The Metropolitan Museum of Art, New York.
Gift of Mr. and Mrs. Robert W. de Forest, 1929
29.157.13-14

121 French, ca. 1550
MACE OF HENRY II OF FRANCE
Steel, gold and silver; 24 x 4½ (60.9 x 11.4)
Lent by The Metropolitan Museum of Art, New York.
Rogers Fund, 1904 04.3.59

122 North Italian, 1570
CURB BIT
Steel; 11 x 4⅛ (27.9 x 10.5)
Lent by The Metropolitan Museum of Art, New York.
Gift of Alan Rutherfurd Stuyvesant, 1951 51.170.5

123 Italian, 1575
HEAD OF A CEREMONIAL WAR HAMMER (Fig. no. 64)
Steel; 8¾ x 12 (22.2 x 30.5)
Lent by The Metropolitan Museum of Art, New York.
Rogers Fund, 1904 04.3.58

124 French, ca. 1600
POWDER FLASK
Gilt bronze, steel and wood; 11⅛ x 8½ (28.2 x 21.6)
Lent by The Metropolitan Museum of Art, New York.
Gift of William H. Riggs, 1913 14.25.1507

125 South German, ca. 1600
STIRRUP
Steel, 4⅜ x 4¾ (11.1 x 12)
Lent by The Metropolitan Museum of Art, New York.
Gift of George D. Pratt,1925 25.188.3

OTHER WORKS IN IRON AND STEEL

126 Italian, 16th century
PLAQUE
Steel inlaid with silver; 6⅛ x 3⅞ (15.6 x 9.8)
Lent by The Minneapolis Institute of Arts.
The Christina N. and Swan J. Turnblad
Memorial Fund 68.19.2

127 German, 16th century
PRESENTOIR (Knife)
Steel, engraved and gilded, rock crystal and semi-precious stones; 21 x 4 (58.4 x 10.2)
Lent by Ruth Blumka, New York

128 Jacopo da Ferrara, second half of 16th century
ARMORER'S VISE (Fig. no. 69)
North Italian, 1588
Iron; 10 3/16 (25.4)
Provenance: Frederic Spitzer, Paris;
Samuel Yellin, Philadelphia
Lent by The Metropolitan Museum of Art, New York.
Harris Brisbane Dick Fund, 1958 58.16.5

129 French, probably 1580-1589
KEY (Fig. no. 70)
Iron; 5 9/16 (14.2)
Provenance: Prof. Luigi Grassi, Florence;
Samuel Yellin, Philadelphia
Lent by The Metropolitan Museum of Art, New York.
Harris Brisbane Dick Fund, 1958 58.16.3

130 Italian (probably Milan), 1545-1547
CASKET (arms of Pier Luigi Farnese) (Fig. no. 71)
Iron, damascened in gold and silver, on wood;
5⅞ x 13⅞ x 8⅞ (14.9 x 35.2 x 20.2)
Lent by The Metropolitan Museum of Art, New York.
Morris Loeb Gift Fund, 1956 56.139 a, b

131 French, 1583
KEY (made for marriage of Ferdinand of Tuscany and Christine de Lorraine at Bar-le-Duc, May 3, 1583)
Iron; 5⅝ (14.3)
Provenance: Brassine, Liège
Courtesy, Museum of Fine Arts, Boston 58.711

132 French, 1550-1600
KEY
Iron, 5⅛ (13)
Provenance: Foulc collection
Lent by Philadelphia Museum of Art. 30.1.146

133 French, 1575-1600
KEY
Iron, 5⅛ (13)
Provenance: Foulc collection
Lent by Philadelphia Museum of Art. 30.1.147

134 German, ca. 1600
SHAPED KNIFE
Wood, bronze, and steel, 12 1/16 (30.7)
Provenance: Foulc collection
Lent by Philadelphia Museum of Art. 30.1.102

TIMEPIECES AND SCIENTIFIC INSTRUMENTS

135 English, 1525-1530
HOURGLASS (Fig. no. 72)
Silver-gilt and glass; 7 (19.3)
Provenance: John Hunt, Dublin
Courtesy, Museum of Fine Arts, Boston
Theodora Wilbour Fund in memory of
Charlotte Beebe Wilbour 57.533

136 Paul Reinmann (act. 1575-1608)
PORTABLE DIPTYCH SUNDIAL (Fig. no. 81)
German (Nuremberg), 1602
Ivory; 4½ (11.4)
Lent by The Metropolitan Museum of Art, New York.
Gift of Mrs. Stephen D. Tucker, 1903 03.21.24

137 School of Erasmus Habermel (d. 1606)
PILLAR SUNDIAL (with screw-out knife and fork) (Fig. no. 75)
German (Nuremberg), ca. 1600
Gilt bronze and steel; 5⅞ (15)
Provenance: W.M. Mensing, Amsterdam
Lent by The Adler Planetarium, Chicago M-306

138 French, ca. 1550-1582
NOCTURNAL AND SUNDIAL (Fig. no. 74)
Gilt brass; 2¾ x 2¼ (7 x 5.7)
Lent by The Metropolitan Museum of Art, New York.
Gift of Mrs. Stephen D. Tucker, 1902 03.21.69

139 Italian, 16th century
SKAPHE SUNDIAL
Gilt bronze; 2¾ x 5⅞ (7 x 14.9)
Provenance: W.M. Mensing, Amsterdam
Lent by The Adler Planetarium, Chicago M-234

140 Christoph Schissler (1530-1608)
COMPENDIUM
German (Augsburg), dated 1559
Gilt brass; d. 3 (7.62)
Lent by The Time Museum, Rockford, Illinois

141 Arsenius Workshop (act. second half of 16th century)
ASTROLABE
Flemish (Louvain), 16th century
Gilt bronze; 16 15/16 x 12⅛ (43 x 30.9)
Provenance: W.M. Mensing, Amsterdam
Lent by The Adler Planetarium, Chicago M-25

Clocks

142 Hans Gruber (act. second half of 16th century)
TABLE CLOCK (Fig. no. 78)
German (Nuremberg), 1570
Steel and gilt brass; 3 11/32 x 5 29/32 (8.5 x 15)
Monogram of Leonhard Danner (1507-1587)
and signature "Hans 1570 Gruber"
Lent by Ruth Blumka, New York

143 German (Augsburg), dated 1568
TABLE CLOCK (Fig. no. 79)
Steel, gilt brass and silver; 8¼ x 4½ x 4½
(20.9 x 11.5 x 11.5)
Lent by The Time Museum, Rockford, Illinois

144 Gerhard Emmoser, 16th century
CELESTIAL GLOBE WITH CLOCKWORKS
(Fig. no. 3)
Austrian (Vienna), dated 1579
Parcel-gilt silver and brass; 10¾ (27.3)
Provenance: Emperor Rudolph II, Vienna; Queen Christina, Stockholm; Charles Mannheim, Paris
Lent by The Metropolitan Museum of Art, New York.
Gift of J. Pierpont Morgan, 1917 17.190.636

145 Caspar Buschmann II (d. 1613)
TABLE CLOCK
German (Augsburg), ca. 1580
Gilt bronze; 5⅞ x 6 19/32 (15 x 16.7)
Provenance: W.M. Mensing, Amsterdam
Lent by The Adler Planetarium, Chicago M-378

146 Bartholomew Newsam (fl. 1568-d. 1593)
TABLE CLOCK AND LEATHER CASE (Fig. no. 77)
English (London), 1580-1593
Gilt brass, silver dial; Clock: 3 (7.6); Case: 4 (10.2)
Provenance: Hilton Price, London
Lent by The Metropolitan Museum of Art, New York.
Gift of J. Pierpont Morgan, 1917 17.190.1514a, b

147 German, ca. 1600
AUTOMATE CLOCK IN THE FORM OF DIANA ON HER CHARIOT (Fig. no. 83)
Wood, gilt bronze and steel; 17⅞ x 17½ x 11½
(45.4 x 44.5 x 29.2)
Lent by Yale University Art Gallery, New Haven, Connecticut.
Gift of Mrs. Laird S. Goldsborough 1951.19.2

148 Probably Italian, 16th century
BOX (possibly a case for a portable clock)
Leather over wood with tasseled cord of silk and metal thread; 2⅝ (6.7)
Provenance: A. Imbert, Rome; Hilton Price, London
Lent by The Metropolitan Museum of Art, New York.
Gift of J. Pierpont Morgan, 1917 17.190.1510b

Watches

149 South German, ca. 1570-1580
TAMBOUR WATCH
Case of gilded brass; movement of iron, with maker's punch mark: A.K.; d. 2½ (6.4)
Provenance: Hilton Price, London
Lent by The Metropolitan Museum of Art, New York.
Gift of J. Pierpont Morgan, 1917 17.190.1538

150 Antonio Arlaud, late 16th century
OVAL WATCH ON STAND SUPPORTED BY HERCULES (Fig. no. 76)
Swiss (Geneva), ca. 1600
Gilt bronze; 10½ (26.7)
Lent by The Walters Art Gallery, Baltimore 58.239

151 French (Paris), early 17th century
WATCH
Case of engraved silver; movement of brass and steel, signed: J. Benard à Paris; 1¾ (4.4)
Provenance: Carl Marfels, Frankfurt-am-Main
Lent by The Metropolitan Museum of Art, New York.
Gift of J. Pierpont Morgan, 1917 17.190.1615

Scientific Instruments

152 School of Christoph Trechsler (ca. 1546-ca. 1624)
GUNNER'S SIGHT
German (Dresden), ca. 1580
Gilt bronze; 4¾ x 2⅝ x ⅞ (12.1 x 6.7 x 2.2)
Provenance: W.M. Mensing, Amsterdam
Lent by The Adler Planetarium, Chicago M-196

153 School of Christoph Schissler
PEDOMETER (Fig. no. 73)
German (Augsburg), ca. 1580
Gilt bronze; 6⅞ x 3½ (17.5 x 9)
Provenance: W.M. Mensing, Amsterdam
Lent by The Adler Planetarium, Chicago M-225

154 German, ca. 1600
SINECAL QUADRANT
Gilt bronze; radius 5¾ (14.7)
Provenance: W.M. Mensing, Amsterdam
Lent by The Adler Planetarium, Chicago M-179

155 Jacob Frölich (act. 1555-d. 1579)
BEAKER ENGRAVED WITH HOROLOGIUM PLANETARE
German (Nuremberg), ca. 1565
Copper-gilt with verre églomisé, enamel; 6⅜ (16.3)
Provenance: Franciscus de Padua
Lent by The Walters Art Gallery, Baltimore 58.220

156 Cristoph Trechsler
ARTILLERY LEVEL (Fig. no. 82)
German (Dresden), dated 1609
Gilt bronze; 11 x 8¾ (28 x 22)
Provenance: W.M. Mensing, Amsterdam
Lent by The Adler Planetarium, Chicago M-200

157 Christoph Trechsler
BEAM COMPASS
German (Dresden), dated 1619
Gilded brass and steel; 11¼ (28.5)
Lent by The Metropolitan Museum of Art, New York.
Bequest of W. Gedney Beatty, 1941 41.160.721

158 French, 16th century
RULER
Steel, 7½ (19)
Provenance: Foulc collection
Lent by Philadelphia Museum of Art, 30.1.157

159 Italian, mid-16th century
INSTRUMENT CASE (Fig. no. 80)
Tooled leather; 13⅛ x 4¾ (33.34 x 12)
Provenance: La Collection Spitzer, Paris
Courtesy, Museum of Fine Arts, Boston.
Hezekiah E. Bolles Fund 1971.214

CERAMICS, GLASS, AND ENAMELS

160 Italian (Florence), ca. 1450
MAJOLICA JAR (Fig. no. 85)
Tin-glazed earthenware; 10½ (26.7)
Lent by Wadsworth Atheneum, Hartford, Connecticut.
Gift of J. P. Morgan 17.416

161 Italian (Florence), ca. 1470
MAJOLICA VASE WITH
THE MEDICI/ORSINI ARMS (Fig. no. 16)
Tin-glazed earthenware; 15½ (39.3)
Probably made for the marriage of
Lorenzo the Magnificent and Clarice Orsini.
Provenance: French & Co., New York
Lent by The Detroit Institute of Arts. Presented to Russel
A. Alger House by the Women's Committee 37.74

162 Italian (Siena), ca. 1510
MAJOLICA ALBARELLO
Tin-glazed earthenware; 8⅞ (22.5)
Provenance: Charles Damiron, Lyons
Lent by The Cleveland Museum of Art.
Gift of the Twentieth Century Club 65.553

163 Italian (Castel Durante), ca. 1540
MAJOLICA JUG
Tin-glazed earthenware; 13⅞ (35.1)
The Fine Arts Museums of San Francisco.
Gift of Jacob Goldschmidt 53.40.9

164 Italian (Castel Durante), ca. 1540
MAJOLICA ALBARELLO
Tin-glazed earthenware; 13⅜ (34)
The Fine Arts Museums of San Francisco.
Gift of Jacob Goldschmidt 53.40.10

165 Italian (Urbino), 1500-1550
MAJOLICA CHRISTENING SET (Fig. no. 91)
Tin-glazed earthenware; d. Bowl: 8½ (21.6);
d. Cup: 5½ (14); d. Cover: 7(18)
Provenance: Baron Nathaniel de Rothschild, Vienna
Lent by The Detroit Institute of Arts.
Gift of Mr. and Mrs. Henry Ford II 59.124

166 Spanish (Valencia), 15th century
MAJOLICA ARMORIAL DISH
Tin-glazed earthenware; d. 16 (40.6)
Lent by Los Angeles County Museum of Art.
The William Randolph Hearst Collection 50.7.3

167 Spanish (Valencia), ca. 1480
MAJOLICA ALBARELLO
Tin-glazed earthenware with lustre decoration;
12½ (31.7)
The Fine Arts Museums of San Francisco.
Gift of The de Young Museum Society 53.36

168 Spanish (Talavera), ca. 1565
MAJOLICA DRUG JAR (Fig. no. 93)
Tin-glazed earthenware; 11 x d. 8 (27.9 x d. 20.3)
Provenance: Boix Collection, Madrid
Lent by John Philip Kassebaum, Wichita, Kansas

169 Spanish (Talavera), ca. 1590
MAJOLICA DRUG JAR
Tin-glazed earthenware; 11¾ x d. 8 (29.9 x d. 20.3)
Provenance: Boix Collection, Madrid
Lent by John Philip Kassebaum, Wichita, Kansas

170 Workshop "Casa Pirota" (act. ca. 1519-ca. 1537)
MAJOLICA PLATE
Italian (Faenza), 1525-1530
Tin-glazed earthenware; d. 9⅝ (24.4)
Lent by The Walters Art Gallery, Baltimore 48.1339

171 Italian, 1526
MAJOLICA DISH (Fig. no. 88)
Tin-glazed earthenware; d. 9⅞ (25)
Lent by The Metropolitan Museum of Art, New York.
Gift of V. Everit Macy, in memory of his wife,
Edith Carpenter Macy, 1927 27.97.25

172 Italian (Urbino), ca. 1530
MAJOLICA PLATE (Apollo and Daphne)
Tin-glazed earthenware; d. 10 5/16 (26.2)
Lent by The Walters Art Gallery, Baltimore 48.1326

173 Italian, 1535
MAJOLICA DISH (Fig. no. 87)
Tin-glazed earthenware; d. 9 3/16 (23.4)
Lent by The Metropolitan Museum of Art, New York.
Gift of Julia A. Berwind, 1953 53.225.80

174 Italian (Pesaro), 1540-1544
MAJOLICA PLATE (Vulcan, Venus and Mars)
(Fig. no. 90)
Tin-glazed earthenware; d. 9¾ (24.76)
Lent by The Cleveland Museum of Art.
John L. Severance Collection 42.624

175 Italian, 16th century
MAJOLICA SALT CELLAR (Fig. no. 92)
Tin-glazed earthenware; 8½ (21.6)
Lent by The Metropolitan Museum of Art, New York.
Rogers Fund, 1904 04.9.15

176 Italian (Faenza), 15th century
OCTAGONAL TILE (Della Rovere arms)
Tin-glazed earthenware; d. 5½ (14)
Inscribed: "I II PM" (for Julius II, Pontificus Maximus)
Lent by Wadsworth Atheneum, Hartford, Connecticut.
Gift of J. P. Morgan 1917.445

177 Italian (Ferrara), ca. 1500
INKSTAND WITH ST. GEORGE
AND THE DRAGON (Fig. no. 89)
Glazed earthenware with sgraffito decoration; 13 (33)
Provenance: R. Langton Douglas, London
Lent by The Detroit Institute of Arts. Founders Society
purchase. Elliott T. Slocum Fund 26.291

178 Italian (Urbino), 16th century
PLATE WITH ARMS OF THE SALVIATI FAMILY
Tin-glazed earthenware; d. 9 (22.9)
Provenance: L. Breitmeyer, London;
Rushton Hall, Kettering
Lent by The Detroit Institute of Arts.
Gift of Mr. and Mrs. Ernest Kanzler
in memory of Mrs. William Clay 61.167

179 Italian (Florence), ca. 1575
"MEDICI" PORCELAIN CRUET (Fig. no. 21)
Soft-paste porcelain; 6¾ x 5¼ x 3½ (17.1 x 13.1 x 8.9)
Courtesy, Museum of Fine Arts, Boston. Gift from the
Estate of Professor Henry Williamson Haynes,
through Miss Sarah H. Blanchard 12.717

180 Attributed to Fra. Xanto Avelli
(act. first half of 16th century)
MAJOLICA WINE CISTERN (Fig. no. 84)
Italian (Urbino), ca. 1540
Tin-glazed earthenware; 8 (20.3)
Lent by Los Angeles County Museum of Art.
Gift of Stanley Mortimer 50.42.2

181 Italian (Deruta), 16th century
MAJOLICA DEEP PLATE
Tin-glazed earthenware; d. 17⅜ (44.1)
Lent by Los Angeles County Museum of Art. The
William Randolph Hearst Collection 50.9.40

182 Italian (Castel Durante), ca. 1570
PILGRIM-BOTTLE
Tin-glazed earthenware; 14¼ (36.2)
The Fine Arts Museums of San Francisco.
Gift of E. John and Rose Magnin. 75.18.55a, b

183 Italian, late 15th century
MAJOLICA DISH (Fig. no. 86)
Lead-glazed earthenware; d. 16¼ (41.3)
Lent by The Metropolitan Museum of Art, New York.
Gift of R. Thornton Wilson, 1943, in memory of
Florence Ellsworth Wilson 43.100.61

184 Italian (Siena), 1518-1522
MAJOLICA PLATE
Tin-glazed earthenware; d. 10⅞ (27.5)
Courtesy, Museum of Fine Arts, Boston.
Harriet Otis Cruft Fund 55.931

185 Italian (Deruta), ca. 1525
MAJOLICA PLATE (Fig. no. 7)
Tin-glazed earthenware; d. 16¾ (42.5)
Inscribed: SAT URNO FOTRE
The Fine Arts Museums of San Francisco.
Gift of Jacob Goldschmidt 54.45.2

186 Italian (Deruta), ca. 1525
MAJOLICA PLATE (unidentified allegorical scene)
Tin-glazed earthenware; d. 16½ (41.9)
The Fine Arts Museums of San Francisco.
Gift of Jacob Goldschmidt 53.40.4

187 Italian (Siena), ca. 1525
PAIR OF VASES
Tin-glazed earthenware; 8½ (21.6)
Lent by William Rockhill Nelson Gallery of Art
and Atkins Museum of Fine Arts,
Kansas City, Missouri. 34.80.1-2

188 French (La Chapelle-des-Pots), 1500-1550
DOUBLE-SPOUTED VESSEL
Glazed earthenware; 10¼ (26)
Courtesy, Museum of Fine Arts, Boston.
Gift of R. Thornton Wilson, in memory of
Florence Ellsworth Wilson 65.28

189 French (Saint-Porchaire), 16th century
SALT CELLAR (Fig. no. 95)
Faïence (tin-glazed earthenware);
4½ x d. 5 (11.4 x d. 12.7)
Provenance: Baron Gustave de Rothschild;
Baron Robert de Rothschild, Paris
Lent by The Cleveland Museum of Art.
Purchase from the J. H. Wade Fund 51.113

190 Manner of Bernard Palissy (ca. 1510-1589/90)
PAIR OF SALT CELLARS (Fig. no. 94)
French, 16th century
Glazed earthenware; 5 15/16 (15.1)
Provenance: Hope Heirlooms; Duke of Newcastle;
George A. Lockett
Lent by Cyril Humphris, London

191 German (Siegburg), ca. 1580
EWER
Stoneware; 9¾ (24.8)
Fine Arts Museums of San Francisco. X71.541

Glass

192 Italian (Venice), 1500-1510
BOWL (Fig. no. 96)
Opaque white glass, enamelled and gilded; 2 5/16 (5.9)
Lent by The Corning Museum of Glass,
Corning, New York 76.3.17

193 Italian (Venice), 1500-1525
GOBLET (Fig. no. 8)
Enamelled glass; 9 15/16 (23.6)
Provenance: Gustave de Rothschild
Lent by The Corning Museum of Glass,
Corning, New York 53.3.38

194 Italian (Venice), early 16th century
TAZZA (arms of one of the Medici popes — Leo X
or Clement VII) (Fig. no. 19)
Glass, enamelled and gilded; 3 x 9⅞ (7.6 x 25.1)
Lent by The Metropolitan Museum of Art, New York.
Gift of J. Pierpont Morgan, 1917 17.190.555

195 Italian (Venice), early 16th century
BOWL
Dark blue glass, enamelled and gilded; 2 13/16 x d. 8¾
(7.2 x d. 22.2)
Lent by The Metropolitan Museum of Art, New York.
Gift of Julia A. Berwind, 1953 53.225.101

196 Italian (Venice), first half of 16th century
TAZZA (Fig. no. 99)
Enamelled glass; 6 x 11⅝ (15.2 x 29.5)
Lent by The Metroplitan Museum of Art, New York.
Gift of J. Pierpont Morgan, 1917 17.190.553

197 Italian (Venice), 16th century
COVERED GOBLET (Fig. no. 97)
Glass; 10¼ (26)
Lent by The Wine Museum of San Francisco.
Franz W. Sichel Collection 739

198 Italian (Venice or "façon de Venise"), ca. 1600
GROUP OF FOUR WINE GLASSES
Glass; a. 6 (15.2), b. 5½ (14), c. 6⅛ (15.6), d. 5¾ (14.6)
Lent by The Wine Museum of San Francisco.
Franz W. Sichel Collection 722, 743, 746, 748

199 Italian (Venice), ca. 1600
VASE
Mold-blown filigree glass; 7¾ (19.7)
Lent by The Corning Museum of Glass,
Corning, New York 53.3.39

Enamels

200 Couly Nouailher (ca. 1514-ca. 1589)
HERCULES CASKET (Fig. no. 4)
French (Limoges), ca. 1550
Enamel and gilt bronze; 5 x 7½ x 4⅞ (12.6 x 19 x 12.3)
Lent by The Walters Art Gallery, Baltimore 44.65

201 Pierre Reymond (ca. 1513-ca. 1585)
PAIR OF SALT CELLARS (Story of Actaeon)
French (Limoges), ca. 1555
Enamel on copper; 3 3/16 x 5¼ (8.2 x 13.4)
Provenance: F. Spitzer, Paris
Lent by The Walters Art Gallery, Baltimore 44.339-340

202 Possibly by Jean de Court (act. ca. 1541-ca. 1575)
PAIR OF CANDLESTICKS (Fig. no. 98)
French (Limoges), 1550-1575
Enamel on copper; 6 x 1½ (15.2 x 3.81)
Lent by The Metropolitan Museum of Art, New York. Gift of Ann Payne Blumenthal, 1939 39.66.1, 2

203 Attributed to Couly Nouailher
PAIR OF SALT CELLARS
French (Limoges), 16th century
Enamel on copper; 2 x 2½ (5.08 x 6.35)
Lent by The Metropolitan Museum of Art, New York. The Michael Friedsam Collection, 1931 31.100.273

FURNITURE AND WOODCARVING

204 Italian (Tuscany), late 15th century
TABLE
Walnut; 27½ x 26 x 55 (70 x 66 x 139)
Lent by The J. Paul Getty Museum, Malibu, California FAC-D.51

205 Italian, 16th century
CASSONE (Fig. no. 107)
Carved walnut; 30 x 22 x 64 (76.2 x 55.9 x 62.1)
Lent by The J. Paul Getty Museum, Malibu, California 68.DA.8

206 Italian (Florence, workshop of Domenico del Tasso), ca. 1500
CASSONE
Walnut with intarsia decoration 43½ x 32½ x 84½ (110.5 x 82.5 x 211.25)
Lent by Los Angeles County Museum of Art. Hearst Foundation Fund 47.8.33

207 Italian (Tuscany), ca. 1500
SGABELLO (Fig. no. 104)
Carved walnut; 40⅛ x 20⅞ x 17 (102 x 53 x 43.2)
Lent by Philadelphia Museum of Art 49.9.1

208 North Italian, ca. 1500
CASKET (Fig. no. 102)
Pastiglia (parcel-gilt wood, molded and carved gesso); 4⅛ x 6¼ x 4⅜ (10.4 x 16 x 11)
Lent by Cooper-Hewitt Museum, The Smithsonian Institution's National Museum of Design, New York 1953.101.1

209 Italian, 16th century
OCTAGONAL TABLE
Carved walnut; 32¾ x 46⅜ (83.2 x 117.8)
Lent by Los Angeles County Museum of Art 46.16.4A, B

210 Italian (Siena), early 16th century
CASKET
Walnut; 5⅝ x 9⅜ x 5½ (14.3 x 23.8 x 14)
Provenance: F.W. Lippman, Berlin
Courtesy, Museum of Fine Arts, Boston. Gift of Eugene L. Garbaty 54.1566

211 Italian (Tuscany), 16th century
STOOL
Carved walnut; 20 x 14½ x 12½ (50.8 x 36.8 x 31.8)
Lent by Philadelphia Museum of Art. Gift of Henry P. McIlhenny 54.83.4

212 Italian, early 16th century
FOLDING CHAIR
Walnut; 39 x 27 (99.06 x 58.58)
Provenance: Bardini, Florence
Lent by The Toledo Museum of Art. Gift of Florence Scott Libbey 56.9

213 Italian, 16th century
BELLOWS (Fig. no. 105)
Carved walnut and bronze; 26¾ x 13 (68 x 33)
Provenance: Foulc Collection
Lent by Philadelphia Museum of Art 30.1.169

214 Italian, 16th century
CHOIR STALL
Walnut; 47¾ x 57¾ x 32 (121.3 x 146.7 x 81.3)
The Fine Arts Museums of San Francisco. Hélène Irwin Fagan Collection 1975.5.47a, b

215 French, 1550-1575
CHAIR (Caquetoire)
Walnut; 45⅛ x 23 x 16⅞ (114.7 x 58.4 x 43)
The Fine Arts Museums of San Francisco. Hélène Irwin Fagan Collection 1975.5.32

216 Italian, 1550-1600
MIRROR
Carved walnut, partially gilt; 32 x 19¾ (81.3 x 50.2)
Lent by The Metropolitan Museum of Art, New York. Bequest of George Blumenthal, 1941 41.190.198

217 French, 1550-1575
CABINET (Fig. no. 9)
Walnut with molded gesso, gilding and marble inlay; 76¼ x 43 x 19¾ (193.67 x 109.22 x 50.16)
The Fine Arts Museums of San Francisco. Gift of the Oakes Foundation, a fund within The San Francisco Foundation 1973.5

218 French, ca. 1550
MIRROR FRAME (Fig. no. 103)
Carved boxwood and glass; 22 x 14¼ (55.9 x 36.2)
The Fine Arts Museums of San Francisco. Gift of Mr. and Mrs. George Wagner 45.27

219 French, 16th century
PANEL
Carved oak; 20⅜ x 11⅜ (51.8 x 28.8)
Lent anonymously

220 French, 16th century
PANEL
Carved walnut; 25¼ x 23¾ (64.1 x 60.3)
Lent by The Metropolitan Museum of Art, New York. Gift of George Blumenthal, 1941 41.100.379b

221 German, 1500-1580
TRAVELING WRITING CABINET
Wood decorated with marquetry; 15½ x 16 x 21½ (39.4 x 46.6 x 54.6)
Provenance: Katherine Schratt
Lent by The J. Paul Getty Museum, Malibu, California FAC-D.31

222 French (School of Fontainebleau), ca. 1550
TWO PANELS (Allegory of Peace and War) (Fig. no. 100)
Carved walnut with marble inlay; 26 x 11¼ (66 x 28.5)
Provenance: Foulc Collection
Lent by Philadelphia Musem of Art. Purchased: John T. Morris Fund 30.1.173.a, b

223 Probably French, 16th century
CHEST WITH BASE (Fig. no. 106)
Carved walnut; 38 x 67 x 27⅛ (96.5 x 170 x 68.9)
The Fine Arts Museums of San Francisco. Hélène Irwin Fagan Collection 1975.5.54a, b

224 French, 1525-1550
PANEL
Carved walnut; 19¼ x 30 (48.9 x 76.2)
Lent by The Metropolitan Museum of Art, New York. Gift of Duveen Brothers, 1912 12.154.1

225 French, 1550-1575
PANEL
Walnut, 21¾ x 21 (55.2 x 53.3)
Provenance: Foulc collection
Lent by Philadelphia Museum of Art. 30.1.201

226 French (Burgundy), ca. 1550
COFFER (Fig. no. 101)
Carved walnut with marquetry; 13¾ x 25¼ x 18
(35 x 64 x 46)
Provenance: Foulc Collection
Lent by Philadelphia Museum of Art. Purchased for the McIlhenny Collection 30.1.189

227 French (Burgundy), ca. 1600
ARMOIRE
Carved walnut; 84 x 24½ x 62½(213.4 x 62.2 x 57.5)
Provenance: C. Servier, Lyons; Lord Wimborne
Lent by The J. Paul Getty Museum, Malibu, California FAC-D.99

228 English, ca. 1600
COURT CUPBOARD
Carved oak with marquetry of various woods;
50 x 49½ x 18½ (127 x 124 x 47)
The Fine Arts Museums of San Francisco. Gift of E. John and Rose Magnin 75.18.36

RENAISSANCE BOOKBINDINGS

229 Probably by Baldassare Scariglio (act. 1451-1497)
Onosander, *De optimo imperatore.* Manuscript, ca. 1485
EARLY EUROPEAN BINDING (Fig. no. 110)
Italian (Naples) ca. 1485
Red morocco, gold-tooled; 8⅝ x 5½ (22 x 14)
Lent by The Pierpont Morgan Library, New York
PML M.449

230 Italian (Milan), ca. 1510
Aristotle, *Opera.* Greek, vol. II.
Venice: A. Manutius, 1497
PLAQUETTE BINDING FOR JEAN GROLIER
Dark brown morocco, gold-tooled, traces of paint;
12½ x 8½ (31.8 x 21.8)
Lent by The Pierpont Morgan Library, New York
PML 19117

231 Attributed to Etienne Roffet or the "Fontainebleau" binder
Horae B.V.M., *Roman Use.* Manuscript, early 16th century
BINDING FOR PEREGRINUS PECCATOR
(Fig. no. 111)
French (Paris), ca. 1540
Red morocco, gold-tooled; 8¼ x 5½ (21 x 14)
Lent by The Pierpont Morgan Library, New York
PML M.31

232 Italian (Bologna), 1545
Homer, *Opera.* Greek. Venice: A. Manutius, 1524
BINDING FOR DAMIAN FLUG
Brown morocco, gold-tooled; 6⅝ x 4⅛ (16.8 x 10.5)
Lent by The Pierpont Morgan Library, New York
PML 55173-4

233 The "Pecking Crow" binder
Decreta concilii Tridentini. Manuscript in hand of Angelo Massarelli, 1547/8
BINDING FOR PRESENTATION TO HENRY II
(Fig. no. 112)
French (Paris), ca. 1548
Dark brown morocco, gold-tooled; 13 x 9⅝ (33 x 24.5)
Lent by The Pierpont Morgan Library, New York
PML MA.225A

234 The "Grolier Cuspinianus" binder
Peter Martyr, *De rebus oceanicis et orbe novo.*
Basel: J. Bebelius, 1533
BINDING FOR THOMAS MAHIEU (Fig. no. 113)
French (Paris), ca. 1550
Brown calf, gold-tooled, enriched with paint; brown morocco inlay; 13 x 8 1/16 (33 x 20.5)
Lent by The Pierpont Morgan Library, New York
PML 44098

235 Claude de Picques (act. ca. 1559-after 1572)
Theophrastus, *Opera.* Greek. Venice: A. Manutius, 1497
GREEK-STYLE BINDING FOR HENRY II
French (Paris), ca. 1550
Olive-brown morocco, gold and silver tooled, with white paint added; 12 9/16 x 8 7/16 (32 x 21.4)
Lent by The Pierpont Morgan Library, New York
PML 34896

236 Claude de Picques
Paulus Jovius, *De Vita Leonis decimi.* Florence: L. Torrentino, 1549
BINDING FOR JEAN GROLIER (Fig. no. 114)
French (Paris), ca. 1552
Brown calf, gold-tooled with painted interlace in gray and black; 13⅝ x 9¼ (34.7 x 23.5)
Lent by The Pierpont Morgan Library, New York
PML 4075

237 Attributed to Claude de Picques
Plato, *Omnia opera.* Greek. Basel: J. Valderus, 1534
BINDING FOR MARCUS FUGGER (Fig. no. 108)
French (Paris), ca. 1552
Black morocco, gold-tooled, with onlays of red, brown and olive morocco; 13¾ x 9 (35 x 22.9)
Lent by The Pierpont Morgan Library, New York
PML 42590

238 French (Paris or Lyons), ca. 1554
Herodian, *L'Histoire.* Lyons: G. Rouille, 1554
ARCHITECTURAL BINDING (Fig. no. 115)
Gold-brown morocco, gold-tooled; 13⅞ x 10⅛
(35.3 x 25.7)
Lent by The Pierpont Morgan Library, New York PML 16102

239 The "Cupid's Bow" binder
Plato *Le Republique,* tr. Le Roy. Paris: S. Nivelle, 1555
BINDING FOR COUNT VON MANSFELD
French (Paris) ca. 1555
Brown calf, tooled in gold and silver, with added painted decoration; 9.64 x c.7 (24.5 x 17)
Lent by The Pierpont Morgan Library, New York PML 15447

240 Italian (Florence), 1555
Pico della Mirandola, *Le sette sposizioni.*
Pescia: L. Torrentino, 1555
BINDING WITH MEDICI ARMS
Olive morocco, gold-tooled; 8⅞ x 5 9/16 (22.5 x 14.2)
Lent by The Pierpont Morgan Library, New York PML 62410

241 French (Paris), ca. 1556
B. Camerarius, *De praedestinatione.*
Paris: M. Davis, 1556
BINDING FOR DIANE DE POITIERS
White kidskin, tooled in dark brown pigment;
9¾ x 6¾ (24.7 x 17.1)
Lent by The Pierpont Morgan Library, New York PML 16137

242 "Dudley-Morocco" binder
Bible, New Testament. London: R. Jugge, 1569
BINDING FOR ARCHBISHOP PARKER (Fig. no. 116)
English (London), ca. 1569
Brown morocco, gold-tooled and blocked;
8⅜ x 6 (21.2 x 15.3)
Lent by The Pierpont Morgan Library,
New York PML 59035

243 Italian (Venice), 1574
Dogal commission to the Podestà of Bergamo, Manuscript, 1574
BINDING IN THE PERSIAN STYLE (Fig. no. 117)
Red morocco, blocked in gold with added gold painting;
9¼ x 6⅞ (23.6 x 17.4)
Lent by The Pierpont Morgan Library,
New York PML M.203

244 Antonio Gentili (ca. 1519-1609)
BINDING FOR CARDINAL ODOARDO FARNESE (Fig. no. 109)
Italian (Rome), 1590-1600
Silver-gilt over wooden boards; 7 x 4¾ (17.8 x 12)
Lent by The Pierpont Morgan Library,
New York PML M.69

PRINTS AND DRAWINGS

245 Giovanni Pietro da Birago, called Master of the Sforza Book of Hours (act. ca. 1470-1513)
THREE ORNAMENTAL PANELS (Fig. no. 1)
Italian, 1505-1515
Engravings; 28 x 22 (71.1 x 55.9)
Lent by University of California, Los Angeles,
Grunwald Center for the Graphic Arts 1961.3.1

246 Agostino Veneziano (ca. 1490-after 1536)
ORNAMENTAL PANEL
Italian, ca. 1520
Engraving; 10½ x 5⅞ (26.7 x 14.9)
Lent by University of California, Los Angeles,
Grunwald Center for the Graphic Arts 1962.26.3

247 Italian (Venice), 1520-1540
DRAWING FOR A TAZZA
Pen and ink; 8⅜ x 5 5/16 (21.4 x 13.5)
Lent by Cooper-Hewitt Museum, The Smithsonian
Institution's National Museum of Design,
New York 1938.88.2636

248 Attributed to Nicoletto da Modena (act. 1500-ca. 1507)
DESIGN FOR A BRONZE CANDLESTICK BASE
Italian (Venice), early 16th century
Pen and ink; 10 5/16 x 7⅝ (26.2 x 19.4)
Lent by Cooper-Hewitt Museum, The Smithsonian
Institution's National Museum of Design,
New York 1956-41-1

249 Perino del Vaga (ca. 1500-1546/47)
DESIGN FOR A BOAT-SHAPED EWER (Fig. no. 54)
Italian (Rome), ca. 1535-1545
Drawing; 7 1/32 x 6 31/32 (17.9 x 15.9)
Lent by Cooper-Hewitt Museum, The Smithsonian
Institution's National Museum of Design, New York
1942.36.6

250 Antonio Fantuzzi (ca. 1508-1550)
DESIGN FOR A EWER
Italian, 1543
Etching; 11¾ x 6¾ (29.8 x 17.2)
Courtesy, Museum of Fine Arts, Boston.
Katherine Eliot Bullard Fund 1970.79

251 Italian, 16th century
TWO DESIGNS FOR A DISH (Fig. no. 49)
Pen and bistre; 10¾ x 16 (27.2 x 40.7)
Provenance: C. Fairfax Murray
Lent by The Pierpont Morgan Library,
New York IV.187

252 Giorgio Vasari (1511-1574)
CEILING DESIGN FOR THE SALA DI LORENZO IL MAGNIFICO (Fig. no. 17)
Italian, (Florence), ca. 1556-1562
Pen and brown ink, brown wash, over faint traces of black chalk; 15½ x 14¼ (69.9 x 66.7)
Provenance: E. Guntrip, Kent;
George H. Fitch, New York
Lent by The Pierpont Morgan Library,
New York D.39b

253 Cesare Vecellio (ca. 1521-1601)
DESIGN FOR LACE (from a book of lace patterns: *Corona delle nobile donne*)
Italian (Venice), 1591
Woodcut; 5 3/32 x 7 7/32 (13 x 18.4)
The Fine Arts Museums of San Francisco,
Achenbach Foundation for Graphic Arts

254 Albrecht Dürer (1471-1528)
COAT OF ARMS WITH A SKULL
German (Nuremberg), 1503
Engraving; 8 21/32 x 6 9/32 (22 x 16)
Provenance: Earl of Aylesford
The Fine Arts Museums of San Francisco, Achenbach
Foundation for Graphic Arts 1963.30.29

255 Albrecht Altdorfer (1480-1538)
THE HOLY FAMILY ON THE FLIGHT INTO EGYPT AT A FOUNTAIN (cover illustration)
German (Regensburg), 1520
Woodcut; 9⅛ x 7 1/16 (23.2 x 17.9)
Lent by Yale University Art Gallery, New Haven,
Connecticut. Gift of Mr. and Mrs. Christopher
Tunnard 1973.156.1

256 German, ca. 1530
DESIGN FOR A DAGGER SHEATH
Engraving; 11 x 2 (28 x 5.1)
Provenance: Friedrich August II, Dresden
Lent by University of California, Los Angeles, Grunwald
Center for the Graphic Arts 1964.9.3

257 Daniel Hopfer (ca. 1470-1536)
ALPHABET OF CAPITAL LETTERS WITH ROMAN AND METAPHORICAL ORNAMENTS
German (Augsburg), early 16th century
Etching; 6 5/16 x 9 1/16 (16 x 23)
The Fine Arts Museums of San Francisco,
Achenbach Foundation for Graphic Arts

258 Heinrich Aldegrever (1502-ca. 1560)
TWO RICHLY DECORATED SPOONS
German (Soest), 1539
Engraving; 3 15/16 x 2 9/16 (10 x 6.6)
The Fine Arts Museums of San Francisco,
Achenbach Foundation for Graphic Arts

259 Jerome Hopfer (act. 1520-d. after 1550)
THREE DESIGNS FOR VASES
German (Nuremberg), ca. 1540
Etching; 11 13/16 x 8 19/32 (29 x 21.8)
The Fine Arts Museums of San Francisco,
Achenbach Foundation for Graphic Arts

260 Hans Sebald Beham (1500-1550)
GROUND PLAN AND ELEVATION OF A CORINTHIAN CAPITAL (first and third state)
German (Nuremberg), 1543
Engravings; 3 15/16 x 5⅞ (10 x 14.9)
Provenance: Duc d'Arenberg
Lent by University of California, Los Angeles, Grunwald Center for the Graphic Arts 1966.18.1A-B

261 Hans Sebald Beham
ORNAMENT WITH SEA MONSTERS
German (Nuremberg), 1544
Engraving: 1 5/16 x 3 15/16 (3.4 x 10)
The Fine Arts Museums of San Francisco, Achenbach Foundation for Graphic Arts 1963.20.373

262 Heinrich Aldegrever
TWO ORNAMENTAL PANELS
German (Soest), 1549
Engravings; 3 9/16 x 1 11/16 (9.1 x 4.4); 3 11/16 x 1 13/16 (9.4 x 4.8)
Provenance: Freiherr von Lanna
Lent by University of California, Los Angeles, Grunwald Center for the Graphic Arts 1962.5.2-3

263 Virgil Solis (1514-1562)
THREE ORNAMENTAL FRIEZES
German (Nuremberg), ca. 1550
Engravings; 1 11/32 x 6 9/16 (3.4 x 16.7)
The Fine Arts Museums of San Francisco, Achenbach Foundation for Graphic Arts

264 Wenzel Jamnitzer (1508-1585)
DESIGN FOR A COVERED CUP
German (Nuremberg), ca. 1551
Engraving; 11¾ x 5 15/16 (29.8 x 15)
Courtesy, Museum of Fine Arts, Boston. Horatio Greenough Curtis Fund M31078

265 Bernhard Zan (act. ca. 1580)
DESIGN FOR A COVERED GOBLET (Fig. no. 51)
German (Nuremberg), 1581
Hand-colored etching on paper; 8⅜ x 4 3/16 (21.3 x 10.6)
Courtesy, Museum of Fine Arts, Boston. Horatio Greenough Curtis Fund 40.100

266 Manner of Bernhard Zan, (act. ca. 1580)
PROJECT FOR AN ORNAMENTED TANKARD
German (Nuremberg), ca. 1580
Pen and ink with watercolor; 6⅛ x 4¾ (15.5 x 12.1)
Lent by University of California, Los Angeles, Grunwald Center for the Graphic Arts 1963.35.31

267 Willem Danielsz Van Tetrode (act. 1550-1600)
DESIGN FOR A SILVER PLATE
Flemish, ca. 1580
Drawing, pen and bistre with reddish wash; d. 24¼ (61.6)
Lent by E. B. Crocker Art Gallery, Sacramento, California D 115

268 Etienne Delaune (1518-1583)
TWO ENGRAVINGS WITH GROTESQUE ORNAMENTS
French, 16th century
Engravings; 2 5/32 x 1 9/16 (5.5 x 4)
The Fine Arts Museums of San Francisco, Achenbach Foundation for Graphic Arts

269 Pierre Woeiriot (1532-after 1596)
DESIGN FOR A SWORD HILT (Fig. no. 67)
French, ca. 1555
Engraving; d. 7¾ (19.7)
Courtesy, Museum of Fine Arts, Boston. Maria Antoinette Evans Fund M36201

270 J. A. Du Cerceau (ca. 1510-ca. 1584)
TWO ORNAMENT PRINTS
French, ca. 1560
Engravings; 4 1/32 x 2⅝ (10.3 x 6.7); 4 3/32 x 2⅝ (10.4 x 6.7)
Lent by Cooper-Hewitt Museum, The Smithsonian Institution's National Museum of Design, New York 1945.6.4a, b

271 Daniel Mignot (act. 1593-1616)
DESIGN FOR A PENDANT (Fig. no. 50)
French, 1593
Engraving; 6½ x 4⅜ (16.5 x 8.6)
Courtesy, Museum of Fine Arts, Boston. George Nixon Black Fund 34.634

272 Taddeo Zuccaro (1542/3-1609)
DESIGN FOR A MAJOLICA DISH (Triumph of Caesar)
Italian, ca. 1560
Pen drawing; 13⅜ x 13⅛ (34 x 33.3)
Provenance: J. Richardson, Sir Joshua Reynolds, A. M. Champernowne, C. D. Ginsburg
Lent by The Walters Art Gallery, Baltimore 37.2440

TEXTILES

273 Flemish (Brussels), ca. 1550
TRIUMPH OF JUSTICE (Fig. no. 119)
Silk and wool tapestry; 173 x 216 (440 x 556)
The Fine Arts Museums of San Francisco. Gift of the Hearst Foundation 1957.125

274 Italian (Florence), ca. 1480
BROCADED VELVET
Silk and metal thread; 38 x 22½ (96.5 x 57.1)
Lent by Los Angeles County Museum of Art. Gift of Mr. and Mrs. Ernest A. Bryant, Jr. M65.9

275 Italian (Venice), 1450-1500
VELVET
Cut and voided silk velvet brocaded in metal thread; 31 x 21 (78.7 x 53.3)
Lent by The Metropolitan Museum of Art, New York. Fletcher Fund, 1946 46.156.118

276 Italian, 15th century
BROCADED VELVET
Silk and metal thread; 18 x 25 (45.7 x 63.5)
Lent by Los Angeles County Museum of Art. Mr. and Mrs. Allan C. Balch Fund M55.12.29

277 Italian (Florence), ca. 1500
COPE
Voided velvet with embroidered orphrey; 56 x 114½ (142 x 290.4)
Lent by Ed Nagel, San Francisco

278 Spanish, 16th century
MAN'S COSTUME
Silk velvet, metallic thread, brass and leather
Lent by Los Angeles County Museum of Art. Costume Council Fund M77.34

279 Marcos Covarrubias (act. ca. 1514-1550)
EMBROIDERED ALTAR FRONTAL
Spanish, ca. 1550
Velvet embroidered in silk and metal thread; 41 x 92¼ (104.1 x 234.3)
The Fine Arts Museums of San Francisco. Gift of the Frederick Talbot Estate 50727

280 Italian, ca. 1550
TEXTILE
Silk velvet; 56 x 41¼ (142 x 105)
Lent by Los Angeles County Museum of Art.
Costume Council Fund M.69.36.1

281 Italian, 16th century
BROCATELLE
Silk; 78 x 21 (198 x 53.3)
Lent by The Metropolitan Museum of Art, New York.
Rogers Fund, 1938 38.77

282 Italian or Spanish, 15th-16th century
END OF A TABLECLOTH
Linen embroidered in silk; 28 x 11 (71.1 x 27.9)
Lent by The Metropolitan Museum of Art, New York.
Rogers Fund, 1908 08.42.132

283 Italian, 16th century
NEEDLEPOINT LACE BORDER
Linen, punto in aria; 108 x 6½ (274 x 16.25)
Lent by The Metropolitan Museum of Art, New York.
Gift of Baroness Fanny Hatvany, 1952 52.55.1

284 Italian, 16th century
BORDER
Embroidered linen; 38 x 8 (95.5 x 20.3)
Lent by The Metropolitan Museum of Art, New York.
Gift of Ann Payne Blumenthal, 1936 36.130.9

285 Italian, 16th century
EMBROIDERED PANEL
Linen and silk; 43¾ x 8¼ (111 x 21)
Lent by The Metropolitan Museum of Art, New York.
Gift of Mr. and Mrs. Harry G. Friedman, 1958 58.119

286 French, ca. 1550
EMBROIDERED PANEL (Scenes from Ovid's Metamorphoses) (Fig. no. 118)
Satin embroidered in silk; 78 x 14¾ (198 x 37.5)
Lent by The Metropolitan Museum of Art, New York.
Rogers Fund, 1956 56.27

Selected Bibliography

General

Burckhardt, Jacob. *Civilization of the Renaissance in Italy.* Vienna, 1937.

Hauser, Arnold. *Mannerism: Crisis of the Renaissance and the Origin of Modern Art.* 2 vols. London, 1965.

Shearman, John. *Mannerism.* Harmondsworth, 1967 and 1973.

Small Bronzes

Wixom, William D. *Renaissance Bronzes from Ohio Collections.* Cleveland, 1975.

Arms and Armor

Blair, Claude. *European and American Arms: c. 1100-1850.* New York, 1962.

Laking, Sir Guy Francis. *A Record of European Armour and Arms Through Seven Centuries.* 5 vols. London, 1920-1922.

Goldsmiths' Work and Jewelry

Evans, Joan. *A History of Jewellery, 1100-1870.* London, 1953.

Hayward, J. F. *Virtuoso Goldsmiths and the Triumph of Humanism 1540-1620.* Sotheby Parke Bernet. London, 1976.

Renaissance Timepieces and Scientific Instruments

Lloyd H. Alan. *The Collectors Dictionary of Clocks.* London, 1964.

Michel, Henri. *Scientific Instruments in Art and History.* New York, 1967. Trans. by R. E. W. Maddison and Francis R. Maddison.

Ceramics, Glass, and Enamels

Honey, W. B. *European Ceramic Art from the End of the Middle Ages to about 1815.* 2 vols. London, 1952.

Honey, W.B. *Glass : A Handbook for the Study of Glass of all Periods and Countries and a Guide to the Museum Collection.* Victoria and Albert Museum. London, 1946.

Liverani, Giuseppe. *Five Centuries of Italian Majolica.* New York and Toronto, 1960.

Rackham, Bernard. *Italian Majolica.* London, 1952.

Verdier, Philippe. *Catalogue of the Painted Enamels of the Renaissance.* The Walters Art Gallery. Baltimore, 1967.

Furniture and Woodwork

Schottmuller, Frieda. *Furniture and Interior Decoration of Italian Renaissance.* Stuttgart, 1928.

Renaissance Bookbindings

Goldschmidt, E. P. *Gothic and Renaissance Bookbindings.* 2 vols. London, 1928.

Miner, D. *The History of Bookbinding, 1525-1950.* The Walters Art Gallery. Baltimore, 1957.